MEETING
THE FOX

MEETING THE FOX

The Allied Invasion of Africa,
from Operation Torch
to Kasserine Pass
to Victory in Tunisia

Orr Kelly

John Wiley & Sons, Inc.

For Mary Davies Kelly
Soulmate and Navigator

Copyright © 2002 by Orr Kelly. All rights reserved
Maps copyright © 2002 by Lachina Publishing Services, Inc.

Published by John Wiley & Sons, Inc., New York.
Published simultaneously in Canada

This publication is designed to provide accurate and authoritative information in regard to the subject matter covered. It is sold with the understanding that the publisher is not engaged in rendering professional services. If professional advice or other expert assistance is required, the services of a competent professional person should be sought.

Library of Congress Cataloging-in-Publication Data:

Kelly, Orr.
    Meeting the Fox / Orr Kelly.
      p. cm.
    Includes bibliographical references and index.
    ISBN 0-471-41429-8 (cloth)
      1. World War, 1939–1945—Campaigns—Africa, North. 2. United States. Army Air Forces. Fighter Group, 33rd—History. 3. United States. Army. Infantry Regiment, 168th—History. 4. United States. Army. Ranger Battalion, 3rd—History. 5. United States. Army. Ranger Battalion, 1st—History. 6. United States. Army. Ranger Battalion, 4th—History. 7. World War, 1939–1945—Regimental histories—United States. 8. Rommel, Erwin, 1891–1944. I. Title.

D766.82 .K45 2002
940.54′23—dc21

                    2001046822

Printed in the United States of America

10 9 8 7 6 5 4 3 2 1

Contents

Maps and Illustrations

Maps

Illustrations

Acknowledgments

Research for *Meeting the Fox* took me to half a dozen archives and libraries. It also took me to the battlefields of Tunisia. Most writers routinely give thanks to a spouse for help, although I suspect the help often involves little more than keeping the kids quiet while the writer communes with his or her muse. In this case, far more than the usual expression of thanks is due to my wife, Mary, for her help during our Tunisian trip.

Acting as navigator, she guided us to the unmarked scenes of battles in rural Tunisia far from the normal tourist routes. When my pocket was artfully picked on our first day in Tunis, she came up with a credit card that was not linked to the ones I had lost and permitted us to continue our research trip. And she proved helpful and supportive even after I drove about ten yards too far on a road in southern Tunisia—just far enough to mire our car to its chassis in the Saharan sand.

My friend Kathryn W. Gest, executive vice president of Powell Tate, which represented the government of Tunisia, put me in touch with Bochra Malki of the Agence *Tunisienne de Communication Extèrieure* in Tunis, who helped me get in contact with Tunisian officials. Nejm Lakhal of the Tunisian Embassy in Washington also helped with contacts in Tunisia.

At the National Archives in College Park, Maryland, I found a great wealth of material on the campaign in North Africa. The records there include not only the after-action reports written in the field, but also the maps and overlays used by the troops. Lifting them out of the folders where they have lain for these sixty years, one can almost feel the lingering grit from the Tunisian battlefields. Sandy Smith, an expert on the naval records, was especially helpful in guiding me to the war diaries of the ships that landed the invasion force.

The papers of many of the officers involved in the campaign are on file at the archives of the Army Military History Institute at Carlisle Barracks, Pennsylvania. Jim Baughman and Dave Keough were very helpful in providing access to those files. Down the hall, in the Institute library, Richard Baker guided me to the library's collection of monographs written by officers soon after the end of the war.

Yvonne Kincaid of the Air Force History Library at Bolling Air Force Base in Washington, D.C., and the staff of the Air Force Historical Research Agency at Maxwell Air Force Base in Alabama provided me with access to many Air Force records.

Aaron Haberman of the George C. Marshall Archives in Lexington, Virginia, guided me through the voluminous collection of the papers of Brig. Gen. Paul M. Robinett, which provided not only factual detail about the battles in which he was involved but an insight into the relationships of the leading American officers with each other and with their British counterparts.

I am also indebted to the veterans of the North African campaign, listed in the bibliography, who shared their memories with me in interviews, gave me access to their diaries and memoirs, and in a number of instances, lent me books, many of them out of print and otherwise unavailable, from their personal collections.

Special thanks are also due, for reading my manuscript and offering a number of valuable comments, to the Rev. Bernard Hillenbrand and Morton Lebow of Washington, D.C., two veteran World War II infantrymen; Col. Robert J. Berens of Springfield, Virginia, who served as a noncommissioned officer with the British Commandos and the American 34th Infantry Division in Tunisia; Col. William R. Tuck of Houston, Texas, a tank veteran of North Africa; and J. Frank Diggs of Arlington, Virginia, who fought in North Africa, was captured in Sicily, and has recently written his own account of life in a German prisoner of war camp.

Essential to making this book possible was the work of Mike Hamilburg, my agent of many years, and Stephen S. Power, my skilled and perceptive editor. At one point, due to the vagaries of the publishing business, Stephen almost got away, but we managed, thankfully, to hang onto him.

Introduction:
Visit to a Forgotten Cemetery

The guidebook to Tunisia warned us: "The detour out to the war cemetery . . . is only for the dedicated."

For my wife, Mary, and me, the route to the cemetery is no detour. The North Africa American Cemetery itself is our goal.

Several years ago, in the course of research for my history of the Air Commandos, *From a Dark Sky: The Story of U.S. Air Force Special Operations,* I came across an Air Force oral history interview with Col. Philip Cochran, who was instrumental in putting together, in Burma, the first air commando operation during World War II. In the interview, he described what happened in Burma, but he also gave a vivid description of his experience leading a fighter outfit in North Africa, in the first confrontation between American and German forces.

His account of those desperate early days stayed in my memory, piquing my curiosity about that almost-forgotten six-month battle. It would eventually become the genesis for *Meeting the Fox.* It is curiosity about those early battles that has, in a sense, made us among the few "dedicated" visitors to this out-of-the-way cemetery.

In our search for it, we drive along the Mediterranean coast east of the city of Tunis past the disappointing ruins of Carthage and the picturesque village of Sidi Bou Said, its sparkling white buildings trimmed in blue, until we find a sign pointing the way up Rue Roosevelt.

1

The parking lot, with space for perhaps a hundred cars and several tour buses, is empty. The only sound is that of the large American flag flapping in the ocean breeze atop a tall flagpole.

An English-speaking Tunisian emerges from the office and invites us in to sign the guest book. His is a lonely job. By his estimate he sees perhaps 3,000 visitors a year—about eight a day. But some days there are none. Most of the visitors come in groups from visiting U.S. Navy ships or an occasional cruise liner. The official U.S. Battle Monuments Commission annual reports put the number of visitors higher: 7,822 in 1997 and 9,163 in 1998. Even accepting those larger numbers, the North African cemetery is a neglected monument to the almost-forgotten crucial first battles between Americans and Germans, receiving far fewer visitors than any other World War II American cemetery.

From the office, we walk out toward the cemetery on a raised platform bordered by a long stone wall. The graves, arrayed on a meticulously trimmed green lawn, are marked by white crosses, with an occasional Star of David, aligned with military precision to form straight lines when viewed from any angle.

There are 2,841 grave markers. As we wander down the lines of crosses, it becomes apparent that there is something strange about this cemetery. Some of the crosses do not carry the names of individuals. They are simply marked "Here Rests in Honored Glory an American Soldier Known But to God."

Then, turning from the burial ground to the long wall—the Wall of the Missing—on the south edge of the cemetery, we see column after column listing the names of 3,724 missing.

In all, 6,565 souls lost.

That the missing and those "Known But to God" so far outnumber those in properly marked graves is startling. And then we stop to realize that the national compulsion to find and identify those missing on the battlefield—a compulsion that has teams scouring the mountains and rice paddies of Vietnam for fragments of bone and teeth that may have lain

Aligned in perfect rows, crosses and a few stars of David mark the graves of 2,841 American dead. (Photo by the author)

there for nearly forty years—is a very new phenomenon in our national life.

Most of the nation's efforts to find the remains of missing service members have focused on Southeast Asia—Vietnam, Laos, and Cambodia—where fewer than 2,000 remain missing. More recently, renewed efforts have been made to find those lost in Korea, where more than 8,000 are listed as such. In the years immediately after World War II, the Army searched the battlefields to recover and identify many of the dead. But the recovery efforts ended in 1951, leaving more than 78,000 still unaccounted for.

The visit to this cemetery in Africa has a special poignancy for Mary and me. We have just finished our collaboration on *Dream's End: Two Iowa Brothers in the Civil War*. In it, we tell the story of my grandmother's two brothers. Andrew, the older one, signed up with the 36th Iowa Volunteer Infantry in 1862, at the age of 17. Barney would join the 8th Iowa Cavalry a year later.

Andrew was killed—shot through the heart, his mother was told—at the battle of Marks' Mills, south of Little Rock, Arkansas, on April 25, 1864. In the cemeteries where some of those killed in the battle were buried, we found no record of Andrew. Perhaps his body was interred in an unmarked grave. More likely, it was consumed in the fire that swept across part of the battlefield after the shooting stopped.

Shortly after Andrew's death, Barney was captured in a raid south of Atlanta and locked up in the infamous prisoner-of-war compound at Andersonville, Georgia. He died shortly after the war of disease contracted during his imprisonment.

Looking out over the rows of crosses here in North Africa, we are comforted to think that at least the bodies of these American soldiers have been identified and properly laid to rest in this monumental site.

But we soon realize that this is not the same kind of cemetery with which we are familiar, a place near home where the bodies of family members or friends are laid to rest. This is, in effect, a "virtual" cemetery, where those who are not buried here outnumber those who are and where some of those who are buried here are not known. It is a place where the bodies of the fallen and, one must acknowledge, body parts have been gathered together from battlefields that stretched 3,200 miles from the Atlantic shore of North Africa to the Persian Gulf.

There is something else unusual about this cemetery. It is the only large cemetery where those who fought and died in North Africa during World War II are commemorated in one place. Other countries whose soldiers died in North Africa—Britain, France, Italy, Germany, Tunisia—have left smaller cemeteries scattered across the land, typically burying the men in small groups near where they fell.

Later in my research I learned that the Americans who fell in battle in North Africa were not, on the battlefields where they died, treated with the care and dignity this cemetery seems to imply. General Paul Robinett, a tank commander involved in all of the major battles in Tunisia, was bothered that the American graves were poorly marked, in contrast to the neat crosses marking German graves. In a

The contrast in the care taken in burying the dead on the battlefield is shown by these two photos: (*top*) American graves near Medjez el Bab on November 22, 1942, and (*bottom*) German graves near Mateur on March 6, 1943. (Source: National Archives)

5

memo to Gen. Dwight Eisenhower, the Allied commander, on February 10, 1943, he complained: "We do not even have a supply of markers and our chaplains have to use ration box boards, sticks, or anything else immediately available."

Later, in our tour of the Tunisian battle sites, we found a small British cemetery on the edge of a lake near Medjez el Bab where personal messages of grief mark the resting spots of those who fell in battle nearby and add a poignancy that is lost in the large-scale perfection of the American cemetery.

By its very size and monumental nature, the American cemetery seems purposely designed not only to memorialize those who fell but to send a message: *Something very important happened here.* It is no accident that the site of the cemetery is on the edge of Carthage, one of the most noteworthy historical sites in all of North Africa. The Phoenicians established their most important African base here in the ninth century before Christ. Hannibal set out, more than 2,200 years ago, in the service of Carthage, to bring his troops and elephants from the Iberian peninsula across southern France and over the Alps in his assault on Rome. The Romans, at the end of the Punic Wars, tore up the city stone from stone, then ploughed salt into the rubble to leave the earth barren. And Romans eventually restored Carthage into their own major city on the southern shore of the Mediterranean.

What happened here at the end of the first half of the twentieth century that was so important to deserve to be remembered in this ancient place? What was so important that the United States took these 6,565 men from their homes and sent them across the ocean to die here, or disappear?

We found the beginnings of an answer at the eastern end of the Wall of the Missing. In the center of a small grotto, open on two sides and with stone walls on the other two, lies a large black stone monument marking the grave of an unknown soldier, sailor, or airman. On the walls, large maps represent the battles fought for North Africa.

Sweeping arrows show how, on November 8, 1942, American and British forces landed near Casablanca on the Atlantic coast of what was then called French Morocco, and at Oran and Algiers in Algeria, also a French colony. Other arrows show how the battle, with astounding quickness, moved more than 1,200 miles to Tunisia, a French protectorate halfway across the continent. And the legend tells how the American and British forces, joined by the French soon after the initial landing, defeated the armies of the German and Italian Axis in Tunisia on May 13, 1943, after a battle of six months and five days.

But the legend does not answer the question: Why here? The shortest route to Berlin, obviously, is not through Casablanca or even Tunis. Neither does it answer a more personal question: Who were these men who came to fight and, many of them, die here? Where did they come from and why were they chosen to be the first Americans to confront the German army, which held sway from the Atlantic coast of France to the Volga, deep in the Soviet Union, and whose troops had swept across North Africa to threaten Egypt and the Suez Canal?

The American part in the battle for North Africa began almost exactly eleven months after the Japanese attack on Pearl Harbor on December 7, 1941, brought the United States into World War II. Although the United States had called up reserves more than a year before, the country was still woefully unprepared to fight a global war. The units that were sent into North Africa to confront the tough, suntanned, battle-savvy veterans of Field Marshal Irwin Rommel's vaunted Afrika Korps were those that happened to be available, regardless of the status of their training, the adequacy of their equipment, or the quality of their leadership. The heaviest part of the burden thus fell to a small number of units: the 34th Infantry Division, a National Guard unit from the Midwest; three regular army divisions, the 1st and 9th Infantry and the 1st Armored; and the Army Air Corps's 33rd Fighter Group. The 3rd Infantry and the 2nd Armored Divisions took part in the initial landings but remained in Morocco while the other four divisions fought in Tunisia.

In the six months of fighting, the 34th Division lost 4,049 men—dead, wounded, captured, or missing; the 1st Armored Division, 3,407; the 1st Infantry Division, 3,196; the 9th Infantry Division, 2,724; and the 12th Air Force, of which the 33rd group was a part, 2,000.

This is the story of those first Americans who suffered a vicious lesson in warfare from Rommel, the Desert Fox. It is the story of how, in those first crucial battles in North Africa, the American army learned how to fight a skilled and tenacious enemy, learned which leaders to trust and which to discard, and prepared itself for victory on the more celebrated battlefields of France, Italy, and Germany itself—battles that might well have been lost were it not for the bitter lessons learned in North Africa.

PART ONE

THE LONG WAY
TO BERLIN

1

The Longest Reach

If modern visitors to the North Africa American Cemetery should ask why the United States, which had been at war with Nazi Germany for nearly a year, chose to make its first move against the enemy more than 1,400 miles from Berlin, in a part of Africa where, except for a few diplomatic personnel, there weren't any Germans, they would be echoing the very question America's Joint Chiefs of Staff had at the time.

The military leaders had a clear-cut and logical plan: They would use the British Isles as a gigantic staging base for a direct assault on Germany, with large-scale daylight bombing raids and preparations for a thrust across the English Channel into France in 1943. Meanwhile, support in the form of bombers and fighters would be sent to help the British in their fight against Rommel's Afrika Korps. U.S. troops would not otherwise be involved in Africa.

As part of that plan, the 34th Infantry Division, the last of the National Guard units to be called to federal service, was the first sent to Northern Ireland, in the late winter and early spring of 1942, to spend at least a year training for the cross-Channel attack. The 1st Armored Division and the 1st Infantry Division followed soon after. About the same time, the B-17 Flying Fortresses of the Eighth Air Force began what were billed as precision bombing attacks on German

11

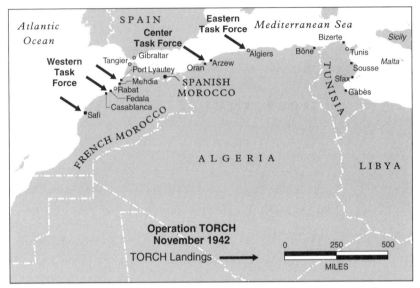

The Allies landed along the Atlantic coast near Casablanca and at
Oran and Algiers, inside the Mediterranean Sea, on November 8,
1942. The action quickly moved far to the east as both sides built up
forces in a battle for control of Tunisia.

military installations and factories. The 33rd Fighter Group,
with its new P-40 Tomahawks, had been sent to the West
Coast immediately after Pearl Harbor to defend against a
Japanese attack, but was called back to the East Coast and
given orders to join the British, where they were trying to
hold the line against Rommel in western Egypt.

Earlier in 1942, serious thought was given to the possibility of a landing in North Africa, but the idea was soon set
aside. There simply weren't enough ships available to put
more than a few thousand men ashore in an initial landing,
and it would take months to build up a force big enough to
be significant.

Two powerful and strong-willed men favored a landing
in North Africa, however, each for his own reasons.

Franklin D. Roosevelt, elected to his third term as president in 1940 when the United States was still at peace but
much of the world was already at war, was determined to get
American ground forces into combat with the Germans as
soon as possible, certainly in 1942. Americans had been fight-

ing the Japanese in the Pacific from December 7, 1941, but ground troops had not engaged in a single exchange of shots with Hitler's armies.

Winston Churchill, the British prime minister, had long favored attacking the Germans through Europe's "soft underbelly" instead of confronting them directly by crossing the Channel. He had, in fact, favored such an approach in World War I, when he served as chief lord of the admiralty.

While the British and American Combined Chiefs of Staff engaged in a transatlantic debate over the best way to pursue the war, Roosevelt and Churchill simply made up their minds. Historians have pinpointed the period of July 25 to 30, 1942, as the one when a firm decision was made to land in North Africa and, unavoidably, delay an attack across the Channel until 1944. The decision seems to have come as a surprise to at least some of the American Joint Chiefs, who thought the possibility of an early cross-Channel attack was still on the table.

Even a quick glance at the map of the world as it stood in mid-1942 is enough to demonstrate why the military leaders were able to keep their enthusiasm for a landing in North Africa so well under control.

In 1940, within months after World War II began, France fell and a French government under German domination was set up in the spa town of Vichy in southern France. The French colonies in North Africa—French Morocco, Algeria, and Tunisia—remained under the control of the Vichy government. Another large chunk of North Africa—Spanish Morocco—was controlled by Spain. And Spain was governed by Generalissimo Francisco Franco, who was friendly toward the Axis.

Aside from their uncertain position in Egypt, the only bits of dry land anywhere near North Africa controlled by the Allies were Gibraltar, at the entrance to the Mediterranean, and the island of Malta, in the middle of the Mediterranean between Italy and Africa. But Gibraltar was too small to serve as a staging area for a major invasion, and besides, it was under both observation and potential attack from Spain, just across the border. Malta, under constant aerial bombardment, was barely able to survive the war, supported only by heroic convoys fighting their way through a gauntlet of bombers and submarines.

Samuel Elliot Morison, the preeminent naval historian of World War II, thumbed back through his books to find a parallel for such an operation. He considered the landing in Turkey's Dardanelles by British, Australian, and New Zealand forces in World War I; the Japanese landing at Port Arthur in 1904; the American landing at Santiago de Cuba during the Spanish-American War in 1898; and the Japanese landings on Pacific islands earlier in World War II. The first was a dismal failure. The others were successful, but all were launched from bases reasonably close to the target. None of them involved moving an army across 4,000 miles of open ocean for a night landing that, the planners had to assume, would be vigorously resisted.

Morison finally found a naval operation whose audacity matched the invasion of North Africa: the Athenian attack on Syracuse, in Sicily, in 415 B.C.E. He uncovered as well an ominous quotation from one Nicias. Although bitterly opposed to the expedition, he was charged with leading it. Before departing, he warned:

> We must not disguise from ourselves that we go to found a city among strangers and enemies, and that he who undertakes such an enterprise should be prepared to become master of the country the first day he lands, or failing in this to find everything hostile to him.

Nicias did not become master of the country the first day he landed and, indeed, did find everything hostile to him. After two years of warfare, his fleet was sunk and his army destroyed while trying to flee from the outskirts of Syracuse. He surrendered and was executed.

Thucydides, the historian of the Peloponnesian War, ended his account of the Syracuse adventure with this dismal summary:

> They were beaten at all points and altogether; all that they suffered was great; they were destroyed, as the saying is, with a total destruction, their fleet, their army—everything was destroyed, and few out of many returned home.

One did not have to be a born pessimist to realize such a fate could befall those attempting a North African landing. The hazards were formidable.

If Roosevelt's demand that Americans confront Germans in 1942 was to be satisfied, ships would have to be assembled, soldiers equipped and trained, Army pilots taught how to be catapulted from ships, and preparations made to support a large army by ships traveling through seas thick with German submarines—and all of this in less than five months.

The forces slated to land inside the Mediterranean at Oran and Algiers would have to pass through the Strait of Gibraltar and confront the same hazards of attack from the air and under the sea faced by the Malta convoys.

Nature also seemed to be in opposition. The surf along the Atlantic coast near Casablanca was notoriously rough— so rough, in fact, that a landing might prove impossible.

Even successful landings would be no guarantee of ultimate victory. The real prize in North Africa was Tunisia, which offered bomber bases within reach of Italy and portions of Germany, and a staging area for landings in Sicily, the Italian Peninsula, or southern France. But Tunisia was nearly 500 miles from the closest landing point in Algiers. Planners concluded reluctantly that an attempt to land farther east, even in Bizerte or Tunis itself, would rule out a landing in Casablanca: There simply weren't enough ships to do both.

While Allied planners focused on preparing for the landings, they could not avoid looking over their shoulders. If Franco permitted German forces to use Spanish bases, Germany could, within hours, fly in enough aircraft to overwhelm the relatively small number of planes that would accompany the invasion fleet. Or the Spanish themselves could decide to join the war, taking Gibraltar and launching attacks against the Allies from their colony in Morocco.

The Allies faced more remote dangers as well. One big worry was what might happen in the east. German armies were deep in the Soviet Union. If Josef Stalin, the Soviet leader, sought peace, Hitler could turn his entire strength toward crushing the Allied beachhead in North Africa. Gathering the forces for the North African operation would also endanger Allied operations in other parts of the world, crippling the American bombing offensive against Germany, just getting under way from bases in England, and drawing ships away from the fight against Japan in the Pacific.

Each of these was a major problem, but all paled in comparison to that of the Vichy French presence in North Africa, with its colonies and protectorates stretching a thousand miles along the southern shore of the Mediterranean. The Americans wanted very much to avoid having to fight the French, not only for practical reasons but because of the emotional ties between the two countries. Those ties had been strong for more than a century and a half, since the Marquis de Lafayette came to help the colonies throw off British rule in the Revolutionary War. In 1917, when Americans landed in France to fight the Germans, an American officer proudly proclaimed: "Lafayette, we are here!" After World War I, many Americans studied at French military academies and became friends with their French counterparts.

Like it or not, though, the Americans were forced to think of the French in North Africa as *the* enemy, at least until the French proved themselves otherwise. The French had been humbled by the German blitzkrieg in 1940 and forced to surrender. The northern part of the country was occupied by the Germans while the southern portion and French possessions in Africa remained under the control of the puppet government set up in Vichy under Marshal Henri Pétain, the great French hero of World War I. Under the terms of the surrender, France retained its army and navy, including troops, ships, and aircraft in North Africa.

The Germans deliberately kept the French armed forces weak, denying them the opportunity to replace equipment lost in 1940 or buy modern arms. But the French forces in North Africa were still strong enough to cause sleepless nights for Allied planners. They had World War I–era tanks, a serious threat, if an obsolete one, until the Allies managed to get their own more modern ones ashore. French fighter planes would actually outnumber Allied aircraft until the Allies seized airfields ashore and flew in fighters from Gibraltar. And French ships would be encountered at each of the major landing points—Casablanca, Oran, and Algiers—including two powerful battleships: the *Jean Bart* at Casablanca and the *Richelieu* further south on the Atlantic coast at Dakar, Senegal.

Even beating the French militarily carried its own risks. The French gendarmes and soldiers maintained tight control over the native peoples all across North Africa. As much as many of the American officers might dislike the French colonial system, they still did not want to fight their way ashore and then find themselves dealing with a series of native rebellions. They needed the French to keep order while they got on with the war against the Germans.

In the frantic months of the late summer and early autumn of 1942, Allied preparations for the North African campaign moved swiftly along two tracks. While the military prepared for the landings on the assumption that they would have to fight the French, diplomats worked just as hard to try to avoid French resistance and, instead, secure French cooperation.

The United States had maintained diplomatic relations with the Vichy regime even after the Japanese attack on Pearl Harbor and the German declaration of war had brought America into the conflict. Robert D. Murphy, counselor at the American Embassy in Vichy, worked hard to convince Pétain to cooperate with the Germans only as much as the French were required to by the agreement that ended the fighting in 1940. He succeeded in convincing the French not to turn their fleet over to the Germans and not to permit the Germans to station their forces in French territories in Africa. He also tried to set the groundwork so that at the appropriate time, the French military would join the Allies in fighting the Germans.

All this diplomatic effort came to a head in the latter half of 1942 as the time for the North African operation approached. At that time, most of the French in North Africa were loyal to Pétain and felt he was doing the best he could for France under difficult circumstances. General Charles de Gaulle, who had set up a Free French government based in Britain, was neither liked nor trusted by most of the French in North Africa. The Allied goal thus became to win over those loyal to Pétain and convince them that aiding the

Allies was what the old marshal—although he could not come out and say so—wanted them to do.

Murphy shifted his efforts from Vichy to Algiers. He got invaluable assistance from a small group of Americans who were dispatched to North Africa to monitor food and other supplies being sent to the Algerian people and prevent it being siphoned off by the Germans. This monitoring activity, giving the Americans daily access to the North African ports, was an important source of intelligence for the invasion planners.

On October 23, 1942, a team headed by Maj. Gen. Mark Clark came ashore from a British submarine about seventy-five miles west of Algiers and met Murphy and French Gen. René Mast, chief of staff of the French Colonial Army. Mast agreed to give orders to the forces under his control not to resist the invasion. But he was not told when or exactly where the landings would be made. Similar contact was made with two officers in Morocco, who also agreed not to resist, but all they were told was the approximate date of the landings.

The discussions went beyond efforts to minimize French resistance to the invasion to the question of how much help the French could provide against the Germans if they actively joined with the Allies. Everyone agreed the French would require a massive infusion of new equipment. But Mast estimated they could quickly put into the field eight infantry divisions, two armored divisions, and a number of separate units—a significant contribution to the Allied war effort.

As another part of their strategy to gain French cooperation, the Allies arranged for Gen. Henri Giraud to be spirited out of France in the hope the French forces in Africa would rally behind him. Giraud was highly respected by the French armed forces. He had fought the Germans—and had been captured and escaped—in both wars. After his escape from the Germans earlier in 1942, he had been permitted to retire near Lyon, in southern France.

Unfortunately, these diplomatic preparations all fell short of guaranteeing a peaceful landing for the invasion force. Much as most French officers might admire Giraud, he was not part of the Vichy government and could not even pretend to speak for Pétain. If they had had their choice, the

Allies would have preferred the help of an officer actually part of the puppet regime. But attempting to enlist the help of such an officer was deemed too risky. Giraud was a second-best choice.

Many, but not all, of the French officers in North Africa probably would have preferred to join with the Allies in fighting the Germans. But this was not an easy decision. Most felt their oath compelled them to obey orders from the French government in Vichy. A few were actually anti-Jewish and pro-German.

The French were also deeply concerned for the welfare of friends and relatives back home. If they aided the Allies, or if they even failed to resist vigorously, they knew German troops would sweep south, completing the jackbooted military occupation of their homeland. Such a move would put the Germans in position to seize the French fleet in the harbor at Toulon.

Even those fully prepared to welcome the Allies harbored the fear of what would happen if the "invasion" turned out to be a hit-and-run commando raid like the ill-fated attack on the northern French port of Dieppe in August 1942. They didn't want to back a loser.

Thus, as troops began moving to staging areas in the United States, Canada, and the British Isles and ships took on loads of ammunition, tanks, trucks, artillery pieces, and aircraft, the Allied generals had to conclude they would have to fight their way ashore, and no one—including the French themselves—knew whether and how much resistance they would face. If the French made a brief show of resistance and then joined the Allied cause, the landing had a good chance of success. If they put up a vigorous defense, the whole enterprise could collapse.

Success in this ambitious undertaking depended heavily on surprise. If the Germans learned of the plans for the invasion in time to oppose it, the landings would almost certainly fail. To preserve secrecy, the soldiers weren't told where they were going, nor were they given any special clothing or equipment they might need for fighting in North Africa. If they knew they were heading for Africa, most of the troops would have imagined a land of sand, palm trees, and hot weather. Their imaginations did not prepare them for reality: high mountains, snow, cold, torrential rains, and mud so thick it would swallow trucks, jeeps, airplanes, even tanks.

Although British units and British commanders would be heavily involved in the operation, a major effort was made to give the landings an all-American look. One reason for this was to let both friend and foe know that the Americans were at last fully involved in the war against Germany. Another reason was the hope that the French in North Africa, who would be inclined to resist the British, might welcome Americans. Although the British and the French had been allies at the time of the German invasion of France, their relationship had turned sour after the French capitulation and especially after the British attacked units of the French fleet at the port of Oran.

As part of this policy, an American, Maj. Gen. Dwight D. Eisenhower, was chosen as overall commander even though neither he nor any of his American subordinates had ever commanded a unit as large as a division in combat. Among his staff, however, were a number of British officers who had been involved in the fighting for several years.

The American units chosen to spearhead the invasion and then to carry the battle to the Germans were not the best trained or the best equipped. They were simply the most readily available. The 1st and 34th Infantry Divisions and the 1st Armored Division were already in the British Isles, training for the invasion of France. They were designated to land at Oran and Algiers. Along with them would come the newly created 1st Ranger Battalion, made up largely of men from the 34th Division. The 3rd and the 9th Infantry Divisions and the 2nd Armored Division, training in the United States, were chosen for the landing at Casablanca. The 33rd Fighter Group's orders to join the British forces in Egypt were abruptly changed, and they were slated to fly ashore as soon as landing fields in the Casablanca area were secured.

The fleet quickly assembled to carry the invading force was one of the strangest ever to put to sea. There was only one real American aircraft carrier, supplemented by a motley collection of escort carriers—tanker ships with aircraft decks hastily welded in place. There were small tankers from a Venezuelan lake that had been converted for landing tanks across beaches—and were to serve as the model for the thousands of tank landing ships to be produced during the war. There were even ferryboats snatched from their routes within the British Isles. They were ordered to fly large American flags as part of the effort to project the image of an all-American operation.

In late October, less than three months after the decision was made to land in North Africa, the ships involved in what was then the largest amphibious operation in history set sail from ports in the United States, Bermuda, and the British Isles. Altogether, there were about 220 ships carrying 107,305 men making their way across the Atlantic, all seeking to arrive off the shores of North Africa at the same moment, prepared to make landings at three points in the Casablanca area, seven—including the first American paratroop drop of the war—in the Oran area, and three at Algiers.

Maj. Gen. George S. Patton commanded the army forces slated to take Casablanca. He was well known within the army for his flamboyant ways and his mystical belief that he was destined to lead vast armies to victory on the battlefield. His picture had appeared on the cover of *Time* and he was becoming familiar to the American public as a dashing armor commander, even though his combat experience was limited to a brief period on the front lines during World War I.

Patton had his doubts, however, about the chances for success in the landings. At a meeting in Norfolk, Virginia, just before the convoys sailed, he gave one of his familiar colorful pep talks: "Never in history has the Navy landed an army at the planned time and place. If you land us anywhere within fifty miles of Fedala [near Casablanca] and within one week of D-Day, I'll go ahead and win . . . "

2

"Things Must Not Be Going So Good"

When crossing the Atlantic, the ships of the Western Task Force weathered a storm so severe some of the heavily laden ships came close to capsizing. And they passed through areas where attack from German submarines seemed almost certain. Fortune favored them, though, and after dark on November 7, 1942, they silently took up their positions off the west coast of Africa.

Pilots of the U.S. Army Air Force's 33rd Fighter Group, aboard the USS *Chenango,* arose well before dawn to prepare to fly ashore as soon as landing fields had been seized—or surrendered. On the crossing, they had spent hours on deck checking over their planes. Scores of propellers churned the air, and it was a dangerous business for a pilot to thread his way to his own plane among the 76 P-40 Warhawks lashed to the deck, wingtip to wingtip.

Dangerous—but essential. The Warhawk's Packard-built Rolls-Royce V-12 engine produced only 1,500 horsepower. Even at top efficiency, the P-40 was barely a match for the French Dewoitine fighters waiting ashore—and outclassed by the German Messerschmitts waiting further east. The pi-

Members of the 33rd Fighter Group posed in front of a P-40 fighter aboard the USS *Chenango* off the North African shore shortly before they were catapulted into the war. (Source: National Archives)

lots and their mechanics listened and tuned their engines, trying to coax every last bit of power from each cylinder.

When they were not working on their planes, the pilots checked over their six .50 caliber machine guns, which they kept wrapped in blankets under their bunks to protect them from the corrosive salt air. A curiously affectionate relationship developed between the humans and their inanimate weapons. "They are my buddies," one pilot wrote in his diary.

Hour after hour passed, and morning wore on into afternoon. Still, no order came to fly ashore. The men aboard the *Chenango*, miles out at sea, had only unfounded rumor and uninformed speculation as a guide to what was happening on the landing beaches.

The inevitable assumption arose. As the hours passed, Lt. James Reed pulled out his diary and noted: "Things must not be going so good."

If the pilots were frustrated by the delay and the lack of information, their feelings were only a shadow of the anxiety felt by General Patton, waiting impatiently aboard the cruiser USS *Augusta* for the signal that a beachhead had been secured and it was safe enough for him to move his headquarters ashore.

If one of the pilots were able to take off and climb high enough to view a 220-mile swath of the North African coast, this is what he would see:

In the center, troop and supply ships were clustered a few miles offshore from Fédala, a town twelve miles north of Casablanca. Protecting the ships were warships on the western and southern sides and a minefield on the north. This was the site of the largest landing—19,364 men—in Task Force Brushwood.

Eighty miles to the north, there was another cluster of ships near the town of Media. This was Task Force Goalpost, including ground crew members of the 33rd Fighter Group assigned to go ashore in the first wave of the landing. Their goal was the French airfield at Port-Lyautey (now Kunitra), a few miles inland from Media. In all, Task Force Goalpost was to put 9,075 men ashore.

One hundred and forty miles to the south were the ships of Task Force Blackstone, hovering off the city of Safi with 6,428 men and 108 tanks of the 2nd Armored Division.

Out at sea was the *Chenango,* part of a naval task force cruising in a 25-mile-long rectangle northwest of Casablanca. At the heart of the formation was the USS *Ranger,* the only genuine American aircraft carrier in the Atlantic, and the *Suwanee* and the *Sangamon,* two converted oil tankers similar to the *Chenango.* Their job was to provide air cover for the landings near Casablanca and Media. Another escort carrier, the *Santee,* hovered off the coast further south to provide support for the landing at Safi.

The frustrating thing for the pilots aboard the *Chenango*—and the commanders of the entire operation—was that the army planes were not expected to play a role in the invasion until there was a safe place ashore for them to land. In other words, they were out of play until the game had been won. Only if things went so badly that their firepower was abso-

Ships of the Operation Torch convoy approach the North African coast in November 1942. (Source: National Archives)

lutely essential to prevent a disaster would they be ordered into the air. If that happened, they could not return to the *Chenango*. The pilots were not trained, and the planes were not equipped, to land aboard a ship. If airfields ashore had not been secured, they would have to land wherever they could when their fuel ran low.

The battle for control of the air would have to be fought and won by the pilots from the *Ranger* and the three smaller flattops. At this point in the war, the United States was still desperately short of aircraft carriers. When the Japanese had struck Pearl Harbor eleven months before, the navy's carriers were absent. But since then the Japanese had sunk the *Lexington*, the *Yorktown*, the *Wasp*, and the *Hornet* and damaged the *Saratoga* and the *Enterprise*. With a full-scale naval war under way in the Pacific, it strained the Navy's resources to provide even the *Ranger* and the small escort carriers for the North African invasion.

Together, they were able to carry 172 planes of various types. But the French were known to have 168 planes based along the Atlantic coast. On paper, it seemed like an even match. But the French had an edge—not only the advantage of flying from unsinkable airfields, but also the skill of their pilots, many of whom had fought the Luftwaffe in the early days of the war. For most of the American navy pilots, this would be their first taste of combat.

Or would it? As the pilots of Fighter Squadrons 9 and 41 soared off from the *Ranger* at dawn, they were not authorized to fire their weapons or drop bombs. In this strange *maybe* kind of war, where political gamesmanship played as much of a role as military power, the orders up and down the 220 miles of the invasion front were to wait: If there was going to be any shooting, the French would have to shoot first.

In a "normal" landing, the beaches would be "softened up" by the 16-inch guns of the battleships in the invading force, the smaller guns of the cruisers and destroyers, and the bombs and machine guns of the carrier aircraft. But because the French might not resist the landing, not a shot was fired. If the French decided to fight, their coastal artillery, their machine guns along the shore, the big guns of the battleship *Jean Bart,* their submarines, all would be undisturbed until the moment they began to fire. The Allies would, essentially, be jumping into a snake pit, hoping the snakes would not strike.

Around midnight the men began to clamber down the cargo nets from the decks of the transport ships into the landing craft bobbing below. In the absence of a naval bombardment, their best hope for success lay in being able to land in darkness and establish themselves onshore before the French realized what was happening. But this very dependence on secrecy may have been self-defeating. The Allies had brought a few French officers in on the plans for the invasion, but they had not given them any details. One pro-Allied French general was alerted during the night that the landing was imminent. He put on his fanciest uniform and hurried down to the docks at Rabat, the capital of Morocco, to welcome the landing force. Before doing so, he warned his superior that a vast invasion fleet was lying offshore. But his boss remained unconvinced, assuming that if anything,

Ships of Operation Torch off the North African coast. (Source: National Archives)

he might be facing a small commando raid. The pro-Allied general might have been able to convince him not to resist this massive invasion force if he had actually made contact with the invaders. But he had not been told where the landings would occur. He waited in vain at Rabat for the sound of landing craft engines while the actual landings were taking place miles away.

The Central Force—First Day

Shortly after six o'clock in the morning machine guns, then the heavy coast artillery near Fédala, opened up. The French seem not to have known whether they were firing at Americans, British, or perhaps even Germans. At this point, they may not have cared. The French had been handily beaten by the Germans in 1940. The French—especially the navy, whose ships had been sunk by the British at Oran and Dakar—may simply have wanted to show that they could

The *Hugh L. Scott,* shown burning, was one of three ships sunk by
torpedoes from the German submarine U-*130,* off Fédala on the
evening of November 12, 1942. (Source: National Archives)

still put up a fight, whoever was out there. Whatever the mo-
tive, those first shots were enough to start the battle.

The signal that shooting had started flashed through the
fleet: "Batter up!" At 6:25 A.M., the *Ranger*'s pilots, circling
offshore, received the signal to begin their attack: "Play
ball!" They moved swiftly to catch French planes on the
ground and then to hit the *Jean Bart.* Even though the battleship had not been completed and could not leave port at
Casablanca, her 15-inch guns were still capable of causing
havoc among the ships clustered offshore.

Early in the day, French planes strafed and bombed the
beaches. But the American navy quickly won the battle for
air superiority—mostly by catching French planes on the
ground: 7 planes on one field, 14 on another, 7 more at
Port-Lyautey. In the biggest air battle, American Wildcats
tangled with 16 French planes near Casablanca. The Americans lost four planes but managed to shoot down eight of the
French fighters and knock out 14 more on the ground. Only
an occasional lone French plane was seen over the beaches
later in the day.

The carrier and its escorts, standing well out to sea, were not endangered by the *Jean Bart* or the shore guns. The artillery was directed at the transports and the destroyers and cruisers surrounding them, the most immediate threat.

The early stages of the landings, in the predawn darkness before the shooting started, went reasonably well. Even though the weather forecast the previous evening called for heavy seas along the coast, the surf turned out to be much calmer than normal. Many of the troops were able to land and take up positions onshore before their presence was detected.

Still, at this early stage in the war, everyone was inexperienced in such a landing. Understandably, many things went wrong and a number of men died before a single shot was fired. Transport ships had difficulty finding their proper places off the beaches; inexperienced coxswains got lost and landed troops on the wrong beaches; landing craft broke up on the shore; army troops moved swiftly inland instead of helping to unload the landing craft; French guns blasted the invasion beaches and targeted the ships offshore; men who were supposed to have landed in the dark did not make it to shore until well after dawn, when the shooting had started.

As men climbed down into their landing craft from the deck of one ship, the cargo net broke loose, throwing those on the net into the water. Heavily laden with weapons, backpacks, and ammunition, they drowned. Others perished a few feet from safety when they were thrown into the sea as their landing craft approached the beaches.

As the GIs said, sometimes things turned to shit. In at least one instance, this was literally true. Robert J. Klein, a mechanic in the 60th Fighter Squadron of the 33rd Fighter Group, was aboard the *Anne Arundel*, a troopship. In those days before environmental awareness, ships routinely discharged sewage at sea through pipes on the side of the vessel. Orders were given to close the toilets while troops were going over the side.

Klein recalls climbing down the net toward the landing craft bobbing below. One moment the boat seemed only a few feet away; the next it was far below. He was afraid he would be hurt if he jumped too soon, and afraid he would be crushed between the boat and the ship's side if he jumped too late. He managed to plop safely into the boat just as someone shouted orders to grab onto ropes dangling from a Jeep overhead and guide it into the boat.

Klein and the other soldiers didn't have much hope of controlling the movement of the Jeep, but they obeyed orders.

At that moment, someone decided to clean out the toilets.

"There I was with my group, waiting for the Jeep to be lowered, faces up to see what was happening, when this cascade came pouring down on us," Klein recalls. "We screamed and yelled, but the commander shouted back to us not to let go or else. Needless to say, we did hang on. The Jeep landed with a bang. I thought it would go through the small boat. We were lucky and were able to tie it down, as the sailors cast off, for they too were subjected to the filthy shower. As we pulled away, we could see another little boat taking our place alongside of the ship. The waste and water was still pouring out of the side of the ship and they had to tie up right under it."

By afternoon, the Americans had a firm foothold at Fédala, but there was a great deal of confusion among the troops. Patton came ashore and strode along the beaches, profanely shouting orders to straighten things out and get supplies and men moving inland.

By nightfall, nearly 8,000 men were ashore and the 3rd Division had taken all of its objectives for the first day. They controlled the town of Fédala and—most important—the harbor where men and equipment could be landed in preparation for the move on Casablanca itself.

Among the prisoners taken near Fédala were a number of French officers who were eager to see the shooting end so they could begin to fight *with* and not *against* their traditional friends, the Americans. They suggested approaches to Casablanca, and whom to contact in the effort to arrange an end to the fighting.

Officers were sent, under white flags, to try to convince the French commanders to end their resistance. But one of these messengers was shot dead by a trigger-happy French gunner. Another tried to contact a French army officer with whom he had gone to school. But he found himself in a navy, rather than an army, post and was coldly rebuffed.

The Northern Force—First Day

While the main thrust of the invasion was aimed at Fédala, just north of Casablanca, with more men than the other two landings combined, the attention of the pilots aboard the *Chenango* was centered on the fate of Task Force Goalpost, eighty miles to the north at Media. It was only after that landing had succeeded in taking the airport at Port-Lyautey that the army pilots would be able to fly ashore.

Geographically, this was the most difficult landing. At both Fédala and Safi, further to the south, the troops could move inland fairly easily as soon as they overcame resistance at the beaches. But the troops involved in Goalpost—members of the 9th Infantry Division and nearly 2,000 air force ground crewmen—faced a series of physical obstacles. The airfield lies in a curve of the Sebou River, which reaches the sea just north of the town of Media. The troops landing both north and south of the river mouth almost immediately ran into trouble, both from the French defenders and from the geography, with either the river or a large marshy area to be crossed before they could approach the airfield.

Shortly after the navy pilots received the word to "Play ball!" they bombed and strafed the field at Port-Lyautey and other fields at Rabat and Casablanca. But enough French planes remained to threaten the troops struggling ashore.

At 7:58 A.M., the *Ranger* recorded an urgent request for "fighter support to repel enemy planes strafing landing craft."

Pinned down on the beaches, the troops had been unable to capture the French coastal guns, as planned. The guns continued to fire—fire so intense that the ships lying offshore were ordered to move fifteen miles out to sea. That meant a 30-mile round trip for the landing craft bringing more men and equipment ashore.

Everything seemed to be going wrong, and the whole operation was falling far behind schedule. Instead of taking the airfield, as they had planned, late in the day the troops were still trying to get a firm hold along the beaches. They faced a stubborn defense, and the French artillery was still firing. And, most ominously, the sea was rising. The forecast: by dawn, 15-foot waves would be crashing on the shore. To complicate matters, communications between the ships and the shore had virtually collapsed when the ships pulled out to sea.

Pilots reported French reinforcements—including tanks—moving toward the beaches, almost certainly preparing for an attack at dawn on November 9. But because of the distance to the supply ships and the rough seas, the Americans were unable to add to the few tanks they had been able to bring ashore.

Any hope of making an end run by sending a ship up the Sebou with a force to take the airfield directly was thwarted by a boom across the river mouth. The boom was protected by the guns of the Kasba, a fort on the south side of the river near its mouth. Repeated efforts to remove the barrier had been foiled by the shore guns and the increasingly rough seas.

By nightfall of the first day, the troops in the northern invasion force were in a precarious position. The danger was very real that early the next day, they would be pushed back off of some of the beaches, not only suffering serious casualties, but endangering the whole operation.

The Southern Force—First Day

General Patton had decided in the early planning stages to avoid a landing at Casablanca itself and to try to take the city with a two-pronged attack from the north and south. The 3rd Division, which had landed at Fédala, was the northern prong. The other prong was the 2nd Armored Division, coming from the south.

While Fédala was only a dozen miles from Casablanca, Safi, the site chosen for the landing of the 2nd Armored, was 140 miles to the south. Safi was just a little fishing village, but it had a port where ships could tie up to take on cargoes of phosphate. It was the only port along the Moroccan coast—with the exception of Casablanca itself—with docks suitable for the landing of Sherman tanks. The assignment of Task Force Blackstone was to get ashore and dash northward toward Casablanca as quickly as possible.

Success at Safi hinged on a daring plan. Two stripped-down destroyers, each carrying 147 soldiers, steamed directly into the harbor. The *Bernadou* led the way. As the ship entered the harbor, crew members set off a spectacular fireworks display that filled the sky with a huge red-white-and-blue American flag. One French soldier said later that at the sight of the flag, he refrained from firing his 75 mm gun. But the rest of the gunners opened up—and the fireworks gave them a good view of what to shoot at. The *Bernadou* managed to blast her way in through a barrage of fire from the French defenders, scrape by a rocky outcropping, and nose onto a sandy beach. The second ship, the *Cole,* faced much less intense fire and managed to tie up at a dock. Within minutes, the troops from the two ships had swarmed ashore and taken over the port.

As we shall see, similar bold landings were attempted at Oran and Algiers with much less favorable results.

Offshore, troops preparing to come ashore encountered the same kind of confusion and delays that hampered the landings at Fédala and Media—with one spectacular addition. A truck being lowered from a cargo ship into a landing craft banged against the side of the ship. A gasoline can on the truck broke open, spraying gasoline onto the engine of the craft below. The landing craft exploded with a flash that was seen by crews of other ships in the area, who assumed they were under attack by French motor torpedo boats. When two American crash boats happened into the area, the ships turned their fire on them. Fortunately, they missed their targets. Crew members of the landing craft, blown overboard by the explosion, were rescued.

When considering the landing at Safi, the planners assumed the French planes based about 75 miles to the southeast at Marrakech would probably not interfere. The word was that the commander there had let it be known that if the Americans didn't attack him, he wouldn't attack them. Therefore, while the *Ranger* and two escort carriers were concentrated near the two northern landing sites, a single escort carrier, the *Santee,* was sent to support the Safi landing. The *Santee* was the newest of the converted tankers. It had put to sea on its shakedown cruise less than two months before the invasion, with men from the shipyard still aboard finishing their work. Many of the crew members had never been to sea before, and most of its pilots were barely out of flight school.

The combination of a newly converted ship and a green crew proved itself an unfortunate combination as soon as the *Santee* began training for the invasion in the waters off Bermuda in mid-October, just three weeks before the ship and crew were to go to war. On October 14, the first plane to be catapulted from the ship took to the air. Later the same day, a plane broke its landing gear on landing. The next day, a torpedo plane crashed off the port bow after a failure of the catapult mechanism. Two days later, a fighter crashed on the flight deck and ended up dangling over the side. The next week, a bomber crashed into the barrier on landing, and on the same day another plane fell while being loaded from a barge.

The most serious accident occurred on October 30 when a plane, while being catapulted, dropped a 325-pound depth bomb on the flight deck. The bomb rolled off the deck and exploded near the port bow of the ship. The entire vessel was severely shaken, a range finder and searchlight base were blown away, and the radar antennae were damaged.

Somehow the *Santee* came through all these accidents with only minor injuries to crew members and a few rivets sprung loose on the ship. But the damage to the ship's reputation was severe. By the time the vessel arrived off Morocco, the admiral in charge of the landing was concerned enough about the performance of the hard-luck carrier that he determined to use the seaplanes based on his battleships for jobs that had to be done.

Planes from the *Santee* did take to the air, but their bad luck continued. Of those on the first sortie, five couldn't find their way back to the carrier. One crashed in the sea, and the others landed at a French airfield and were captured. Another flight ran low on fuel and tried to land on the short runway at the small Safi airfield. Most of those planes were so badly damaged in landing that they could not take off again. The pilots were forced to abandon their planes and board small boats for the ride out to the *Santee*.

Through the initial stages of the invasion, the French air force remained on the ground. But then a pilot from the *Santee* reported that as he circled over the French airdrome at Marrakech, he was fired on by antiaircraft guns. He dropped two bombs, neither of which went off. The French, who had seemed content to sit out this phase of the war, took to the air early on the morning of November 9. Those on the ground at Safi heard the roar of many aircraft engines passing over the port above a low overcast. One plane found its way under the clouds and dropped a single bomb before being shot down. The bomb hit an ammunition storage area and set off a spectacular explosion, but caused far less damage than if the entire formation had unloaded on the dock area. The other planes flew away and were not seen or heard from again.

But they might come back. A squadron from *Santee* attacked the airdrome and destroyed twenty planes on the ground. On the way back, they found and struck a 40-truck convoy of French ground troops on their way from Marrakech to Safi.

By the afternoon of that second day, Maj. Gen. Ernest Harmon, the commander of the 2nd Armored Division, decided that the situation was well enough under control at Safi that he could set off on his dash for Casablanca. His tanks had been quickly unloaded from a ship that had followed the two destroyers into the harbor, and a small American unit had been sent to pin down the survivors of the French truck convoy that had managed to take up positions on a hill line east of Safi.

But there was a slight problem: Harmon's tanks could not carry enough fuel themselves to make the 140-mile trip, and there were not enough trucks ashore to bring fuel along with them. The navy came to the rescue. The *Bernadou* and the *Cole,* carrying ammunition and other supplies, set off for the north, accompanied by a fleet of small landing craft carrying five-gallon cans of gas to meet the armored column at the small port of Mazagan and supply it for the final 60-mile dash to Casablanca.

Harmon later recounted an incident along the way that seemed to capsulize this strange parody of a war.

At some point during the night, the column came to a halt. Harmon hurried forward to see what was wrong. In the middle of the road, standing beside a large rock, was an elderly man with a huge mustache, holding a lantern. On his chest was an array of combat ribbons and awards for bravery. The soldiers couldn't understand his French and were not sure how to deal with this roadblock.

Harmon, who had served in France in World War I and spoke French, asked the man why he was there. He replied that he had received orders to put up a barricade to slow the Americans' advance. His rock, he explained, was a *barricade symbolique,* since obviously he couldn't hope to stop an armored column.

Harmon assured him he had done well, shook his hand, and sent him back to his farmhouse nearby. But before he left, Harmon asked why he had been holding a lantern.

"He replied—with candor and simplicity—that he was hoping to provide enough light so my young Americans wouldn't injure themselves," Harmon recalled.

Center Force—Second Day

While the southern task force landing at Safi had gone remarkably well, both the northern and central task forces had run into trouble of different kinds.

In his planning for the attack, Patton had avoided a direct assault on Casablanca. But that still left the problem of the powerful French naval force in the harbor there. In addition to the *Jean Bart,* there were 11 submarines, 10 destroyers, and a light cruiser, plus a powerful shore battery that had an advantage in range over the American ships.

Almost as soon as the shooting started, the French navy began moving out to do battle. In the next few hours, a swirling naval clash took place in the waters outside the Casablanca harbor. Three French submarines were sunk in the harbor, and the uncompleted *Jean Bart* was not able to leave the port. But eight submarines, a light cruiser, and 10 destroyers sailed out to engage the American ships. In two major battles during the day, they were unable to penetrate into the area where the troop and cargo ships were concentrated. However, they managed to score hits on two cruisers, two destroyers, and the battleship *Massachusetts.*

Despite an impressive display of seamanship, the outgunned French fleet suffered more severe casualties. Four destroyers were sunk, eight submarines were sunk or missing, and the *Jean Bart,* the cruiser, and two destroyers were disabled.

Northern Force—Second Day

In the north, the threat came not from the sea, but from the land. Early on the morning of November 9, French infantry and tanks were spotted coming northward up the road from the capital city of Rabat, moving into position to block a major route from the invasion beaches to the airfield.

Seven tanks that might have been used for a thrust on the airport were hurried over to deal with this threat. As the tanks reached the Rabat road, the Americans saw a column of French tanks, with infantry, approaching. They counted fourteen to eighteen tanks, giving the French an advantage of at least two to one. Fortunately for the Americans, the approaching tanks were World War I–era Renaults with relatively small 37 mm guns.

The Americans pulled into position behind a slight rise in the earth and waited. Both sides found themselves at a disadvantage. The guns on the old French tanks were not powerful enough to penetrate the frontal armor of the American tanks, but the Americans had not had time to adjust their sights since coming ashore. Their aim was maddeningly inaccurate. Still, with the help of gunfire from an American cruiser offshore, they were able to break up the infantry formation, knock out four of the French tanks, and force the French to withdraw.

A short time later, the French regrouped and tried again. The battle went on for most of the day, gradually lessening in intensity and ending the immediate threat to the landing beaches.

Late that second night, a raiding party of sailors—the predecessors of today's Navy SEALs—set off up the Sebou in a small Higgins boat loaded with explosives. This was their second try at cutting the cable that blocked access to the river. The night before, they had been driven off by the machine guns and 75 mm cannons of the Kasba and almost drowned by the heavy seas at the mouth of the river. On this second attempt, they managed to avoid detection, clamped explosives to the cable, and cut it. But a smaller cable hanging above the water was apparently hooked to an alarm. As soon as they cut it, the guns above them opened up. Their boat took 13 hits, but none of the men was lost.

Cutting of the cable opened the way for a daring attempt to raid the airfield. The *Dallas*, a World War I–era destroyer, had been stripped of her masts and much of her superstructure to make her lighter and her draft as shallow as possible. With a raiding party of 75 soldiers, she started up the river in the dark at 4:00 A.M. It was raining heavily, and the rough seas near the mouth of the river made it difficult for the crew to steer. At one point, shortly after entering the river, the ship ran aground and had to use all of its power to break free. As the ship approached the point where the net had been cut, it became obvious that the barrier still blocked part of the river. As the *Dallas* rammed its way through, guns of the Kasba opened up.

The ship sailed on up the river, sometimes scraping bottom, working its way past two ships that had been scuttled in the channel. At 7:30 A.M., after a three-and-a-half-hour journey, she came to a stop beside the airfield, her keel cutting a groove in the soft mud. The raiders went ashore in small rubber boats to take over the airfield. Despite its ordeal by fire, no one aboard the *Dallas* was wounded.

Waiting anxiously aboard the *Chenango*, the pilots of the 33rd Fighter Group finally received word to take off and fly to the Port-Lyautey airfield.

Lieutenant John ("Jack") Bent was one of the most experienced pilots aboard the escort carrier. He had earned his license before the war and liked to fly. But being hurled into the air by a catapult was not something he looked forward to.

Back in the States, three of the senior pilots in his squadron had disappeared for a few days. When they came back, they wouldn't say where they had been. Bent and the other pilots later learned that they had gone off to see if a P-40 could be catapulted safely from a carrier. Navy planes are built much more ruggedly than army planes, to take the stresses of the catapult and landing on a carrier deck. The air force keeps its fighters as light as possible to give them an edge in a dogfight. Until someone tried it, no one was quite sure whether a catapult would get the plane up to flying speed, or tear the bottom out of it. The army pilots decided the P-40, with minor alterations to give the catapult something to hold onto, was strong enough to survive being catapulted.

Bent and the other pilots were sent to the navy yard at Philadelphia to learn to catapult.

"The first time I didn't mind because I didn't know what the hell the score was," Bent says. "The second time I didn't like it at all. The third time was for real. I disliked that very much, too."

Over the next two days, the 76 planes aboard the *Chenango* were hurled into the air for the short flight to the field at Port-Lyautey. Although there were other French airfields further south, the planes were stationed at Port-Lyautey because it was closest to the border with Spanish Morocco, from which the next danger might come as soon as the French stopped fighting.

Bent landed safely at Port Lyautey. But his brakes malfunctioned and he ran into a hole made by an American bomb during attacks on the field a few days before. Several other planes were also damaged on landing. One pilot ran off into the mud, flipped over, and was killed. Major William Momyer, the group commander and probably the most experienced pilot in the group, ran into a navy plane as he tried to maneuver his plane into a hangar.

By the time the planes came ashore, a cease-fire had been arranged. The French did not surrender. They continued to fly the French flag, kept their weapons, and maintained control over the native population. But the shooting stopped and many of the French immediately began preparing to join with the allies in resuming the fight against Germany. Word was sent to Harmon that his tanks would not be needed for an assault on Casablanca.

It was at this point, on Armistice Day, three days after the first landings and once peace of a sort had come to

French Morocco, that the Germans took a hand in the fighting—with devastating effect.

As the invasion force approached North Africa on November 2 and again on November 5 and 6, there were several reports of submarine contacts, and the ships changed course a number of times to throw off the aim of any nearby submarine skipper. No actual attacks occurred.

Berlin had been slow to recognize the size and purpose of the flotillas of warships, cargo ships, and transports moving toward North Africa. As the time for the landing approached, there were only seven German submarines in the area. But then 25 more were dispatched from bases in France or diverted from attacks on the North Atlantic convoys.

Late on the evening before the landing, as the carriers moved into position for the operation, lookouts aboard the *Ranger* reported a torpedo wake crossing the ship's bow from port to starboard (left to right.) It was the first solid evidence that a German submarine "wolf pack" had caught up to the carriers. Traveling at 14 knots during their Atlantic crossing, the ships presented difficult prey for the subs. But now, maneuvering offshore, they were tempting and vulnerable targets for the submarine skippers.

The *Ranger* itself could probably absorb a strike by one or more torpedoes and continue to stay afloat and even operate its aircraft. But the *Chenango* and the other two escort carriers were much more vulnerable than those aboard cared to think about. They were, after all, converted oil tankers, so in addition to the planes on their improvised carrier decks, they also carried a full load of fuel for the other ships in the fleet. A single torpedo could literally blow one of these ships out of the water. In fact, a few days later, the *Avenger,* an escort carrier flying the British flag, was torpedoed. Almost all hands were lost when it exploded and sank.

Over the next three days, the ships in the carrier group were forced to change course frequently in response to sightings of submarine periscopes and, often, torpedoes in the water. In response to each sighting, destroyers and planes from the carriers dashed to the scene to drop depth charges.

The threat to the carriers from submarines came to a head on the morning of November 10. The log of the *Ranger* gives this account of a frantic 3-hour-and-39-minute wolf-pack assault:

> 0630. Radar surface contact, port bow, 9000 yards. Disappeared from screen at 5000 yards.
>
> 0857. Submarine 700 yards on port beam—periscope sighted; sighted torpedo wakes approaching *Ranger*—the wakes passed close astern—periscope submerged. Two more torpedoes broached in our wake about 100 yards astern and narrowly missed *Cleveland* which was astern of *Ranger*. Executed emergency turn to the right and made emergency full speed ahead, maneuvering to escape attack. A fighter plane strafed the periscope.
>
> 0904. Destroyer reported submarine on our port quarter and dropped depth charges.
>
> 0906. *Cleveland* reported torpedo fired at her.
>
> 1009. Submarine periscope sighted 2000 yards on the starboard bow. Executed emergency left turn and made emergency full speed. Destroyer on starboard bow attacked with depth charges.

Perhaps because the ships in the carrier task group had the freedom to maneuver, not a single torpedo found its target. They were much more fortunate than the transport ships sitting at anchor off the invasion beaches.

When the cease-fire went into effect, the admiral in charge of the naval part of the operation had a difficult decision to make: Should he move the 15 ships that were still discharging cargo and men offshore into the Casablanca harbor, or should he save the spaces in the harbor for a fast convoy rapidly approaching from the west?

He opted to leave the transport ships where they were and keep the harbor open for the new arrivals. The captains of the ships were also ordered to remain anchored. This order made sure they wouldn't mill around and run into each other. But it also meant they had no chance to maneuver to avoid submarine attack.

At the very moment the admiral was making his fateful decision, the U-*173*, whose skipper was 27-year-old Hans-Adolph Schweichel, was working its way through the destroyers protecting the anchored ships. At 7:48 P.M., on November 11, a torpedo struck the *Joseph Hewes,* a transport ship. Less than 10 minutes later, the *Winooski,* a tanker, was struck, and so was the *Hambleton,* a destroyer waiting to be refueled by the tanker.

The *Hewes,* which had unloaded most of its cargo and men, sank within an hour, taking with it her captain; most of the crew members were picked up by other vessels. The *Winooski* was fortunate. The torpedo hit a fuel tank that had been filled with water. The ship was able to resume operations the following day. The *Hambleton* was more seriously damaged, with 20 men killed, missing, or fatally wounded. But the ship remained afloat and was towed into Casablanca for repairs.

That night, the question of whether to move the remaining ships into Casablanca was again considered. Again, the answer was to leave them where they were.

Although the American officers had no way to know it at the time, another U-boat, the U-*130,* was inching its way along the coast toward the invasion anchorage. Instead of trying to slip through the antisubmarine warfare screen, the commander, Ernst Kals, decided to slip inside the Allied minefield, scraping along through 60 feet of water—barely enough to cover his vessel. Just before 6:00 P.M. on the night of November 12, Kals fired four torpedoes from his bow tubes, then turned and shot another from the stern.

The transports *Edward Rutledge, Tasker H. Bliss,* and *Hugh L. Scott* were each struck, each burst into flames, and each sank. Of the more than 1,600 men aboard the doomed trio, 115 lost their lives. Most of the rest were rescued by landing craft that swarmed into the area. Much of the ships' cargo was lost.

Both Schweichel and Kals managed to get away. On the morning of November 15, the USS *Electra* was torpedoed while approaching Casablanca by Schweichel in U-*173.* The survivors were rescued, and the ship was beached near the city and later repaired.

By this time, the whole area was criss-crossed with destroyers and antisubmarine warfare aircraft. One German submarine skipper later reported he had had to remain sub-

merged for 20 hours, unable to surface to recharge his batteries or air out the boat. Another U-boat commander told
how he had been depth-charged and bombed for three days.
At one point, the crew listened, horrified, as a mine scraped
the entire length of the hull and then exploded, causing a
fuel leak that forced them to limp back to port in France.

Schweichel and his crew in the U-*173* had only five days
to enjoy their triumph. On November 16, three American
destroyers detected the submarine off Casablanca and sank
her with a barrage of eleven depth charges. The U-*130* got
away again, only to be sunk in the North Atlantic on March
12, 1943.

Meanwhile, thousands of American and British troops
had come ashore inside the Mediterranean on the Algerian
coast. The French resistance to the landings on the west
coast of Africa, brief as it was, had cost the American army
and navy 337 men killed, 637 wounded, 122 missing, and 71
captured. The Allies also did some damage to themselves—
strategically. The landings near Casablanca had involved the
most experienced regular army infantry divisions and the armored division most favored in men and equipment, thus
putting them farthest from Tunisia—where Rommel and his
Afrika Korps would soon be waiting.

3

Oran: Seize the Airfields

$\mathbf{B}$ ill Tuck, a Georgia farm boy, joined the army before the war, in 1939, when, as he says, "frankly, times were tough: three-cent cotton and five-cent cattle. I thought I'd go in for a few months and then go back to the farm. I liked it, so I stayed in."

Tuck's decision to stay in as an officer in the regular army gave him an insider's view as the army raced to field an armored force to match—and, hopefully, defeat—the panzer divisions that were leading the German blitzkrieg victories across the face of Europe and North Africa.

When he was assigned to the 1st Cavalry Regiment (Mechanized) at Fort Knox, Kentucky, barely two years before the United States entered the war, the regiment was at peacetime (Depression) strength.

"There were only four tank companies in the regiment, whereas nine companies were authorized in the tables of organization and equipment," Tuck recalls. "These companies were manned at no more than 75 percent of the authorized strength and this strength was further reduced by the daily requirements to furnish details of men to maintain Fort Knox, repairing roads, cutting roads and building maintenance. Training was very limited, consisting mainly of road marches and company tactics.

"When we met an enemy, we were taught to lay down a base of fire with one platoon behind a hill, in a defilade position, to fire at the enemy and hold him down while the other two platoons of the company assaulted, usually from a flanking position. Of course there was no live fire. There was no infantry at Fort Knox, so we never trained with infantry. And although there was one battalion of artillery there, we never trained with them. So during the first year I was there, I really spent most of my time doing housekeeping work for the post."

In the winter of 1940-41, the regiment formed the nucleus of the new 1st Armored Division, stationed at Fort Knox, Kentucky, which has since become home to the armored force. At the same time, the 2nd Armored Division was established at Fort Benning, Georgia, traditional home to the infantry. Old-line cavalry officers at Fort Riley, Kansas, continued to insist that the army would always have to rely on the horse for mobility—not noisy, gas-guzzling mechanical contraptions. At the same time, old-line infantry officers argued that the role of the tank was the same as it had been in World War I—to make holes in the enemy lines for the infantry and then get out of the way.

Maneuvers in Texas, Louisiana, and the Carolinas kept Tuck and his fledgling tankers constantly on the move through much of 1941. He recalls arriving back at Fort Knox on the evening of December 6, cleaning up the tanks, putting them away, and then dropping into bed exhausted, with orders that he not be disturbed for any reason. But he was awakened the next morning to hear the news that the Japanese had bombed Pearl Harbor and the United States was at war.

A few months later, the 1st Armored Division was sent to the British Isles, the second army unit and the first armored division to be deployed across the Atlantic. At that time, in the spring of 1942, the plan was to build up forces in the British Isles and continue their training for an eventual landing in northern France. It did not matter that the 2nd Armored Division, still back in the states, had been issued new radios while the 1st Armored went overseas with radios adapted from those used by the Connecticut State

Police. The 1st Armored and the 34th Infantry Division, which had arrived in Ireland even earlier, would, everyone assumed, have plenty of time to train and be supplied with first-rate new equipment.

But then, as Tuck recalls it, his boss, Lt. Col. John Waters (who happened to be married to General Patton's daughter), ordered him to meet him at a location off their training base. He gave him directions and insisted that he tell no one where he was going.

When he arrived, Waters was there with a tall, distinguished-looking British officer. Waters introduced them: "Captain Tuck, I'd like you to meet Lord Louis Mountbatten."

Mountbatten, a great-grandson of Queen Victoria, had pursued a career as a naval officer, rising to command of an aircraft carrier. At this point in 1942, he was Chief of Combined Operations, which meant that he was in charge of the British commandos.

In their meeting with Mountbatten, Tuck and Waters became two of the first American combat commanders to learn that they had only a few weeks to prepare to land in North Africa, rather than nearly a year to prepare for the invasion of France, and that they would most likely be among the first Americans to go into combat against the German army.

Mountbatten gave them the broad picture of the invasion plan: the Western Task Force, under Patton, landing on the west coast of Africa near Casablanca; the Center Task Force, under Maj. Gen. Lloyd Fredendall, landing near Oran, on the Mediterranean coast of Algeria; and the Eastern Task Force, under Maj. Gen. Charles Ryder, commander of the 34th Infantry Division, landing at Algiers, further east in Algeria.

He pointed to Oran. This was where elements of the 1st Armored Division would land, at two points separated by some 50 miles, east and west of the city. Their first goal, he explained, was not the city itself but two airfields just south of the city, Tafaraoui and La Sénia. There were believed to be nearly a hundred French planes on those two fields and at a seaplane base at Arzew. The British would have one true aircraft carrier and two escort carriers with 57 planes to support the landing. Until the airfields were in Allied hands, the French would have air superiority over the landing beaches.

Mountbatten explained the crucial role Waters and Tuck would play in this effort. Their light tanks would be loaded on landing craft converted from tankers used on a lake in Venezuela. They could nose up onto the sand and deliver the tanks onto the beach, ready for a dash to the Tafaraoui airfield. The bulkier medium tanks were deep in the holds of transport ships and could not be unloaded until a port was secured. Waters and Tuck, with their light tanks, would be on the way to Tafaraoui—and, if everything went smoothly, would have it under control—while the new and bigger Sherman medium tanks were still being extracted from the cargo ships.

Tuck, by now a professional soldier, was comfortable with the plan. He was confident his light M-3 tanks, sporting a relatively small 37 mm gun, and the tactics he had practiced over and over in the months before the war would get the job done. He didn't dream how much he would soon learn about the defects of his tanks and the tactics he had practiced so earnestly.

Although Waters, Tuck, and the other tankers of the 1st Armored Division would play a crucial role in the invasion, some two-thirds of the division, including its commander, Maj. Gen. Orlando Ward, would remain back in England until the Algerian ports had been secured.

The portion of the division assigned to the operation was known as Combat Command B. It was headed by Brig. Gen. Lunsford E. Oliver, who would be in charge of the units landing east of Oran. His deputy, Col. Paul McD. Robinett, was in charge of the units landing west of the city. Robinett was a skilled horseman from the army's old cavalry. He had been a member of the Army Equestrian Team at the 1924 Olympics in Paris and trained General Patton in horsemanship. Now, as a tanker, rather than a horseman, he would begin an odyssey that would place him at virtually every critical point in the coming six months of battle for control of North Africa.

The bulk of the invading force would be made up of members of the 1st Infantry Division, the Big Red One, a unit very different from the similarly named 1st Armored Division, with whom they would cooperate closely on this operation and later in the fighting in Tunisia. The 1st Infantry was a regular army unit led by two of the most flamboyant American military leaders to emerge during the war, its commander Maj. Gen. Terry de la Mesa Allen, a close friend of both Eisenhower and Patton; and his deputy, Brig. Gen. Theodore Roosevelt Jr., the son of the 26th president, a writer, an explorer, a World War I hero, and a gregarious man much like his father. He claimed that every soldier in the division knew his voice. One night while standing with Maj. Gen. Omar Bradley beside a road where a blacked-out convoy was moving by, he proved it by shouting: "Hey, what outfit is that?" Out of the dark came the immediate response: "Company C of the Eighteenth Infantry, General Roosevelt."

Both Allen and Roosevelt were skilled at motivating their soldiers, but neither was a strict disciplinarian of the kind that an infantry outfit probably needs, at least as deputy commander. The flavor of their leadership was perhaps summed up in the general instructions Allen gave as the division prepared to go into combat: "Nothing in Hell must stop the 1st Division."

The 1st Infantry, along with the 1st Armored's Combat Command B, would land at Arzew, a small city with a good port about 25 miles east of Oran, and on beaches west of Oran. Then they would assault the primary target in a pincer movement.

Meanwhile, three other smaller, specialized units were training for their role in the North African campaign. One of the units was designated as the 2nd Battalion of the 503rd Parachute Infantry. Actually, the battalion was the only one in the regiment, which was sometimes referred to as the 503rd Parachute Infantry Battalion. Shortly after landing in North Africa, the name was changed to the 509th Parachute Infantry, which still consisted of the single battalion. This change in names succeeded in confusing the Germans, who later tortured a captured officer in an attempt to learn what had happened to the 503rd.

As the parachutists trained in the British Isles, they were not told where they were going; only a few of the top brass knew. The best guess pointed them toward Norway, which

Maj. Gen. Terry de la Mesa Allen, commander of the 1st Infantry Division, is shown with his staff in November 1942. (Source: National Archives)

had been under German occupation for two years. Only shortly before they took off did most of them learn their real goal and the details of their risky mission: They would fly all the way from England, nonstop, and make the first assault, ever, by American paratroops. Their target was the same as that assigned to Tuck: the critical airbase at Tafaraoui, plus the field at La Sénia. If the former had been taken by the time they got there, they would land and secure the area. If the French were still in control, they would parachute onto the field and attempt to seize it. If the field were still in hostile hands when the time came to take off, they would receive a coded signal telling them to leave early enough to make their jump in the dark. If the field were already in American hands, they would receive no message and should plan to land at the field in daylight.

While the paratroops focused on the Tafaraoui airfield, a brand-new volunteer outfit drawn largely from the 34th Infantry Division, with a few from the 1st Armored, was tapped to be the first ashore to take out the big French coastal guns that posed a mortal threat to the invasion fleet. This was the 1st Ranger Battalion, known more familiarly as Darby's Rangers, named for Maj. William O. Darby. A 31-year-old native of Fort Smith, Arkansas, Darby graduated from West Point in 1933 and spent the next eight years at Fort Bliss, Texas, in the army's only unit of horse artillery. He went overseas as assistant to the commander of the 34th Infantry Division but was soon selected to create his own specialized battalion.

The Rangers were the American equivalent of the British Commandos, who had already made a name for themselves in daring raids against German targets. Training for the Rangers, under veteran British Commandos, was rigorous, but brief. Unlike today's commando-type units, such as the Army's Special Forces and the Navy SEALs, who spend a year or more in training before they are considered ready for combat, Darby's men had less than five months from the time the new 575-man battalion was activated on June 19 until they were to go ashore on a hostile beach. Despite their later gung-ho reputation, many of those who volunteered for the Rangers were not looking for action and glory.

Most were probably like Carl H. Lehmann, who was building Chevrolets at a plant in Baltimore when he was drafted just before Pearl Harbor. After basic training, he was assigned as a private to the 34th Division. He felt like a stranger, out of place in an outfit where most of the men were from the same little towns back in Iowa and many had been friends back home.

"That's why I joined the Rangers," Lehmann says. "They said: 'Fall out and police up. Noncoms to the rear.' And then I'm all by myself picking up all the butts because everybody with one stripe was a noncom. So I figured I'd get out of that goddamn National Guard unit."

Two-thirds of the Ranger battalion, under Darby, would land outside Arzew and take out the Batterie du Nord, on a hill overlooking the harbor. The other Rangers, under Darby's executive officer, Maj. Herman Dammer, would land at Arzew itself and take out the smaller Fort de la Point.

The third specialized part of the Oran invasion plan was almost a carbon copy of the landing on the Atlantic coast at

Safi, where two stripped-down destroyers were assigned to shoot their way right into the port to deliver an infantry team to take control before the facilities could be sabotaged. In this case, the *Hartland* and the *Walney,* two British corvettes—U.S. Coast Guard cutters that had been given to the British before the United States entered the war—were assigned to slip into the harbor at Oran as the landing was getting under way, carrying two infantry companies from the 1st Armored Division.

This was one of the most controversial elements in the whole invasion plan, bitterly opposed by senior American officers. In a message to Eisenhower three weeks before the invasion, Rear Adm. A. C. Bennett, an amphibious force commander, warned that the plan was "suicidal" and predicted that "this small force will be wiped out." General Ward, the commander of the 1st Armored Division, spoke out against the plan on at least two occasions. But then, believing that "when a decision has been made it must of necessity be carried out as one's own," he saw the battalion off, "wishing them good luck and God speed, behind what I hoped was a cheerful and confident mien."

The convoys carrying the forces for both the Oran and Algiers landings sailed from British ports on October 26 and November 1 and swung far out into the Atlantic before turning toward the southeast and heading toward Gibraltar. Darby's Rangers were aboard H.M.S. *Ulster Monarch, Royal Scotsman,* and *Royal Ulsterman.* To call them "His Majesty's Ships" was really pretentious. They were actually three ferryboats taken from the Glasgow-Belfast run and probably should not have been going to war at all, although they were large ships—a city block long—fully capable of handling the often rough water of the Irish Sea. After passing through the straits into the Mediterranean, the three ferryboats had to circle for three nervous days, waiting for the rest of the convoy, before heading on to the east.

Lehmann saw Gibraltar and recognized it instantly. "It looked just like the rock on my insurance policy," he recalled.

On the evening of November 7, the convoy sailed past Oran in the hope that the Germans would think it was another group of supply ships trying to break through to resupply allied forces on the island of Malta. Then, after dark, the ships carrying the troops for the Oran landing turned back and headed toward their actual destination.

The Rangers Attack

The Ranger officers studied their target on a plaster of paris mockup of the Arzew area. The other Rangers pored over maps and photographs until they knew the area well enough to find their way through the dark.

About midnight, four companies of Rangers in Darby's force made their way quietly across the decks of the *Ulster Monarch* and the *Royal Ulsterman* and climbed into five landing craft hanging from davits on each ship. Then, at a signal, they were lowered into the water. It was a much better way to go to war than having to climb down cargo nets to small craft far below. But there was one hitch. The lines on one davit got caught, tipping a landing craft over and dumping occupants and its contents into the water. The men were quickly hauled aboard the other boats. But the loss of that one craft would cause big problems later.

Darby's men landed without opposition on a beach north of the town of Arzew and set out on a four-mile hike to their objective: a gun emplacement and a fort overlooking the town. The four-gun battery, capable of hurling shells five miles out to sea, posed a serious threat to the fleet offshore if it was not silenced.

Dammer, leading two companies from the *Royal Scotsman*, brought his men ashore in boats equipped with a ski-like attachment to enable them to jump over a cable that was sometimes stretched across the entrance to the port. But the cable was not in place. The boats sailed serenely into the harbor, pulled up at the dock, and dropped their landing ramps. As the Rangers stormed ashore, they discovered one vital gap in their intelligence. They found the sloping ramp leading up to the dock covered with slime. As they struggled up through the muck, their cursing should have been enough to alert the enemy. Fortunately, it didn't.

As they cut through barbed wire protecting the fort, a French sentry called out to ask who was there. A French-speaking Ranger replied, and the sentry wandered down for a closer look. He was hit from behind and knocked out before he could give the alarm. The Rangers dashed through the opening in the wire, jumped over a low wall, and, after firing only a few shots, took possession of the guns and rounded up about 60 prisoners. The whole operation had taken only about 15 minutes.

As soon as they had secured the dock area, Dammer's men took up defensive positions near a cemetery. Clarence W. Eineichner looked around. "We were so well rehearsed," he says, "I almost felt like I had been there before."

Suddenly a machine gun began to fire at them. Carl Lehmann dropped to the ground.

"I hit the dirt in front of this tombstone," he recalls. "And then there was another burst that straddled me. That convinced me I was on the wrong side of the tombstone."

Lehmann scooted around to the other side of the monument. As he lay there, he looked up and saw a picture of a French soldier attached to the stone. Under the man's name was the legend *Morte de Verdun*. He was one of the thousands killed in the bloodiest siege of World War I.

The machine gun, which was a long distance away, let off a few desultory rounds and then ceased firing.

Dammer got on the radio and reported to Darby, who was still two miles from his objective, that he had completed his assignment. Darby thought he sensed a note of one-up-manship in Dammer's tone.

Darby's task, as it turned out, was more difficult. As his men approached the fort, one company, with four 81 mm mortars, set up in a hollow that had been picked out from aerial photos. The three rifle companies crept forward until they found their way blocked by a tangle of barbed wire 8 feet high and 14 feet deep. As quietly as possible, they snipped the wires and twisted them aside. It was not until they had reached the last strand of wire that machine guns opened up. Darby signaled for his men to pull back while he sent one platoon to capture a lookout tower.

As soon as the tower was taken, Darby ordered the mortar company to fire one salvo. They purposely aimed long to avoid hitting their fellow Rangers. As the shells burst, the lookout in the tower corrected the aim. The next barrage brought 80 shells crashing down on the French positions. Darby later reported that the machine guns stopped firing "as if someone had pulled a switch."

The Rangers dashed through the wire, vaulted over a parapet, and jammed Bangalore torpedoes in the muzzles of the big guns. At the same time, another group of Rangers shot their way through the main entrance of the battery. The French defenders, mistaking the mortar rounds for aerial bombs, had retreated into an underground bunker. They refused a shouted request, in French, to come out, so a torpedo was pushed down the ventilator shaft. Moments later, 60 men emerged, their hands in the air. The battle for Batterie du Nord and Fort de la Pointe was over. The cost to the Rangers had been two men killed and eight wounded.

Darby's Rangers had secured the guns and the fort above the town by 4:00 A.M. and they had vital information for Fredendall, waiting offshore to send in the armor and infantry. Under the plan, as soon as the guns were in American control, the Rangers would radio news of their success and confirm the message by firing four green Very lights followed by four white star shells. (*Very lights* are colored flares fired from a special pistol invented by E. W. Very, an American ordnance expert.) But both the long-range radio and the white rockets had been stored in the landing craft that had spilled its occupants and its contents into the ocean. The rockets were at the bottom of the Mediterranean—along with a radio powerful enough to contact the fleet offshore.

The Rangers at Batterie du Nord fired off a dazzling display of green lights. Fredendall and Allen saw the lights and then waited, puzzled, for the white star shells that were supposed to confirm that the Rangers had completed their mission. It was not until two and a half hours later that Allen received confirmation, by a radio message transmitted by a British forward observer party through a British destroyer, that Darby had taken the coastal guns. But by that time, assuming that the green flares were a signal for success, he had dispatched his troops toward the shore. By dawn, two regimental combat teams from Allen's 1st Infantry Division were firmly ashore.

The *Hartland* and the *Walney* Attack

About the same time Darby's Rangers were making their foray against the defenses at Arzew, the *Hartland* and the *Walney* cruised through the darkness for their dash into the harbor at Oran.

Their maps showed a harbor stretching from west to east, protected on the seaward side by a 3,000-foot-long breakwater. The eastern end of this narrow anchorage was nearly enclosed by a jetty that left only a 200-yard-wide gap. And across this gap was a floating boom that the leading ship would have to crack through.

The entire harbor was covered by big coastal defense guns, field artillery, machine guns, and the weapons of a number of French ships in the harbor. Realistically, the only chance that these two converted Coast Guard cutters, with their thin skins and light armament, had was to surprise the defenders.

But as they approached the harbor, the *Walney* in the lead, they could hear sirens ashore. Then the lights went out. It was an unmistakable sign that their arrival would not be a surprise. Even before she reached the boom across the harbor entrance, the *Walney* came under heavy fire. Her skipper swung around in a circle and picked up speed to enter the harbor at full speed.

He brushed past the boom and slowed for the passage toward the other end of the harbor. Suddenly the guns ashore shifted to the *Hartland*, following close behind. The *Walney* cruised slowly to the west in eerie silence. A small landing party slipped into three canoes and began paddling for the shore. Suddenly, a French destroyer loomed out of the darkness, heading directly toward the small cutter. His mission already in deep trouble, the skipper of the *Walney* tried to ram the destroyer but just missed. As the destroyer scraped past, it raked the *Walney* at point-blank range, killing and wounding many of the soldiers and crew. As the *Walney* proceeded into the western end of the harbor, it came under even more intense bombardment. Fires sprang up and ammunition began to explode. Finally, the order to abandon ship was shouted from man to man, and those still able to move clambered off the doomed vessel. She ended up a burning, semi-submerged wreck near the western end of the harbor. The survivors huddled ashore, waiting for other units to secure the city.

Even before the *Hartland* entered the harbor, her captain had been wounded in one eye by a shell fragment. The ship went off course and slammed into the jetty, blocking the entrance to the harbor. Despite the heavy fire he was receiving, the skipper ordered another attempt to enter the anchorage. This time, the tiny ship slipped through, only to come under the guns of a French destroyer. Fires erupted at several points and the ship drifted helplessly out of control. The survivors climbed down into two motor launches and escaped out to sea.

Admiral Bennett had been right on the mark in his warning to Eisenhower. This had been a suicide mission. The 6th Armored Infantry had 393 men aboard the two vessels. Of those, 189 were killed and 157 wounded. The navy lost five killed and seven wounded and the Royal Navy, which provided most of the crew members, lost 113 killed and 86 wounded.

This futile effort was by far the costliest of the entire Oran operation. And yet it contributed nothing at all to the eventual success of the landings.

The Paratroops Take Off

For the paratroopers, preparations for their first combat mission began the day before the invasion as they gathered at two airfields, St. Eval and Prelernack, at Land's End on the southern tip of England. They had trained for the "war plan," which called for them to jump and seize both the Tafaraoui and La Sénia airfields. If the war plan was in effect, they would receive the code phrase "Advance Alexis" by

4:30 P.M. from Eisenhower's headquarters on Gibraltar. If they didn't receive the signal, it meant the French would not resist their landing—and might even welcome them. The time for the war plan message came and went without word. They switched to the "peace plan," which called for arrival at the airfields at dawn instead of in the dark. The men were thus in a fairly relaxed mood as they took their places in the 39 twin-engined C-47 transport planes. Takeoff began at 9:30 P.M., and by 10:00 P.M. all the planes were in the air.

Almost as soon as they took off, things began to go wrong. Heavy fog forced the pilots to break up their formations and spread out to avoid running into each other. The men ate a late dinner and then settled down to sleep as well as they could in the canvas seats attached to the sides of the planes.

By dawn, the largest formation consisted of only half a dozen planes. The crews of more than half of the planes didn't know where they were. Three planes ran low on fuel and landed in Spanish Morocco. The men were interned. One plane, with engine trouble, landed at Gibraltar. Another reached La Sénia and landed. Those men were imprisoned.

As other planes reached the two airfields, they were fired at by antiaircraft guns and French fighters. They swung away from the airfields and landed in the Sebkra, a dry lake west of Oran.

Colonel Edson D. Raff, the battalion commander, approached the dry lake in a formation of five planes. Circling the area, he saw that some of the planes had already landed, but were under fire from a column of armored vehicles on a nearby road. Raff ordered the men in the five planes accompanying him to jump and try to stop the shelling. The troops gathered at a jump zone picked out by Raff and sneaked up on the armored column, only to discover that it was made up of American vehicles with large white stars on their sides. Americans had been firing on Americans. Fortunately, they hadn't done any harm.

Raff assembled his men and set off to march toward the airfields on foot. The men were tired from the long flight from England and were wearing winter clothing with heavy underwear. Although the Sebkra was supposed to be a dry lake bed, parts of it still contained enough water to form a layer of sticky mud. One of the men called the march in the desert heat one of the toughest ever made by the battalion.

The Landings at Arzew

By the time the paratroops had begun to sort themselves out, men and equipment were streaming ashore at Arzew and at beaches west of Oran.

As soon as his light tanks were ashore, Bill Tuck and his company formed a flying column and raced toward Tafaraoui on a road that looped down to the south of Oran.

"We got on the field without any resistance," Tuck recalls. "We're heading across it and they started shooting at us with antiaircraft guns. Luckily, they were made to shoot in the air and they couldn't depress them enough to get at us. We had a lot of small arms fire and we were strafed and bombed by French planes. It was inconsequential. The action there only lasted an hour and it was not very intense. We considered it intense at the time. We were there all by ourselves, my company. We had one antitank platoon attached to us but that's all. At that time, we hadn't trained to have infantry with us. We didn't even know anything about that. We had a lot to learn."

A short time later, the rest of Colonel Waters's tank battalion arrived. By then, the action in that sector was pretty well over.

Raff's paratroops, emerging from the mud of the Sebkra onto a hard surface road, intercepted a radio message in which Waters reported that his forces had taken Tafaraoui.

The battle for Oran itself was far from over, however. Allen's 1st Infantry Division ran into unexpectedly stiff resistance at St. Cloud, a little town southeast of Oran, as his infantry moved on Oran after landing at Arzew. By 9:00 A.M., one battalion found itself in a bruising battle for the town, taking heavy casualties. A second battalion joined the battle, but at midnight they were still bogged down. The regiment's third battalion arrived during the night. The town was hit by a 15-minute artillery barrage and then, at 7:00 A.M., the three battalions attacked, only to be thrown back.

Allen, who had been occupied several miles away, hurried to the scene. The regimental commander had already asked for a barrage by all of the division's available artillery to prepare for another assault at 2:30 P.M. Allen looked over the situation and noted that there were many civilians, including hundreds of women and children, trapped in the town. He canceled the barrage. "We don't need the damned place anyway," he said. He ordered the regimental commander to leave one battalion to pin down the defenders in St. Cloud and then send the other two battalions around the town, to the north and south, toward Oran. He also ordered that all movements be made in the dark. This was the beginning of a technique the 1st Division used effectively on a number of occasions later in the war: While the enemy hunkered down for the night, the Big Red One moved or struck in the dark.

A constant worry during the entire landing operation was the possibility that French reinforcements would be able to arrive from nearby forts before the Americans had built up enough strength to hold their ground.

On the day after the landing, Tuck's tank company was in reserve, resting at the Tafaraoui airfield, when a radio message reported a column of French Foreign Legion tanks approaching from the south. Tuck and his men hurried out to meet them.

Tuck's light tanks were small, but he had a potent force: three platoons of five tanks each. He met the French tanks at the edge of a tiny village. The French had had time to camouflage themselves and were waiting among the trees atop a small hill about 500 yards away across an open field.

Tuck followed a textbook tactic that was the standard American army approach to such a situation at that time. He had practiced it many times over the last three years. While one platoon laid down a base of fire, the other two platoons attacked from the right.

The French World War I–era Renault tanks were no match for Tuck's M-3s. The shells from the American 37 mm guns penetrated the French armor, but the French shells bounced off the American tanks. The battle ended quickly with the virtual annihilation of the French force.

But Tuck was not pleased with himself. As soon as he gave the order to attack, he realized that he had made a potentially fatal mistake. "Boy, if those guns had been effective, they would have wiped us all out," he says. "I never did that again."

He resolved to fight smarter in the future. If he faced a situation like that again, he would use smoke and maneuver and call for artillery rather than dashing headlong across an open field into the muzzles of the enemy guns. He would soon have a chance to try his hand against tanks much more formidable than armor left over from the last war. In those later battles, the commander of the French unit defeated by Tuck formed a new unit equipped with American tanks and fought skillfully with the allies against the Germans in Tunisia.

The Landings West of Oran

Robinett, with about a third of Combat Command B, was in charge of the landings on two beaches about 25 miles west of Oran. Because he would be separated by almost 50 miles from General Oliver and the remainder of Combat Command B, Robinett was ordered to report directly to Fredendall, in charge of the whole operation on a ship offshore. This was to set a pattern for much of the North African campaign in which Robinett, who later took over Combat Command B, reported directly to Fredendall instead of his own division commander, almost as though he were running his own little independent division.

The remainder of the 1st Infantry Division, under Roosevelt, landed at nearby beaches, also to the west of Oran. Together, the elements of the armored and infantry divisions moved toward Oran and the airfields to its south.

The most tenacious opposition to the landings came on the other side of Oran where the French, seeking to block Allen and his infantrymen, fought more tenaciously and longer than at any of the other landing sites in Morocco and Algiers.

On the third day, Allen prepared for an air and artillery barrage before driving into the city from the east. But Waters, riding with Tuck's tankers, entered the city from the south and paraded through the center of town, past the cathedral, in a show of force. They met little resistance, except for a number of snipers. Several of the tanks ran out of gas because they had outrun their fuel supplies. Several of them reached the eastern edge of the city in time to warn Allen to call off his barrage and attack. The French soon agreed to an armistice.

The Americans, going into combat for the first time, quickly learned that war, among other things, can often be tedious, even boring. Men tend to remember the moments of fear, and also humorous incidents, standing out against such a background.

Edmund M. Paige, a rifleman in the 1st Infantry Division, recalls trying to sleep beside the road on the evening of the first day ashore. From time to time he was awakened by other soldiers trading the challenge for the day, "Hi-yo, Silver!" followed by the response, "Away!" The next day, he passed an old Algerian riding down the road on a donkey, greeting everyone he passed with a hearty "Hi-yo, Silver!"

Paige had not yet been in combat, but he was worried about his rifle: the front sight was broken. As he walked down the road, he saw the body of an American soldier lying in a ditch beside the road, his rifle lying beside him. Paige stepped down into the ditch and exchanged rifles with the dead man.

A few minutes later, his formation reached another unit that had set up its position along the road. Paige asked why no one had recovered the body they had just passed.

"We couldn't get near him," one of the soldiers said. "He was lying across a high-tension wire. Didn't you notice that when you passed by?"

Paige glanced down at his new rifle and shuddered.

The shooting had barely stopped when American salvage crews moved in to begin cleaning up the Oran harbor. They found a mess awaiting them. The hulks of the partially submerged *Walney* and *Hartland* still smoldered. And because of the failure to seize the port early on the morning of the invasion, French crews had had time to scuttle 23 of their ships. All this wreckage, along with three large "floating" dry docks that were no longer afloat, blocked the harbor. The salvage crews, with the full cooperation of the French, quickly opened a 20-foot-wide corridor through the harbor, but it would be two months before the port was opened to normal traffic.

Oran, with a large harbor at the city itself and two major ports at Mers El Kebir to the west of the city and Arzew to the east, quickly became the most important staging area for the next phase of the war, the effort to seize Tunisia before the Germans could fly in enough troops and planes to hold it. Now that the port was secure, the 1st Armored Division's Combat Command B, still operating independently from the rest of the division, which was not due to arrive from England until the port had been secured, was to be headed in the direction of Tunisia within days.

4

Landing at Algiers

Sergeant Milo Green later earned a Silver Star for removing wounded men from the battlefield, but his most vivid memory of the Allied landings at Algiers was watching other men go into combat.

Green, who wrote a series of chatty reports under the heading of "Brickbats," for the newspapers of two small towns in southwestern Iowa—the *Villisca Review* and the *Adams County Free Press* of Corning—gave this account for the readers back home of how he sat on the top deck of a troopship off Algiers early on the morning of November 8 and watched British—and a few American—commandos come trooping up the stairs from their quarters down below:

> Their be-smeared faces framed with olive green, steel helmets have an appearance not unlike Al Jolson made up for a turn of Mammy songs. In their eyes were the mingled emotions and expressions of anticipation, apprehension, confidence, and just a wee bit of fear. They knew well that theirs was a mission of great danger and tremendous responsibility.

In many ways, the landing at Algiers was a carbon copy of the landings at Casablanca and Oran: the commandos would come ashore early to take out the coastal guns; troops would avoid the city of Algiers itself and instead land to the east and west before moving in to encircle and capture the city; and two destroyers would crash through the barrier at the entrance to the Algiers harbor to land troops and try to prevent sabotage of the port.

The landing at Algiers was also, in many ways, the most critical of the three landings being carried out on November 8. Algiers was the administrative headquarters for the French in North Africa, and important leaders were known to be there that day. Success in the landing could lead to a quick end to French resistance all the way across North Africa, as well as give the allies their closest port and airfields to the critical future battleground in Tunisia.

Many of the troops waiting to go ashore at Algiers were, like Milo Green, from a cluster of small towns in southwestern Iowa—Atlantic, Council Bluffs, Glenwood, Red Oak, Villisca, Shenandoah, Clarinda, and Corning—which had contributed companies to the 34th Division's 168th Infantry Regiment. The 168th, whose history could be traced back to the Civil War and through the Spanish American War, the Philippine insurrection, the border conflict with Mexico in 1916, and World War I, formed the core of a force specially tailored for the American landings at Algiers. Called the 168th Regimental Combat Team, it represented only about a third of the 34th Division. But it was fleshed out with the 175th Field Artillery Battalion plus small medical, engineer, and military police units.

The remainder of the division stayed in the British Isles for the time being. Although the army has a formula for dividing up its forces—building from squad, platoon, company, battalion, regiment, division, and corps to army and even to group of armies—it is not uncommon for a combat team to be created out of various units, not even necessarily from the same division, for a special task. We will see much more of this in the ensuing battles in Tunisia.

In its few months in Ireland and Scotland, the Red Bull Division, as it called itself, had gone through a rapid transformation. When the division was called to active duty in February 1941, many of its officers were veterans of World War I who had continued to serve their country by remaining in the National Guard during the lean peacetime years. But they were now in their forties or older, content to ride around in staff cars while the men marched. By the time the 168th was sent off to combat, most of the old-timers were gone.

The division commander already had been replaced once and was replaced again while they were in the British Isles. The man who would be in command of the Algiers landing and lead the division into combat was Maj. Gen. Charles W. "Doc" Ryder. He was a tall, lanky, hump-shouldered regular army officer. The men were quick to notice his striking resemblance to Abraham Lincoln. Ryder was one of that small group of officers whose names had been carefully entered in a little black book kept by General George Marshall during the peacetime years. When war came and Marshall became chief of staff, those names—Eisenhower, Patton, and Bradley among them—moved into positions of command. Ryder had a reputation as a very good tactician, although Bradley later faulted him for not being tough enough in replacing weak subordinates.

During the invasion, Ryder remained offshore on the HMS *Bulolo*. The man who led the 168th ashore was its commander, Col. John "Iron Mike" O'Daniel, another World War I veteran who had been brought in as a replacement regimental commander. O'Daniel quickly won the admiration and loyalty of the regiment. Here was a man who looked and talked and acted as though he could take them into combat and give them a good chance of coming back out alive.

When they first saw him, the troops could not help but notice the long scar arcing across his cheek. Perhaps it was only imagination but it was not hard to picture him in a bayonet duel with a German soldier in the trenches of World War I, emerging bloodied but victorious.

Captain Larry McBride recalls how O'Daniel assembled the regiment in a muddy field shortly after he had taken command. Standing with a rifle gripped across his chest, he said: "Men, when the enemy shoots at you, the thing to do is hit the ground. You'll do this without anyone telling you to, but some of you won't hit it fast enough or flat enough."

"Iron Mike" then proceeded to demonstrate the proper way to hit the ground, first slowly, by the numbers, and then abruptly, as though he were being shot at—all this while wearing his dress uniform. When he ordered the regiment to "hit the deck," some of the officers, worried about how to get their clothes cleaned again, exchanged nervous glances—and then dropped into the mud.

Of the three regiments in the 34th Division, the 168th was the most nearly ready to go to war. But only a few veterans of World War I, a quarter-century before, had ever been shot at or fired a shot in anger. Their training in Ireland and Scotland had been tough and intense. But O'Daniel had plenty to worry about as the landing craft worked their way through the darkness toward the invasion shores.

A couple of days before leaving for Africa, the regiment had held a final dress rehearsal of the landing. As O'Daniel later recalled, "we were landed unsatisfactorily over wide areas on unscheduled beaches."

O'Daniel set out from HMS *Karen* about 1:00 A.M., leading a part of his assault force. The British had stationed a submarine off the invasion beach and the landing craft were supposed to follow the stern lights of the sub toward the correct beach. But the element of surprise was so great that people ashore were still behaving as though there weren't a war on. When they eventually got ashore, one group of soldiers found a couple nestled on the beach making love. One of the men handed the blushing girl a pack of LifeSavers and sent them on their way. As the landing craft groped toward the shore, lights from a few houses and an occasional automobile shone brightly—so brightly, in fact, that the coxswains couldn't pick out the lights of the submarine

"We became lost and cruised about all night following one light and then another," O'Daniel recalled. Finally, about daylight, they found a beach where the British had landed. They stepped ashore, got directions from the British, climbed back in their boats, and found their correct landing spot about 7:00 A.M.

Meanwhile, other members of the regiment had already made it ashore—some where they were supposed to be, others as much as 15 miles from where they should have been.

After the war, O'Daniel, by then a major general, said the confusion didn't surprise him. "We had planned and rehearsed for such an eventuality, however, and my orders before leaving Scotland covered the matter thoroughly by directing all persons, in case of being landed on incorrect beaches, to look as quickly as possible for the shortest route . . . to Algiers."

The regiment's 1st Battalion reported it was pulling itself together and beginning to move toward Algiers. But the 2nd Battalion was still badly scattered, and O'Daniel could not contact its commander. He radioed to the commander of the 3rd Battalion, waiting aboard ship, to hurry ashore.

By that time, the timetable was badly disrupted and the delay was beginning to have a serious impact on the entire operation.

Actually, the men of the 3rd Battalion were supposed to begin leaving their troopship as soon as the landing craft returned from the beaches to pick them up after delivering the first wave. But a fog enveloped the invasion fleet. Instead of wandering around in the dark until they ran out of fuel, the coxswains of the landing craft wisely turned off their motors and drifted until the fog began to lift with the coming of dawn. It was thus after 7:00 A.M. when the men of the 3rd Battalion headed toward the beaches and broad daylight when they came ashore.

Through much of the night, General Mast, the French officer who had met secretly with General Clark and promised his support for the invasion, had been trying desperately to make contact with the landing party. In his meeting with Clark, Mast agreed to throw in his lot with the allies, ordering his troops to welcome the invaders rather than to resist them. A small group of brave French officials put their careers and their lives on the line by taking control of key points in Algiers and detaining pro-German officials and officers still taking orders from the French government in Vichy.

There are several dramatic accounts of Americans coming across Mast as they landed or moved inland. Although the circumstances vary, in each case his message was the same: "You're late."

Sergeant Elmer Popejoy was a draftee, not a member of the original National Guard unit, but he felt at home in the 34th Division because members of his family had been Iowa pioneers and there was even a little town in Iowa named for one of his ancestors. He came ashore with Capt. Edward W. Bird, commander of B Company of the 1st Battalion, as a member of an advance unit.

"I was in the point of the advance party . . . a bunch of shock troops," Popejoy recalls. Suddenly a French soldier popped up out of a hole in the sand and tossed his rifle to Popejoy.

"He waved with his hand, to follow him," Popejoy recalls. "He turned his back to me and hurriedly went up the beach. I followed him and there, standing in a clearing—Bird later told me what his name was—was General Mast, there on the beach with his aide. If you've ever been around the French high officers, they're something to see. They're a picture of grandeur.

"We had a young officer who knew how to speak French. This young officer jabbered in French to this haughty French general. Mast stood there and looked at him for a little bit. That's when he turned to me and said—in English—'A pleasant surprise, but you're an hour late.' "

Bird gave a different and even more dramatic account of his encounter with Mast.

Unable to contact his battalion commander, he ordered his company to move toward Algiers. As they started out, a vehicle approached from the direction of the city. When the driver failed to follow shouted orders to stop, a soldier shot out its tire. General Mast was one of four French officers who climbed out of the vehicle. He chided Bird for being "one hour late" and then ordered Bird to head for the nearby Blida airfield. He said he had trucks waiting to carry the American soldiers.

Bird, knowing that a British unit was under orders to take the airfield, declined the offer. Mast then took a lieutenant and two enlisted men to arrange for the surrender of a nearby fort.

A third account of an encounter with Mast was given by O'Daniel after the war:

"The prearranged code word for contacting those in the know ashore was 'Whiskey.' As I moved my jeep toward Algiers, someone hailed me from the roadside with 'Whiskey.' It was General Mast with Colonel Joost, both French, and a member of the U.S. State Department. They were concerned of course in the demand for speed due to the fact . . . that the situation was in friendly hands in Algiers at about midnight, but they were afraid that it might have been taken over by the regularly appointed officials before we could arrive there."

That is exactly what had happened. Mast had given orders to his troops not to contest the invasion. But his superior had countermanded that order. Worse for the pro-Allied French, while they had taken over key points in Algiers during the night, they weren't strong enough to hold on when the Allies failed to arrive. Many were arrested, and a few were killed.

The delay also threw into disarray Allied plans for seizing the port of Algiers to prevent sabotage. As at Safi, on the Atlantic coast, and at Oran, two ships, the British destroyers *Broke* and *Malcolm,* carrying members of the 34th Division's 135th Infantry, were given the antisabotage task. The plan here made more sense than at Oran: The ships were not scheduled to enter the harbor until three hours after the landings had begun and the defenders—it was hoped—had been drawn away from the port area. But because of the delay and confusion in the landings, the troops were just making it ashore or were still afloat when the *Broke* and the *Malcolm* charged toward the barrier at the harbor entrance about 4:00 A.M. and missed it—twice.

They had neither the element of surprise nor the help of friendly forces ashore. By the time they circled for a third try, the city lights had gone out and searchlights, groping through the darkness, had caught them in their glare. The *Malcolm* was hit and caught fire. She pulled back out to sea with 10 men dead and 25 wounded.

The *Broke* made it into the harbor on the third try, landing the infantrymen at a little after 5:00 A.M. Even without the additional troops from the *Malcolm,* they made rapid progress in taking over the port, an electric power station, and a fuel storage facility. Firing gradually died out. While some of the soldiers began to extend their perimeter to a nearby seaplane base, the others settled down to wait for O'Daniel's combat team to arrive. They even entered into some tentative peace negotiations with several civilians, but they knew they were still surrounded and substantially outnumbered by potentially hostile French forces.

Then, about 8:00 A.M., a harbor gun began firing on the *Broke*. Her captain moved to a more sheltered area, but another gun zeroed in. The skipper sounded his siren as a signal to withdraw. About 60 of the infantrymen who were near the ship clambered aboard. But the others were too far away to get there for several minutes. Their commander decided he could hold out ashore until the arrival of friendly forces. The *Broke* managed to make it out to sea about 9:40 A.M., but she was so badly damaged she had to be taken under tow.

The men ashore found themselves in a gun battle with French Senegalese troops. They held their own for a while, but then they ran dangerously low on ammunition. The situation got even worse about 11:30 A.M. when several tanks and armored cars joined the French infantry. At 12:30 P.M., with not even any firing in the distance to indicate rescue was near, the American commander surrendered.

While the men from the 34th Division were attacking Algiers from the west, the British 1st Commando was landing on a cape to the east of the city. With the British was a platoon of Americans headed by Lt. Mark T. Martin, a Des Moines newspaperman in peacetime. Most of them were Iowa boys, members of the 34th Division who had been attached temporarily to the commando unit. The commandos' job was to try to silence the big coastal defense guns in two French fortifications on Cap Matifou.

Private First Class Robert J. Berens of Neola, Iowa, was a member of the commando landing team. He and other members of Martin's platoon had just left the USS *Leedstown* when the shore batteries began firing on that ship and others lying offshore, making their assignment to silence the guns even more urgent. But the commandos ran into trouble even before they reached the beach: their landing craft grounded on a sandbar, the men dashed into the water and immediately found themselves up to their necks.

Forming a chain by holding hands, they managed to get ashore safely, but all of their equipment, including their ammunition, was wet. They looked for the French guide who was supposed to meet them. He was nowhere to be found, but it was no problem for the men to follow the sound and the muzzle flashes to find their way to the guns.

Martin led his men up a steep incline onto a broad plain crossed by a macadam road leading to Batterie de Lazeret. As his men crouched in a defensive perimeter, Martin and an interpreter strode up and banged on the gate. The interpreter shouted: "*Je suis Americain!* We have come as friends." The reply was a burst of machine gun fire.

Martin quickly pulled back and had his men set up their two-inch mortar and begin shelling the fortification while other members of the platoon spread out to look for an opening in the wire around the battery. The French fired furiously, their bullets kicking up the sand and ricocheting off the barbed wire. Two of the Americans were hit. One of them was killed; the other suffered a stomach wound and died a few hours later, before he could be evacuated for treatment by a doctor.

By that time, dawn was beginning to break and the British commandos, having taken Fort D'Estrées, moved up to where the Americans were pinned down outside the Batterie du Lazaret. The unit's commander decided to try again to get the French to surrender. He tied a white handkerchief to a stick and walked up to the gate. This time, the French commander came out to talk to him and the two men could be seen in heated conversation, both gesturing with their arms. The Frenchman refused to surrender. The British officer called in a bombardment from HMS *Zetland,* a British destroyer. The French still held out, so the British officer radioed for planes to bomb the fortification.

As Albacore bombers from HMS *Formidable* dived in to release their bombs, one of the Americans slipped a bangalore torpedo under the gate and lit the fuse. But the device failed to go off, perhaps because of the drenching when the men had plunged into deep water during their landing.

Suddenly the gate swung open. The Americans were not sure what was going on. Had the French commandant finally decided to surrender? They didn't wait to find out. Instead, they charged in, firing at fleeing Frenchmen and tossing hand grenades after them into an underground tunnel.

By the end of the day, the entire area east of Algiers, including the important Maison Blanche airfield, was in Allied hands. As it turned out, the commandos had accomplished a good deal more than they were supposed to have done.

Under the invasion plan, while the 168th Regiment was landing west of Algiers and the commandos were taking out the guns on Cap Matifou, elements of the 9th Infantry Division were scheduled to come ashore on Cap Matifou along with the commandos. But the landing on the east had begun to go wrong hours before, far out in the Mediterranean.

Milo Green, aboard a ship in the convoy, recorded what happened:

> Our worst scare came just before dawn one morning when two terrific explosions in the water shook us all from the lethargy of sleep and the ship's alarm bells began their dreaded jangling for "action stations." A lone German plane had dived out of the sky and deposited two aerial torpedoes just behind the stern of a vessel some two hundred yards from our own. In a few minutes' time we learned that its rudder had been damaged and many of its passengers badly shaken up, but no troops were reported killed. However, the ship was forced to fall behind in the convoy and had to be towed in.

The target of the attack was the USS *Thomas Stone*, which was the best equipped for a night amphibious landing and was carrying a 1,400-man battalion landing team and a number of landing craft destined for the beaches east of Algiers. Just what happened to the ship is not clear. George F. Howe, the official historian of the North African campaign, agrees with Milo Green that the ship was torpedoed by a plane. But Samuel Eliot Morison, the official naval historian, says she was actually hit by a single torpedo from a submarine and that the plane seen by many observers was an Allied aircraft making an attack on the submarine. However, neither German nor Italian records, examined after the war, mentioned an attack on the *Thomas Stone.*

In any event, the ship was dead in the water at dawn on November 7 about 155 miles from Algiers. Under strict rules laid down before the ships had left port, the rest of the convoy sailed on and left her there, motionless and vulnerable, with a single corvette remaining to provide whatever limited protection it could. The skipper of another troopship offered to take the damaged vessel in tow, but the captain of the *Thomas Stone* said that was against his orders. Similarly, he turned down an offer to transfer the troops from his vessel to the other ship.

The commander of the assault troops aboard the *Thomas Stone* knew his men were needed and might even make the difference between success and failure in the landings. He loaded 800 of his men, all that would fit, into the 24 landing craft carried by the ship and set off for Algiers about 7:00 P.M. the night before the scheduled landings. The British corvette came along as an escort, leaving the *Thomas Stone* alone until two destroyers arrived from Gibraltar several hours later.

At six o'clock the next morning, by which time the invasion was well under way, the boats were taking water and running low on fuel and the men were wet and miserable. They and their equipment were all taken aboard the corvette. The ship attempted to tow a few of the small boats, but all of them were eventually scuttled.

When the corvette finally arrived off Algiers, it was 20 hours after the troops should have gone ashore. They had missed the invasion, but they had also missed a ferocious attack by German bombers and torpedo planes on the troopships anchored offshore.

The most seriously damaged was the USS *Leedstown,* which was hit in the stern by a torpedo. Her steering mechanism was damaged and the rear portion of the ship was flooded. About one o'clock the next afternoon, she was hit by two torpedoes and the order to abandon ship was given a few minutes later. She was bombed again about four o'clock and sank a short time later. Although most of the damage was done by the Axis bombers, *Leedstown* was also hit by a torpedo fired by the German U-*331* in one of the few successful U-boat attacks.

The order to abandon the stricken ship apparently came just in time, with 500 men still aboard. Some of them had the strange experience of jumping into the ocean and then being forced to jump a second time after being sucked back in through a gaping hole in the side of the vessel. Even after the men got away from the *Leedstown,* they were still in trouble. Most of the lifeboats collapsed in the heavy surf, tossing the men into the water where a strong undertow threatened to pull them out to sea. Crew members of other ships, joined by French and Algerians, saved a number of lives by bringing the survivors ashore. Most of the ship's cargo had already either been unloaded or was salvaged. But the Americans with 1st Commando lost all of their backup equipment, so when they were ordered to Tunisia a few days later they had only the gear they carried with them in the initial assault.

The loss of the *Leedstown* was a minor one compared to what might have happened if the Germans had managed to bring the full weight of their submarine force to bear on the invasion. But faulty intelligence, a belated realization of what was happening, and intense Allied antisubmarine warfare operations had a devastating effect on the U-boat resistance to the landings. A line of submarines was set up west of Gibraltar after the bulk of the invasion force had passed through. There were 18 U-boats inside the Mediterranean. But their commander concluded the landings would be at Bougie Bay, about a hundred miles beyond Algiers, so his force was concentrated far from the actual landings.

For Berlin, the use of U-boats to resist the invasion was a dismal failure. The subs managed to sink 11 Allied ships and damage five others. But of the subs in both the Atlantic and the Mediterranean, the Germans lost eight boats with all hands, and fifteen others were forced to abort or suffered damage. Even worse, by concentrating its U-boat force against Operation Torch, Berlin gave Allied convoys an almost free run across the North Atlantic.

On the western side of Algiers, where the 168th Combat Team had landed, the reception accorded the Americans by the French and their colonial troops reflected the conflict within the French leadership.

Captain Larry McBride was a member of the 3rd Battalion, the reserve battalion that did not come ashore until well after daylight. Because he spoke a little French, he had been given the job of trying to tell the defenders that they came as friends.

"During the last few days," he recalled later, "my imagination had worked some grisly details out of the prospect of wading ashore at night, under fire, trying to stop a war by shouting such phrases as *'Nous sommes vos amis'* (we are your friends), *'Nous sommes les Americains'* (we are the Americans), *'Cessez le feu'* (cease firing), and other soothing bits of stilted French to a bunch of possibly irate and bloodthirsty Berber Colonials and French Marines."

The reality was startlingly different.

"There was no firing. We were close to a villa of some sort. Frenchmen in berets rushed to the scene, clasped the hands of American soldiers, and exclaimed, *'Bon! Bon! Vive les Americains!'*

"The African sun was shining brilliantly. Here were the grape arbors, the supporting wires of which we had trained to cross cautiously in darkness. Here were the beaches which we had anticipated crossing at a full run with bullets kicking sand in our faces. We looked at the peaceful French villas surrounded by eucalyptus and prickly pear trees. Here and there were groups of staring, curious French. A little further on were several more unconcerned Arabs in dirty, flowing robes . . . A long, red-fezzed Senegalese soldier, unarmed, accepted a cigarette from an American soldier."

The men set off on foot toward Algiers, about 12 miles away. About halfway there, they passed through the town of Cheraga, where the streets were lined with French and Arabs. The French shouted *"Vive les Americains!"* while the Arabs silently observed the scene. When one of them was hit by a motorcycle, the crowd dragged the man out of the way and berated him for holding up the advance.

As the Americans were passing through the town, Maj. Robert R. Moore of Villisca, Iowa, drove by and informed them that his unit, which had landed hours earlier, was about two miles to the rear. This thus put the 3rd Battalion—the reserve unit—in the advance toward Algiers.

Later in the afternoon, members of the 2nd and 3rd Battalions took up positions near the town of El Biar, which lay on their path toward Algiers, just below the commanding presence of Fort L'Empereur. As they spread out, a small Arab boy approached one of the soldiers and handed him a note in French. McBride translated it:

To the Commandant Americain:
    We have nobody here but small children. We are frightened. Please do not fire on the convent.

It was signed, "Sister Marie. The Convent of the Good Pasteur."

McBride picked out the convent on his map. He sent the message back to the commander of the pack howitzers who had begun firing on the village. No shells fell on the convent during the fighting around the city.

The Americans first ran into resistance at a housing project under construction just outside the town but managed to push on through. "Iron Mike" O'Daniel arrived about that time and drove on to the center of El Biar. Suddenly a French tank or armored car appeared and began spraying the street with machine gun fire.

"We all ducked into doorways and stairways," O'Daniel recalled. "I leaned out and saw two or three men lying in the street. One ducked across the street to a doorway and was hit by a sniper from a building on my side, the left side, of the street. There was a light machine gun crew near me, and I directed them to fire on the tank. They rapidly set up their gun and began firing in long bursts at the ports of the enemy tank, which was about 400 yards away. After a few bursts from our gun, the tank hurriedly backed away and disappeared around a bend. Our men began moving forward again, and one company moved to the right to attempt to outflank Fort L'Empereur."

The men of the 168th Regiment thus found themselves not only in combat for the first time but in combat of the worst kind: house-to-house street fighting.

"Jumping from doorway to doorway, using stone stairs and curbings as ramparts, the men of the 2nd and 3rd Battalions moved through the village," McBride wrote later.

> Bullets ricocheted off trees and drilled neat, round holes in the metal lampposts. 1st Lt. Kenneth Ames, 3rd Battalion chaplain, was with the forward elements as they battled in the street. The enemy fire was sporadic but deadly. Snipers were located in houses along the main street and the side streets. Machine guns fired crossfire from avenues branching off the main thoroughfare. At one point, which we dubbed "the fire lane," we had a traffic control system. An H Company sergeant, in the scant cover of a shallow doorway . . . motioned the men on, singly and at irregular intervals, as they crossed the open area on the run.
>
> Earlier, 2nd Lt. Carl F. Ruth of L Company had turned into this narrow, high-walled corridor . . . in an attempt to get around to the left of the main avenue. With two or three men Lt. Ruth advanced down the passageway for a distance of about fifty yards when enemy fire of snipers, in the houses above the lane, and a machine gun at the end of the lane . . . opened up on the little group. Lt. Ruth was hit from almost directly above by a sniper at one of the windows. His men managed to evacuate him and he was given first aid treatment within a few minutes after being hit but died, later on, of internal hemorrhage.

Much of the fighting at El Biar took place in the town's marketplace. The American soldiers, crouching in the doorways and niches in the walls, were nonplussed to see the natives tending their stalls, doing their shopping, and trundling through the narrow streets with their donkey-drawn carts as though this fight had nothing to do with them. And they were probably right: whichever side won, their condition was unlikely to get any better—or any worse.

While the 168th Regiment was still fighting for El Biar, Capt. Ed Bird and Lt. Col. Edward J. Doyle, commander of the regiment's 1st Battalion, bypassed the town and worked their way down into the center of Algiers. They reached the governor's palace, and while they were arguing with a French soldier who barred their entrance, Bird noticed a man, two women, and a child leaving the nearby German Consulate. When the German, who identified himself as the vice consul, tried to drive away, one of Bird's men shot out the tires of his car. Despite his protests that he had diplomatic immunity, Bird took him prisoner.

Doyle, meanwhile, had taken a few men and gone looking for an American who reportedly lived nearby. Bird heard firing from the direction in which they had gone. When he arrived on the scene, he found that Doyle and an enlisted man had been hit by a sniper. The bullet had struck Doyle in the chest, near the heart, and he had obviously been seriously injured. As Bird attempted first aid, a French ambulance drove up. The crew loaded Doyle aboard and sped off. Bird later learned that Doyle had been taken to a French hospital, where he died of his wounds—one of the first members of the 168th to fall in battle.

While Doyle and Bird were making their way down into Algiers, Maj. David V. Rosen, an American who had landed with the British 5th Northamptonshire Battalion, worked his way around the fighting in El Biar toward Fort L'Empereur, running into William H. Stoneman, a war correspondent, on the way.

"I found that the lieutenant colonel in charge of the fort had been killed and that the major, named Chanson, wanted to surrender, but only to an American, and not to the British major with whom he was negotiating," Rosen recalled after the war. "Bill Stoneman suggested that I take the surrender, but not wishing to deprive the 168th Infantry of that privilege after having fought for it all afternoon, I conducted a brief search for an officer of that outfit."

Finding only a chaplain, Rosen decided the matter was urgent and accepted the surrender himself while fighting was still going on down below in El Biar.

Not until late in the afternoon were the defenders driven out of the town back toward the fort. General Ryder had come ashore about 9:00 A.M. on the day of the invasion and set up his command post in a small town west of Algiers.

About 4:00 P.M., an American diplomat arrived at his head-quarters and asked if he would be interested in receiving the surrender of Algiers.

"I will go anywhere to talk to anyone who wishes to surrender Algiers to me," he replied.

The diplomat drove off and returned about 5:15 P.M. Ryder and several aides joined him in his official car.

As they drove toward El Biar, they were stopped by a sergeant of the 168th Regiment who was not at all impressed by the car full of brass hats. Only after an argument did he let them proceed to the center of El Biar, where they found a French general's automobile, flying a French tricolor and a white flag, waiting to take them to Fort L'Empereur.

They set off through the French lines with a French trumpeter continually blowing the "cease fire" call. At the fort, Ryder met with the French general and they agreed that all French troops would be confined to their barracks—although they would be allowed to retain their arms—and that the Americans would enter the city of Algiers at eight o'clock that evening.

Although Ryder referred to this agreement as a "surrender," it should more accurately be termed an armistice or just an arrangement for what might be only a temporary cease fire. There was still a great deal of confusion about who was in charge on the French side and considerable uncertainty about whether the French would continue to resist, agree to a kind of armed neutrality, or actively join the Allies in fighting the Axis forces.

Allied hopes then turned to Adm. Jean François Darlan, commander of the armed forces of Vichy France. By chance, at the time of the invasion, Darlan was in Algiers to be with his seriously ill son. More than a year earlier, Darlan had met with an American diplomat and indicated that he might be willing to order the French armed forces to cooperate with the Allies in driving the Germans out. But the Allies remained suspicious of him.

Ryder met with Darlan later that night and failed to reach an agreement on the surrender of French forces. Darlan was in a tough position. If the French continued to resist, many people on both sides would be killed or wounded and the

French would lose. But if the French did not resist, the Germans, who had occupied only the northern part of France, would take over the entire country. Darlan insisted that he could end resistance only with the approval of Pétain. He told Ryder they would meet again the next morning. But before the meeting ended, he made a significant concession. Ryder later described what happened:

"I informed Admiral Darlan that I wished to move my transports into the harbor of Algiers where they could be protected, as rapidly as possible. . . . Everything was arranged so the leading ship could enter the harbor any time after four o'clock in the morning of November 9. It is interesting to note that the ships moved from their places off the landing beaches at dawn, were bombed as they left by the first German air raid, entered Algiers harbor, and as they were entering the harbor, the second German air raid began and in that raid all Allied guns opened up, including all of the French fixed antiaircraft defenses, in the attempt to drive off the Germans."

As the time neared for Ryder's meeting with Darlan the next morning, there was a good deal of apprehension among the Allied troops. The French were confined to their barracks but still had their weapons (although Ryder had arranged for most, if not all, of their ammunition to be locked up), and it was feared that fighting might break out again if Ryder and Darlan failed to reach an agreement.

On the morning of November 9, Major Rosen was told by a British artillery commander that if the discussions fell through, he had orders to bombard, attack, and capture Fort L'Empereur. Rosen went to the fort and found 15 men from the 168th Combat Team there—along with about 250 French soldiers.

"As the morning wore on and the presumed ultimatum deadline passed, I became concerned," Rosen recalled. "At about 1100 hours, I gave Major Chanson a routine to the effect that the French and Americans were brothers and friends, that we had no desire to fight each other regardless of the outcome of the deliberations, and that I thought it would be an excellent idea and would eliminate many casualties and other unpleasant consequences if he would move his arms and ammunition out of the fort, with his personnel of some 250 remaining inside.

"I added that the installation was surrounded, as he already knew, that resistance would be futile in any event, and that he could eliminate such an unhappy occurrence by complying with the suggested action. He replied agitatedly that he could not do so without permission of his division commander. . . . "

Failing to reach his commander, Chanson made Rosen a counteroffer: that all arms and ammunition be locked in the arsenal room and that the Americans be given the key.

"Since this was considerably more than I had expected . . . I accepted with alacrity. I also had the breech blocks of the four artillery pieces removed and stored with the other material, and later directed privately to the American captain that all available grenades be furnished the guards. If the negotiations collapsed, the matériel could be blown and we could hold the fort with our 14 men. . . . "

It was not until two weeks later that Darlan finally agreed to end French resistance, not only in Algiers but in the Casablanca and Oran areas as well, and to begin cooperating with the Allies. Under the deal, he became High Commissioner and Commander in Chief of Naval Forces. Almost all the other high-ranking posts went to officials who had resisted the invasion, rather than to those who supported the Allies.

Darlan's order was disavowed in a radio broadcast from Vichy. But Darlan said he had long had a secret agreement with Pétain to resume resistance to the Germans when the opportunity arose. This was enough to ease the consciences of those officers who felt bound by oath to obey Pétain.

Supporters of General Charles de Gaulle, the leader of the Free French, based in London, were alarmed at the deal with Darlan. They watched in growing anger and consternation as he seemed to be trying to set up in North Africa a French government that would replace Vichy and, after an Allied victory, establish a fascist government in mainland France.

Perhaps, in the interest of military efficiency, the arrangement with Darlan made sense. It secured the cooperation of French forces in fighting the Axis and provided for the

French to use their police and military forces to maintain control over the restive native population. But it also put the Allies in the company of a very unsavory lot—French officials who ran a secret police operation that rivaled the German Gestapo in its brutality and contempt for human rights, and who carried out anti-Jewish policies that mirrored German anti-Semitism. Worse was that a number of high-ranking American officers accepted the hospitality of these French officials while ignoring the brave officers and officials who had thrown in their lot with the Allies, only to be locked up when the invasion fell so badly behind schedule.

Jews, Moslems, men who had served in the Foreign Legion, and former concentration camp inmates were all turned away when they tried to enlist to fight the Germans. Instead, they were segregated in a special unit called the Corps Franc d'Afrique, separate from the regular French army.

A. J. Liebling, *The New Yorker* magazine's boxing writer turned war correspondent, arrived in Oran shortly after the Allied landings and was shocked at the mess things were in.

"It was as if continental United States had extended statehood to Puerto Rico and Hawaii, and had then itself been occupied by an enemy power, leaving the untypical new states to carry on pro tem as the United States of America, and the sugar companies had then been left free to run Puerto Rico and Hawaii," he reported.

When he moved on to Algiers at Christmastime, things were no better. Although the correspondents were prevented by their censors from giving a detailed report about the political situation to their readers, the reporters made it a point to confront both French and American officials, asking angry questions about the arrest of those who had helped pave the way for the invasion.

It was not until after word of what was going on in Africa worked its way back to politicians in London and Washington that the situation changed and many of the pro-German, even fascist, officials were replaced and some degree of political freedom was established in North Africa.

Darlan's reign wouldn't last long. He was shot to death on December 24. A 20-year-old Frenchman was arrested, tried by court-martial as the assassin, and executed by a firing squad on December 26. In the days immediately after the invasion, Darlan had been a major source of worry to the Allies because of his pro-Nazi leanings. There were, of course, rumors, buttressed by the unseemly haste with which the alleged assassin was dispatched, that the Allies had used this method to get rid of a problem. But by the time he was killed, Darlan had proved himself a trustworthy agent of the Allies, and Eisenhower described him as "the source of all our practical help."

Upon Darlan's death, Giraud took over as Commander in Chief of French Forces and Governor of North Africa. By that time, however, French resistance had ceased and the French were already cooperating with the Allies against the Axis.

While the generals and the politicians worked things out with the French, members of the 168th Regiment set up camp near Algiers and prepared for their coming battles with the Germans in Tunisia. At the end of December, "Iron Mike" O'Daniel, who had become highly popular with the troops in the brief time he had commanded the regiment and taken it into combat for the first time, was reassigned to command the 5th Army Invasion Training Center near Oran.

His replacement was another regular Army officer, Col. Thomas D. Drake. Like O'Daniel, Drake was a veteran of World War I, where he had won a Distinguished Service Cross. After the war, he left the army but rejoined in 1923. One student of the regiment called him "a dynamic if somewhat rash regular army commander." Eager for a go at the Germans, he trained the troops hard and was seen as a strict disciplinarian. Perhaps resenting the replacement of the popular "Iron Mike" by this newcomer, at least some of the men were notably cool toward Drake, referring to him behind his back as "Quack Quack."

Regardless of their feelings toward him, it was Drake who would soon lead them into their historic confrontation with Field Marshal Rommel, the Desert Fox, in the dry hills of Tunisia.

On November 5, only three days before the Allied landings, Rommel had begun a long retreat toward the west after losing two battles to the British near the Egyptian city of El Alamein, only 60 miles west of Alexandria.

It is easy, looking back, to see Rommel, short on tanks, short on fuel, and encumbered by Italian divisions without motor transport, as a beaten warrior, fleeing from a vastly superior British Eighth Army.

But from the American view, Rommel might be retreating—but he was retreating *toward them.* No one, from Eisenhower's headquarters down to the rawest recruit, was inclined to write Rommel off as a threat or to underestimate the trouble he could cause.

By the fall of 1942, Rommel had gained a mythical, almost superhuman, reputation, aided enthusiastically by Hitler's propaganda chief, Joseph Goebbels.

Goebbels had a lot to work with. In the spring of 1940, as a 48-year-old new general with his first command of an armor division, Rommel, often standing in the turret of his Panzer III tank, spearheaded the German blitzkrieg as it swept across Belgium, through a northern extension of the Maginot line, and then across northern France, cutting off the British and forcing their desperate withdrawal at Dunkirk.

His Seventh Panzer division penetrated so deeply behind Allied lines and moved so fast—more than 200 miles on several days—that the French dubbed it "the spook division." After the fall of France, Rommel's exploits became the subject of a book, *The Spook Division,* and his troops went back to the battlefield to reenact their exploits for a Goebbels film called *Victory in the West.*

As a result of his performance in the invasion of France, Rommel became one of Hitler's favorite generals. In February 1941, the führer sent him to Libya with a two-division Afrika Korps to help out an Italian army that had suffered a series of defeats at the hands of the British and was on the brink of collapse.

Almost always outnumbered in men and tanks, Rommel succeeded, through a series of daring, unexpected maneuvers, in stopping the British. He even drove them back on several occasions. In May 1942, he left a thin line of Italian troops to hold the British while he made a bold five-division end run around the British position. It was a typical Rommel maneuver—and it failed miserably. In a few hours, Rommel lost a third of his tank force.

But then he did something quite untypical. He hunkered down in a defensive position that came to be known as the Cauldron and beat off wave after wave of British tank attacks. In less than two weeks, he whittled the number of British tanks from some 900 down to fewer than 200. On June 11, 1942, Rommel roared out of the Cauldron and set the British fleeing toward the Egyptian frontier.

At Churchill's insistence, however, the British left 30,000 men to try to hold onto the Libyan port city of Tobruk. On June 21, Rommel took Tobruk and with it a vast store of military equipment. It was a catastrophe that rivaled, for the British, the loss of their Far Eastern bastion at Singapore. When Rommel took up his pursuit of the fleeing British units, most of his troops were driving or riding in captured British vehicles. It seemed only a matter of days before Rommel would be in Cairo and then on to the Suez Canal.

But the British finally halted their retreat near El Alamein. There they were able to stop the Germans, exhausted by the fighting and hampered by lack of fuel, equipment, and supplies. A new British commander, Gen. Bernard Law Montgomery, was placed in charge of the Eighth Army and began methodical preparations for his offensive with a massive buildup. By the time he was ready to attack on the night of October 23–24, 1942, he outnumbered the Axis force 230,000 men to 80,000, 1,230 tanks to 210, and 1,500 planes to 350. In the face of these odds, Rommel began his retreat—or, as it might have seemed to the Americans, his advance to the rear—on November 5.

In the heady days immediately after their successful landings, the Allies hoped for a quick victory that would give them control of Tunisia and catch Rommel between the jaws of their force and Montgomery's advancing Eighth Army. But everyone knew that Rommel was still dangerous—perhaps, like a wounded animal, even more dangerous than ever.

5

The Axis Reacts

On November 8, 1942, the very day that the Allied armies landed in North Africa, Adolf Hitler made a long speech to the Nazi "Old Combatants" in the Burgerbraukeller in Munich—the cellar beer hall from which his Nazi party had begun its rise to power.

In a remarkably upbeat account of the battle for Stalingrad, then reaching its climax along the Volga River deep in the Soviet Union, he gave no hint that he realized how sweepingly the tides of history were changing, if not on that very day, then certainly in those few weeks in mid-November of 1942. From that time on, it was no longer a question of whether Hitler's dream of a thousand-year Reich would come true, but how long it would be before the Third Reich collapsed and Germany itself lay in ashes.

When large numbers of Allied ships were seen in the waters near Gibraltar on November 6 and 7, Hitler and his generals were not surprised—at least, not very surprised. They had been assuming for some time that the Allies would attempt a landing somewhere in the Mediterranean. But they assumed that the landings would come in 1943 and in southern France, Sicily, or mainland Italy rather than in North Africa. That the Allies had been able to move a vast army across the Atlantic and down from the British Isles without the enemy knowing it was coming or where it was headed was a remarkable achievement of wartime secrecy. It was also, on the Axis side, a colossal failure of intelligence.

Even when it became apparent the ships were heading for North Africa, there was confusion in Berlin over where the troops would land and how many of them were involved. While some of his advisers expected only one or two divisions to be landed, Hitler himself concluded that the landing would involve four or five divisions, and he was more nearly right than his generals. But he and his advisers then made the critical mistake of assuming that the landings would be far to the east, at the Libyan ports of Tripoli and Benghazi. If that was where they were headed, they would have to pass through—or try to pass through—the relatively narrow section of the Mediterranean between Sicily and North Africa. There, the Germans were confident, their picket line of submarines and aircraft flying the short distance from bases in Sicily and Italy would take a devastating toll before the convoys reached their destinations.

Thus, it was only after the landings were well under way that submarines were assembled to attack the ships at anchor near Casablanca and bombers were dispatched to attack the vessels anchored off the beaches at Algiers. The initial reaction of the Axis was both too little and too late to prevent, or even to seriously impede, the landings.

Once the scale of the Allied operation became clear to the Axis leaders, they realized they faced a host of problems:

Rommel, retreating out of Egypt across Libya, warned time after time that he could not resist the British offensive unless he received dramatically increased shipments of guns, tanks, other equipment, and especially fuel. Despite Hitler's promises to Rommel that he would get what he needed, the threat from the Allied landings meant Rommel would continue to be shortchanged—and that he would have to continue his retreat.

The French were a great worry. Under the armistice signed in 1940 after the Nazi defeat of France, the French agreed to defend North Africa. But the armistice also limited French armaments, restricting their ability to resist the Allies even if they wanted to. Within hours after the landings, the Germans moved into the southern portions of France that had not been occupied in 1940, and the Italians took the island of Corsica and a section of southern France. This meant a larger area for occupation troops to monitor.

In the east, the German Sixth Army was engaged in a battle to the death with Stalin's Red Army over the city named for him—Stalingrad. Initially, some troops slated to reinforce the army on the Volga were diverted to Tunisia. But then the Soviet Union struck a devastating and totally unexpected blow with its Operation Uranus on November 19. Troops that might have gone to Tunisia were hurried to the eastern front.

Despite this array of problems pressing in from all sides, the Axis reacted with remarkable speed and clearheadedness to the threat in North Africa. It was as obvious to the German and Italian leaders as it was to the Allies that control of Tunisia was the key to victory or defeat in North Africa.

Within hours of the Allied landings, German transport planes began depositing troops at the airport at Tunis. General der Panzertruppen Walther Nehring was placed in charge. Nehring was an experienced combat leader, until recently the commander, under Rommel, of the Afrika Korps. He had barely recuperated, at his home near Berlin, from injuries suffered on August 31 when a British fighter-bomber struck his command vehicle, killing several of his associates and riddling him with shell fragments.

The first Germans off the planes faced a dicey situation. The airport was immediately surrounded by French troops, and there was an understandable fear that the French could— and might—take the first Germans prisoner and prevent the arrival of reinforcements. Maneuvering for time to continue the buildup, Nehring issued a proclamation asserting that the Axis troops had come as guests of the French and that their only purpose was to defend French territory.

A more candid statement of German intentions is contained in the war diary of Col. Hans Lederer, a division commander under Nehring. His operations diary noted: "Colonel Lederer thinks that, the division being still so weak, we are not in a position to offend the French by a manifestly hostile attitude and would force them to go over to the other side. We first have to be strong enough so as to be master of the situation."

The French themselves were divided on which side to take. The admiral in charge at Bizerte cooperated with the Germans and even ordered his anti-aircraft crews to fire on Allied planes bombing the harbor. But French Gen. Georges Barré, commanding army units in the Tunis area, pulled his troops back into the chain of mountains to the west of Tunis and south of Bizerte. The Germans were disturbed to see that when Barré's troops dug in, they were prepared to confront an attack from the east, not from the west.

Supplies, which Hitler had promised to Rommel but never seemed to deliver, came pouring into the Tunisian ports and airfields. The equipment included four of the giant Panzer VI Tiger tanks, one of Hitler's secret new weapons. New anti-aircraft guns designed to bring down the highest-flying Allied bombers were borrowed from the defenses of Berlin and sent to Tunisia.

But the troops were of a mixed bag. The 10th Panzer Division and the Hermann Göring Division were competent. But some of the troops, moved directly from occupation duties in France, arrived with only their hand weapons—none of the machine guns, mortars, and artillery of a proper infantry unit.

At first the French resisted the introduction of Italian troops, but as soon as the German buildup had reached a significant level, Italian units came flooding in. When the fighting began, however, the Germans wondered whether they were more of a problem than an asset. When the Axis unit in Bizerte sent a patrol out on November 21, it ran into a French outpost. The division operations diary tells what happened:

"An Italian assault gun was destroyed by a direct hit from an antitank gun, whereupon two other assault guns were abandoned by their crews in a mad hurry and the advance could not be continued because the Italians could not be brought forward. The lack of German infantry is the greatest weakness of the present conduct of operations. Italian infantry can be committed to attack only when combined with German infantry; otherwise it will not face the enemy."

As Nehring deployed his forces, it was obvious that geography would dictate strategy and tactics on both sides. Tunis and Bizerte, the two most important port cities in northern Tunisia, each lie on its own coastal plain, separated by a low range of hills. To the east is a range of mountains that begins near the Mediterranean coast west of Bizerte, forming the tail of an inverted letter Y. To the south, the two arms of the Y form what are called the Eastern Dorsal and the Western, or Grand, Dorsal. These are rugged mountain ranges, each of them pierced by only a few passes carrying rail and road traffic. A striking characteristic of the Tunisian landscape is the tall, rocky outcroppings that rise from the surrounding plains like islands or stand out above other mountains.

These *djebels,* as they are called, were created some ten to twenty-five million years ago, during the Miocene and Pliocene periods, when broad rivers flowed from south to north through Tunisia. The landscape was much more lush during that period than it is today, and scientists have found fossils of a number of wet-climate animals such as antelopes, turtles, and a dog-sized horse. As the rivers flowed through the area, they wore away the soil from around the harder stone, thus creating the rocky outcroppings—the military's favored high ground—that were to be the sites of some of the most vicious and difficult fighting in the battle for Tunisia—some of the most difficult in all of the fighting in World War II, for that matter.

The German plan was to hold the mountain passes protecting the Tunis and Bizerte beachheads while also moving as rapidly as possible to secure the coastal corridor stretching to the south—the route by which Rommel would approach if his retreat took him that far.

By mid-November, when the first British and American troops arrived in Tunisia, Nehring had at least the basic framework of a defensive system that would permit a continued rapid buildup of Axis forces. Perhaps most important of all, he had a series of airfields with paved runways within minutes of the mountain passes where the first battles for Tunisia would be fought.

6

First Blood

It was a lonely feeling for the troopers of Lt. Col. John Waters's battalion as they unloaded their light tanks after an uncomfortable, week-long train trip from Oran to Souk Ahras, Algeria, and headed across the border into Tunisia.

Bill Tuck, who commanded Waters's Company B, recalls the feeling:

"We were the first Americans out there—the first unit. We headed out toward Tunis the first day. We never saw a British unit. We would have British officers come out and give us orders. But we were all by ourselves, one battalion out there. Fortunately, the Germans weren't there yet, either."

The Germans weren't there yet on the ground, but their Stuka dive bombers and ME-109 fighters dominated the air.

"Those first days, it was almost total German air superiority," Tuck says. "They would come bomb and strafe us, go back and fill up and come bomb and strafe again. They had Stukas. I can still hear those screaming things coming down. They were really very poor shots. But we were scared, no doubt about that. Of course anything shooting at us got us scared in those days. It sure did."

The Stuka—Junkers JU-87—was a gull-winged two-man dive bomber that had begun its service with German forces fighting on the side of Generalissimo Francisco Franco in

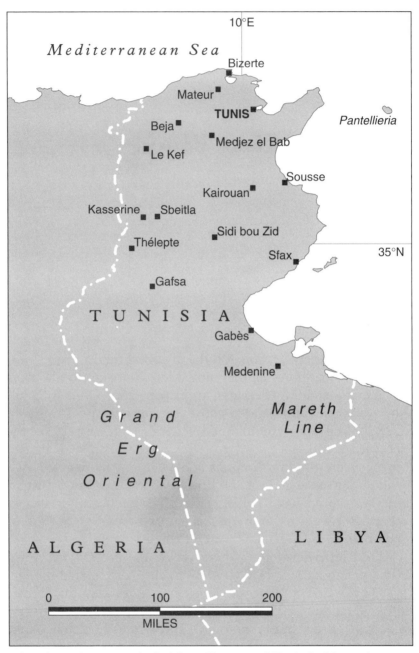

After the Axis success in holding Bizerte and Tunis in November and December, the fighting spread into the center of the country. The 33rd Fighter Group began operations near the small town of Thélepte, the closest point to the front lines and enemy bomber bases. In February, as Field Marshal Erwin Rommel, retreating from Egypt, took up defensive positions on the Mareth Line, the Allies suffered serious defeats at Sidi Bou Zid and Kasserine Pass.

92

Spain in 1936 and helped spearhead the Nazi blitzkrieg attacks on Poland, France, and the Low Countries in 1939 and 1940. One of the best-known terror weapons of the war, the planes were equipped with sirens that produced an eerie scream during a dive-bombing attack. By the time of the North African campaign, it had become obvious that the Stuka was extremely vulnerable both to ground fire and to hostile fighters. But in Tunisia in late 1942, there were few Allied fighters available to deal with the Stukas.

"In the first few days, we were in nice columns of tanks going down the road. Just like a parade," Tuck recalls. "We learned quickly to get away from that. We scattered out and got in smaller units."

British engineers soon planted warning signs along the roads: "Don't sit and die—jump and run." "If in doubt, get out."

Within hours of the landings at Algiers, the pretense—for the benefit of the French—that this was an all-American operation was dropped. General Eisenhower, who was soon to transfer his headquarters from Gibraltar to Algiers, remained in overall charge. But key battlefield commands went to British officers.

This change in leadership acknowledged the sizable British troop commitment to the campaign. It also recognized that the British, who had been at war since 1939, presumably knew more about fighting than did the Americans, who were just entering the war and had yet to exchange a shot with the Germans.

General Ryder, the commander of the 34th Infantry Division, who was in charge of the landing at Algiers, turned over command to British Lt. Gen. Kenneth A. N. Anderson, who was designated commander of the British First Army— the army that was supposed to capture Tunis and Bizerte in short order. Eisenhower, in his memoirs, praises Anderson as a "gallant Scot" and says he had "real respect for his fighting heart."

General Harmon, who later served under Anderson as commander of the 1st Armored Division, had a much less favorable view of the British general, whom he referred to as "that dour Scot." He described him as "a disagreeable man disliked by practically everyone."

The choice of Anderson for the command position was an unfortunate one, dictated more by coalition politics than by a search for the best man for the job. Anderson, who was fifty years old, had been in the army since 1911 and had served in World War I, but his previous highest command had been that of a division in France in the disastrous early days of the war, ending with the British retreat from Dunkirk.

By contrast, General Nehring, his German counterpart in the first phases of the battle for Tunisia, was a literally battle-scarred veteran of some of the bitterest fighting of the war as commander of Rommel's Afrika Korps.

News that the allies were sending the "First Army" into combat stirred a wave of optimism in England and the United States. It shouldn't have. The word "army" is a technical military term used to describe a unit consisting of two or more corps, each made up of two or more divisions. If all the bits and pieces Anderson was able to deploy in Tunisia in November and December were added together, they would barely amount to two divisions—at best an understrength corps, and hardly an army.

And even though the British had been at war for more than three years, most of the troops they sent into Tunisia were not veterans of recent fighting—or were not veterans at all. True, some British soldiers had been involved in battles with the Germans and Italians in Africa and with the Japanese in Asia. But most of those sent into Tunisia were either relatively new recruits or had been involved in the rebuilding of British military strength after the escape from Dunkirk two years before. Thus, while the Americans were totally inexperienced, the British, despite the air of superiority with which many of their top officers clothed themselves, were not very experienced either.

It did not require a great deal of experience, however, to see how this battle for Tunisia should be fought. The key, as in most military engagements, was geography.

In the north, two hill masses—Djebel Azag and Djebel el Adjred, which the troops quickly named Green Hill and Bald Hill—blocked the route toward Bizerte.

In the center, the route led past an imposing hill mass that was later to become infamous as Hill 609, then across

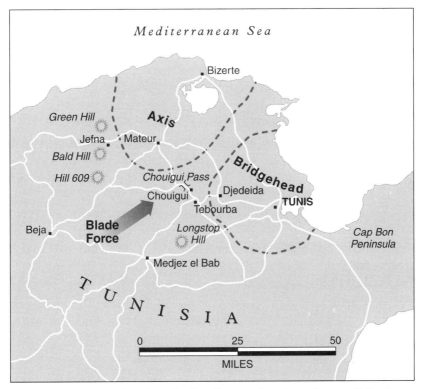

In November, shortly after the landings, a few Americans of the 1st Armored Division joined with the British in Blade Force in a thrust toward Tunis. The Allies suffered losses at Chouigui Pass, Longstop Hill, and Bald and Green Hills before giving up hopes for a quick victory.

the Tine river valley and through Chouigui Pass, which the troops of course referred to as "Chewy Gooey Pass." Once through the pass and the towns of Tebourba and Djedeida, it was a clear shot to Tunis.

In the south, the way was blocked by a hill mass known as Longstop Hill. On the eastern side of Longstop Hill lay the town of Medjez el Bab. Although it was just a dusty little Tunisian town, it was an important crossroads and river crossing and thus worth fighting for. Once the town was taken, the attackers would swing north to join the unit attacking in the center for the dash toward Tunis from Tebourba.

Waters's battalion, the only part of the American 1st Armored Division's Combat Command B ready to go into combat, was attached to one part of the Blade Force, a predominantly British unit under British officers. While two spearheads of the force struck toward Medjez el Bab in the south, Waters's battalion was part of the task force that took the center route toward Chouigui Pass and Tebourba.

The orders to Waters were simple: create a "tank-infested area" in the Tine River valley and then speed through Chouigui Pass to reconnoiter the bridges across the Medjerda River on the other side of the pass.

Given the U.S. Army's inexperience in armored warfare, Waters may not have realized it at the time, but his force was woefully ill equipped for this assignment. He had his headquarters company and three other companies of light M-3 tanks—a total of some 60 tanks—plus an 81 mm mortar platoon and an assault gun platoon with three 75 mm pack howitzers. But aside from the pack howitzers and the mortars, he had no artillery, no antitank guns, and no engineers. Even more important, he had no infantry. As the Americans were to learn the hard way, a tank, for all its earthshaking mass, cannot survive for long without foot soldiers to protect it. Ironically, the North Vietnamese were forced to learn this same lesson at the hands of the Americans when they introduced tanks into the fighting in South Vietnam nearly thirty years later.

The Allied advance kicked off on November 25, just 17 days after the landings hundreds of miles to the west.

Waters's American battalion brushed past small units of Germans and Italians, who were reconnoitering the area between the forces but had not yet set up serious defensive positions, and moved into Chouigui Pass. Tuck and his tankers of Company B dug in to defend the pass. Maj. Carl Siglin and his Company A, without infantry to help them, tried unsuccessfully to dislodge a group of German paratroops and an Italian antitank unit holed up in a nearby farm. Maj. Rudolph Barlow and his Company C reconnoitered along the Medjerda River, knocking out troops guarding one bridge across the river. They then found themselves behind a low ridge. On the other side was an airfield alive with German warplanes.

A First Armored Division crew rested beside their M-3 tank at Souk el Arba on November 23, 1942. (Source: National Archives)

While Barlow ventured out into enemy territory, Tuck stayed in touch with him by radio. But as Barlow moved further away, it became more difficult to communicate. Tuck began to climb a barren hill—it reminded him of places he had seen in Southern California—so he could relay messages from Barlow back to Waters.

"I could see him," Tuck recalls. "I could see him going up there. And then I could see an airfield up there. When I got to the top, I could see the airfield very clearly through my field glasses. There were planes taking off and landing. Rudy called me and said, 'We're laying down a base of fire now and we'll be attacking.'"

As Tuck watched from his grandstand seat, Barlow's tanks swept across the field, shooting up the airplanes, blasting the buildings, and gunning down the defending troops. The Germans had somehow neglected to provide for security of this vital installation.

"If I remember correctly, I saw twenty-one Messerschmitts burning at one time," Tuck says. "It was really a unique experience."

It was also particularly gratifying for the Americans, who seldom saw a friendly plane in the sky except for formations of heavy bombers passing by five miles overhead.

Barlow's company suffered two men killed, several tanks damaged, and one tank and its crew missing. At Nehring's headquarters, an account of this attack, coupled with a false report that American tanks were within nine miles of Tunis, caused a good deal of anxiety.

During the night, both sides pulled back. Waters's battalion spent the night in the Tine River valley and then moved back into Chouigui Pass early the next morning. In Tunis, Nehring got a lecture from Field Marshal Albrecht Kesselring, who chastised him for pulling back and assured him the Allied advance would be slow and cautious. At Kesselring's urging, Nehring sent a probing force including six Panzer IV tanks with high-velocity 75 mm guns and at least three Panzer IIIs with 50 mm guns.

The Germans spotted Carl Siglin's Company A and moved to attack. What they didn't see was Tuck's tanks hidden behind a rise in the earth.

"We crawled up where we could watch the German tanks," Tuck says. They held their fire as four tanks came into view. Then one of Tuck's tanks opened fire.

"I've got a hit! I've got a fire!" the tank commander shouted.

"Where did you aim?" Tuck demanded.

"Right back of the sprocket."

Tuck's other tanks opened up, aiming near the front of the tank, just behind the sprocket that drives the track.

"Sure enough," Tuck says, "we found that it was armor, but it was thin. The shell would go right through it and get a fire. If you get a fire in a tank, it's gone. We got four tanks that day."

Veterans who fought in the Sherman medium tank, with its 75 mm gun, will tell you that such precise aiming is impossible. They felt themselves lucky to hit an enemy tank anywhere. But Tuck has this explanation:

"These little 37 mm guns—I wouldn't advise anybody to go to war with them again but they were most accurate out to, if I remember correctly, out to about three thousand yards [about 1 3/4 miles]. We did a lot of tests with them to determine how accurate they were and they were very accurate. We could also move our turret much faster than a medium tank and much faster than the Tiger [the big new German tank with a high-powered 88 mm gun]. That 88 was like a telephone pole. It traversed at a very slow rate. We found out we could go into defilade and get out of the way of them if we found them facing the wrong way."

All together the Americans knocked out seven tanks before the Germans pulled back. The Americans lost six of their light tanks and suffered several casualties, including the death of Major Siglin.

The American tankers were much too busy, of course, to be concerned about their place in the history books. But historians would later write that that clash between Waters's battalion of the 1st Armored Division and the 190th Panzer Battalion on November 26, 1942, was the first battle between American and German tanks in World War II.

Although the encounter was a victory for Tuck's well-hidden little tanks, the overall score was probably a draw, with both sides suffering roughly comparable losses. If Major Barlow's spectacular assault on the German airfield is counted in, that first encounter in the center was probably a plus for the Allied side. But the other arms of the offensive, in the north and the south, got off to a much less promising start.

Just as Waters's battalion of light tanks had been stripped off from the 1st Armored Division and attached to the British Blade Force, the 175th Field Artillery Battalion had been stripped from the 34th Infantry Division and attached to the part of Blade Force attacking along the southern axis toward the town of Medjez el Bab. This made more sense than some of the other ad hoc commitments of forces in those early days in Tunisia. The 175th, a Minnesota National Guard outfit, fit right in with Blade Force because it was equipped with a British weapon, the 25-pounder gun-howitzer, so named because its projectile weighed about 25 pounds. This was an excellent weapon with a unique feature that made it especially useful in fighting tanks: It came equipped with a circular metal platform. When the gun was in position, its rubber tires rested on the platform. One man could lift the trail extending back behind the weapon and swing it around to a new firing position in seconds.

The 175th, commanded by Col. Joseph E. "Ed" Kelly, arrived in Tunisia on November 18 after a two-day journey by truck from Algiers, and was sent forward toward Medjez el Bab almost immediately. To the surprise of the artillery-men, they were able to move into and through the town. The only soldiers there were a few French, who had so little am-munition that they offered no resistance—but they couldn't offer much help either. At daybreak on November 19, the artillerymen spotted German tanks and artillery parked east of Medjez. They opened fire on machine gun nests with their antitank guns and followed up with a barrage from their 25-pounders.

It was another historic moment—probably the first artil-lery rounds fired by an American battery against German positions in World War II. Captain Norman Kinsley realized the significance of the moment, saved the shell casing from the first round, and sent it home to be displayed at the Min-nesota National Guard Armory in Minneapolis.

The Germans responded with the first of four attacks that day by Stuka bombers. Machine gunners hit one plane, which was seen heading east trailing smoke. The Americans soon received word from people in the neighborhood that the plane had crashed.

"The Arab 'telegraph' was our best intelligence source," wrote John Glendower Westover, a member of the 175th, after the war. "Arab criers would shout from hilltop to hill-top. The message always started, 'Oh-ho, Mohammed.' Some-times we would get a warning of German activities. There were times when we saw Allied bombers heading for the Tunis harbor and we'd get a report of German ships hit long before it was reported on the evening BBC news."

Throughout the North African campaign, the Americans referred to the desperately poor natives with whom they came in contact as "Arabs." But most of those they referred to as "Arabs" were members of Berber tribes who had tended their sheep and camels in this area for countless centuries. They were descendants of the ancient Numidians, in a way analogous to the Native Americans of North America, the

Aborigines of Australia, and the Maori of New Zealand. This was not their first encounter with armed foreigners. They had survived the Phoenicians, who came in the 8th or 9th century B.C.E.; the Romans, who conquered Carthage in 146 B.C.E.; and the Arabs, who didn't arrive until late in the 7th century A.D.

The encounter between Colonel Kelly's artillerymen and the Germans was a kind of accident, what soldiers call a "meeting engagement" in which two hostile forces happen upon each other. Without infantry to help protect them, the artillerymen pulled back from Medjez.

By the time the Allied offensive kicked off in the middle of the night of November 24–25 and the 175th moved forward once more, the Germans had not only taken control of the town but also held the important river crossing at Medjez. Getting back to where they had been a week before would prove a daunting challenge for the Allies.

A British infantry battalion began the attack with a moonlight assault across a barren plain toward the town. Caught by machine guns and artillery and then attacked by infantry and tanks, the British fell back in a disorganized retreat. Casualties were heavy.

The American artillerymen, along with a British infantry battalion, attacked from the southwest and captured a hill overlooking the town, only to lose it again when the Germans counterattacked with tanks.

By the end of the day on November 25, it was clear that the Allied assault on Medjez had failed. But Nehring, the German commander, was worried about what might happen the next day. He ordered his troops to abandon the town during the night—a decision for which he was sharply criticized by Kesselring. The next day, after an Allied artillery bombardment, an American tank unit led British infantry into the town. They found the Germans gone, having demolished one span of the bridge across the river.

The Allies swung north toward Tébourba and Djedeida, the site of the airfield attacked by Major Barlow a few days before. If they could take those two key positions, they would be in place for the final assault on Tunis, only 12 miles away. By this time, the Germans had moved new planes into the

Djedeida field and held almost complete air superiority over the battlefield.

Allied reinforcements also continued to arrive on the ground, but not in the air. General Oliver showed up with the bulk of Combat Command B of the 1st Armored Division late in November after overcoming a curious bureaucratic hazard. When Oliver landed in Oran, he was under orders—and eager—to hurry to the scene of conflict in Tunisia. But a staff officer, thoroughly schooled in the penny-pinching ways of the peacetime army, refused to let him go because the 700-mile road trip would use up half the life of his half-track vehicles. Only after a personal appeal to Eisenhower did Oliver get permission for the trip. He arrived just in time to see the devastating effect of the German air attacks. He described what it was like in an interview with Army Air Forces officers in February 1943:

> [British] Spitfires would fly around in a sweep, but they could be over the particular area where we were for a matter of only 15 or 20 minutes. While they were there, we saw no enemy planes . . . But the moment that those Spitfires went away, the German planes came right out and were on us again. One of our battalions was dive-bombed as many as 22 times in one day . . .
>
> The actual material results of that dive bombing and strafing were not very great, but the effect on morale was pretty bad. I stood about a mile away on one occasion while one of our artillery batteries was being dive-bombed, and it looked to me like (or sounded like) everything in that vicinity would be wiped out. Actually, one of our guns was hit, and the ammunition carrier for that gun was hit and both were destroyed. A few men were wounded, but nobody was killed. After the men had been subjected to those attacks a few times, and found out that the material damage was not as great as it sounded, they got so they were not quite so disorganized by the dive-bombing.
>
> The nearest a bomb ever dropped near me was about 300 yards away. When it dropped, I was certain all the time that it was going to land right in the middle of my back, and was very much ashamed of myself when I found out that it did drop as much as 300 yards away.

In their rush to reach Tunis, the Allies had taken the risk of pushing their ground forces out beyond their air cover. The closest allied field was 70 miles away, while the closest German field was within minutes of the battlefield. It would have taken a superiority of three-to-one in fighters to make up for that disadvantage in distance, and the Allies didn't have anything near that many fighters. To make matters worse, the Allied planes that did arrive over the battlefield sometimes failed to distinguish friends from foes on the ground.

On November 26, Thanksgiving Day, as the first Allied offensive reached its climax, 11 American P-38 fighters appeared over the battlefield. They drove off a flight of Axis planes and then turned their attention to the forces on the ground. In five low-level strafing runs, they hammered Company C of the American 701st Tank Destroyer Battalion, killing five men, wounding 11, and damaging most of the unit's guns and vehicles. The whole attack took only about three minutes. The troops on the ground, recognizing the distinctive twin-tailed P-38s, or perhaps too shocked by the sudden attack by friendly planes, didn't shoot back. This restraint was to change, however, as some American ground units adopted an "if it flies, shoot it!" policy, whatever the nationality of the planes overhead.

One officer, writing later about this early phase of the battle for Tunisia, had this caustic comment about the Thanksgiving Day attack: "When the planes had used up their ammunition and left, Company C had ceased to exist as a fighting unit at a most critical moment in the race for Tunis. This terrible blunder by our own air force may be traced directly to the lack of air-ground training in the American army."

The Allies, including a dozen newly arrived tanks of the American Combat Command B, launched a new attack on Djedeida on November 29 after a half-hour artillery barrage. But the Germans hunkered down while the artillery shells were falling and then fought back with artillery, antitank guns, and heavy machine guns. Air attacks were the most intense so far. By nightfall, the attack had petered out.

In the northern sector, focusing on Bizerte, the Allied offensive had started out on a positive note on November 28. The British 36th Brigade, made up of a dozen Bren gun carriers and two companies of infantry, moved eastward through the valley of the Sedjenane River on the direct route toward Bizerte. The Brits paused as they approached the two hills flanking the road, Bald Hill and Green Hill. To bypass the hills through the brush-covered land on either side would take time, if it could be done at all through that rough terrain. Officers scanned the two hills with their field glasses. Green Hill was covered in green brush. The lower slopes of Bald Hill were also brush-covered, but the top quarter was gray and bald. From what they could see, there was no sign of the Germans.

The men climbed into their vehicles and rumbled forward into the pass between the two hills. The infantry came marching behind. It was quiet as they entered the pass. They moved on toward the open roadway on the other side. And then, as they reached the center of the pass, heavy German machine guns, hidden on the slopes above, opened up. Within minutes, 10 of the 12 gun carriers were blazing, 30 men were dead, and another 50 were wounded. The survivors rallied and tried to get at the enemy machine gun nests, but without success. As night fell, the survivors pulled back out of the pass, leaving 86 prisoners in enemy hands. It was to be another five months before another Allied force got that close to Bizerte.

Blocked on all fronts and suffering from severe air attacks, the British general in charge called off the offensive until something could be done about the almost total German control of the air.

About the time the offensive came to a halt, on November 30, the Allies were setting in motion two daring operations designed to hit the Germans from behind.

The British 1st Commando, including two platoons of Americans drawn from the 34th Infantry Division, sailed in landing craft from Tabarka, on the Mediterranean coast near the Algerian border, to a beach a short distance west of Bizerte. Their landing, on the morning of December 1, was unopposed. But they were almost immediately spotted by two

German planes that attacked one of the landing craft as it pulled back out to sea. The commandos set off to the south, marching eight miles cross-country through brush-covered hills. Their job was to block the road between Bizerte and Bald and Green hills to prevent reinforcements from reaching the Germans guarding that pass and to harass them as they retreated. Although the commandos didn't know it at the time, the battle for the hills had already been fought and lost. Only as it became obvious from the lack of traffic on the road that the Germans were neither rushing up reinforcements nor retreating did the commandos realized what had happened.

One of the American platoons was caught in an ambush. Their platoon leader concluded the situation was hopeless and ordered his men to lay down their weapons. But Sgt. "Chief" Sessions refused.

"No sir," he told the lieutenant, "I'm fighting my way out and anyone else is welcome to join me." He and two other men fought their way out of the trap and by sundown had joined the other American platoon. The men they left behind were captured.

Bob Berens, by this time promoted to corporal, was in the other American platoon and was there when Sessions and his two colleagues approached from the direction of Bizerte about sundown. So far, their platoon had seen one German command car whiz past and had stopped a motorcycle with a sidecar with fire from a Browning automatic rifle (BAR).

That relatively peaceful situation changed dramatically the next morning. Berens later described what happened next:

"An infantry-tank team approached from the south and stopped just out of range of our weapons, where the infantry detrucked and fell in behind the tanks, mounting 75 mm guns. Lieutenant Martin took them under fire as they neared the bridge. The infantry dispersed to the sides of the road while the tanks continued. The lead tank stopped short of the bridge, apparently because the commander was not sure the bridge would bear the load.

"Lieutenant Martin decided to strike back. He sent Sergeant [Leo] Taylor and the two men with shaped-charge grenades down the west side of the road, which was screened by trees. The BAR man sprayed the front of the tank with bullets while Sergeant Taylor's team launched a grenade that struck the turret and exploded but with no apparent effect. The tank responded by driving slowly onto the bridge, shooting as it advanced. The other three tanks and infantry also advanced. Even the intrepid Lieutenant Martin began to have second thoughts at that point."

The lightly armed commandos were no match for tanks and infantry armed with heavy machine guns.

Martin ordered his men to "slide westward along the river bank." They had gone only about a hundred yards to some woods when they discovered they had left their radio behind. Taylor dashed back, scooped up the radio, and returned with their only link to the other commando units.

By that time, 1st Commando had held the road for three days. But it was obvious now that the British were not going to come marching triumphantly down the highway from the direction of Bald and Green hills. The commandos, traveling as lightly as possible, had not even taken blankets with them. Their food consisted of a few tins of sardines, biscuits, and tea. When they ran out of water purification tablets, they drank from the streams with no ill effects. Almost out of food and low on ammunition, the remnants of 1st Commando walked back across the hills and mountains, arriving in friendly lines five days after they had landed almost within sight of Bizerte. The operation had cost 134 casualties, including 74 Americans.

The other attempt to hit behind German lines met with even less success. On the afternoon of November 29, 500 British paratroops jumped from American transport planes about 25 miles south of Tunis and made a nighttime attack on an airfield at a town named Oudna. But their intelligence was bad: the field was not in use by Axis planes. The paratroops shot up the installation and then set off, carrying their wounded, to work their way cross-country back to Medjez el Bab. More than half the force was lost: 19 killed, four wounded, and 266 missing.

Thus, by the end of November, the Allies had been stopped all along the line.

Eisenhower reported to the Combined Chiefs of Staff that his forces desperately needed a breathing space, primarily to try to do something about the German dominance of the air. Allied air forces were already so overworked, he warned, that in another week they would be at or near a complete breakdown. In the next few days, he said, air activity would be limited to attacks on German ports and lines of communication, with occasional fighter attacks against German airfields, while the air commanders sought to build up their forces. He set December 9 as the tentative date for a new offensive.

"The principal objective will be the capture of Tunis, to throw the enemy back into the Bizerte stronghold. There we will try to confine him closely while bringing up additional means for the final kill," Eisenhower wrote.

But the Germans had no intention of providing the Allies with the breathing space they so badly needed. At 7:45 A.M. on December 1, they launched a determined offensive aimed at the center of the Allied line, in the area of Tebourba, Djedeida, and Chouigui Pass.

If Eisenhower knew how worried the German commanders were as they mounted this offensive defense, he might have felt better about having his plans so rudely disrupted.

Generalmajor Wolfgang Fischer was in charge of the December 1 offensive. He had some good troops, especially the members of his own 10th Panzer Division, who were just then arriving in Tunisia. But he also had some men scraped together from various sources and hurriedly sent to the front. As his offensive got under way, he complained to Nehring:

> . . . not the slightest interest existed, no aggressive spirit, no readiness for action, so that I was forced to lead some companies, platoons, even squads, and to assign them a sector on the battlefield. I consider it my duty to point out this critical condition as it is impossible to fight successfully with such troops. It is also true that their command is inadequate. I have warned one captain who failed several times to execute his missions that in case of a repetition I would have him relieved. I had another officer relieved on the spot and demanded that he be court-martialed because he and his men lurked under cover for hours. . . .

On the Allied side, Paul Robinett—freshly promoted from colonel to brigadier general—rushed forward on December 2 with more elements of the American 1st Armored Division's Combat Command B. He arrived on the front line just as everything seemed to be coming apart. One unit of 30 light tanks, attacking without artillery support, had just been thrown back with heavy losses. A column of Sherman medium tanks tried to go to the rescue of a tank unit that had been cut off and quickly lost eight of its tanks to enemy antitank fire. Robinett called off a planned attack and decided to go on the defensive until British and American forces could be reinforced and better arrangements made for coordinating the two countries' forces.

Robinett later sized up the situation: "We had reached the front too late, with too little, without a balanced force, without proper command arrangements to insure coordination, and failed to employ available forces so that they were mutually supporting. But the folly of all follies was the intermingling of the forces of three nations in the same sector. Tactical coordination could only be accomplished by cooperation and responsibility could not be fixed. Communication was limited to personal visits, liaison officers and messengers."

By the time the German offensive ended on December 4, Tunis, which once seemed so tantalizingly close, was beginning to seem almost inaccessible. General Fischer estimated that his forces had knocked out 55 tanks, destroyed or captured scores of artillery pieces and smaller guns, and captured more than 1,000 Allied soldiers. Although the Germans had not seized a great deal of land, they had stopped the Allied attack on Tunis.

Most important, however, the terrain the Germans had seized gave them defensive positions all along the hills that lay between the First Army and Tunis and Bizerte. Experts were flown in from Germany and spent the next few days establishing sites where a few men, armed with machine guns and heavy mortars, could hamper the movement of enemy forces through the passes leading out onto the Tunis and Bizerte plains.

The German defense was greatly aided, too, by a decision made by the British after World War I—the war to end all wars. The British infantry had been ordered to turn in their heavy Vickers machine guns and replace them with lighter weapons. The decision must have seemed brilliant at the time. It gave the soldiers lighter weapons, easier to carry. It enabled them to carry more ammunition. And it probably saved some money. But all along the hill lines in those dreary days of December 1942, the British found themselves facing skillfully hidden German machine guns that fired heavier, more destructive bullets than their weapons—and fired them farther. It was like boxing against an opponent with bigger fists and longer arms. In the coming battles, the plebeian machine gun was to give the Allies at least as much trouble as the Stukas that worried them so much.

As the German offensive came to an end, the British general on the scene proposed pulling his forces back, abandoning Medjez el Bab. He realized a quick capture of Tunis seemed increasingly unrealistic and argued that it would be better to give up some territory while conserving and building up his forces for a later offensive. The French argued against the pullback and Eisenhower agreed—with considerable reluctance. In a letter on December 7, he expressed his misgivings:

> I think the best way to describe our operations to date is that they have violated every recognized principle of war, are in conflict with all operational and logistic methods laid down in textbooks, and will be condemned in their entirety by all Leavenworth and War College classes for the next twenty-five years.

Whatever hopes Eisenhower may have had for a resumption of the march toward Tunis were shattered on December 10 by yet another German offensive.

Waters and his battalion of light tanks were dug in—but not very deeply—on a hill to the east of Medjez el Bab. In midmorning, Waters and Major Barlow were standing beside their tanks, talking. Bill Tuck was in the turret of his tank. They could see German tanks moving toward them down below and were looking for something to shoot at. And then suddenly they were taken under fire from enemy tanks that had slipped around to the side, unseen.

"I heard a loud bang," Tuck recalls. "The next thing I remember I was being taken out of the tank and I was wounded. That's all I remember. They shot me full of morphine and took me by train to Algiers.

"They told me later that some German tanks, probably about a platoon of them, had gotten to the south and were shooting at us from the rear or side. We thought we had the hill protected but they got back there and started shooting at us. That's when they got me. The shell went through the turret, killed . . . my tank commander. I was in the left-hand side, he was on the right. It killed him immediately, took his chest out. It hit me a glancing blow on the chest and went through the other side of the tank."

Tuck was badly hurt. The concussion of the shell passing through the tank had caved in his chest, causing what he was told was blast pneumonia. The whole right side of his body was riddled with splinters from the interior of the tank, torn loose as the shell passed through the turret. The other two members of his crew, down below, were not harmed.

In short order, the Germans knocked out five of Waters's light tanks and five half-tracks. The surviving Americans pulled back. Later in the day, another unit of American light tanks was caught by heavier German tanks as they came over a ridge. As the Americans tumbled out of their burning tanks, the enemy tankers on the high ground above them sprayed the area with machine gun fire. The survivors crawled to a dip in the earth and hid until they could begin the walk back to friendly lines. By this time, rain had been falling for several days, turning the ground into seemingly bottomless mud—which was fortunate for one of the Americans, who survived being run over by a Panzer III tank by being only pressed into the mud.

That night, the order was given for a general retreat of Combat Command B. During the withdrawal on December 11, a column of tanks and half-tracks took a wrong turn, became mired in the mud, and had to be abandoned. All together, Combat Command B lost—to the enemy and the mud—18 tanks, 41 guns, 132 other vehicles, and 19 trailers.

George Howe, who wrote the official history of the North African campaign for the Army, also wrote the generally admiring *The Battle History of the 1st Armored Division.* He was forced to describe the events of December 10 and 11, involving the division's Combat Command B, as "a humiliating and costly misfortune after a series of frustrations and disappointments in action against the enemy."

Waters's battalion, which had been the first American armored unit into combat with the Germans a little over two weeks before, was so badly battered that the survivors were ordered to turn their tanks over to another unit and return to Oran to prepare for combat later in the campaign.

In early December, Generaloberst Juergen von Arnim was recalled from the Russian front, where he commanded a panzer corps. He stopped for a meeting with Hitler at the führer's eastern headquarters and then flew on to Tunis to take over from Nehring. In the process, his command was upgraded to become the Fifth Panzer Army, its new title matching in grandiosity the British First Army. Despite repeated raids by heavy bombers against the docks in Bizerte and Tunis, the Germans had managed to continue their buildup of forces in Tunisia. But, like its British counterpart, the Fifth Army was an "army" only in name. As the first battle for Tunisia neared its climax, the Germans had about 25,000 combat troops, plus 10,000 service troops, facing 20,000 British, 11,800 Americans, and 7,000 French.

When von Arnim arrived on the scene, he had some reason to be gratified by what Nehring had accomplished. The Germans had a strong defensive line running from the sea west of Bizerte down through the hill line and across to another point on the shore south of Tunis. Von Arnim even had enough troops to begin building a defense of the coastal area, the vital link between his army and Rommel's when the Desert Fox had completed his withdrawal into Tunisia. The weather, which is cold and rainy in northern Tunisia in the winter, was on von Arnim's side, turning Allied airfields and roads into bottomless muck. And yet his pilots brought him reports of preparations on the other side of the hill for a renewed lunge at Tunis.

The British commander on the scene had become increasingly skeptical of the chances of taking Tunis anytime soon. But orders came down from above to put in motion one more offensive. One major obstacle remained between his troops and Tunis. It was called Longstop Hill. Lying about seven miles north of Medjez el Bab, it is only a little more than 900 feet high, in contrast to the much higher mountains that rise behind it to the north. But it was the high ground from which artillery and air strikes could be coordinated on any Allied forces attempting to bypass it on the way to Tunis.

As the time for the attack came on the night of December 23, the situation looked remarkably promising. The rains had stopped two days before, and the ground was rapidly drying out. A bright moon was shining as the British Coldstream Guards battalion made its attack on the hill. American and British armor massed for the dash to Tunis once the hill was taken.

The Guards fought their way to the top and then turned the job over to an American unit, which almost immediately came under heavy fire from a nearby hilltop whose significance—perhaps even its very existence—had somehow been overlooked in planning for the attack. The Guards battalion hurried back. By that time, it was raining heavily. Together with the Americans, they held on through Christmas Day. But without heavy machine guns and more soldiers, they couldn't stay there. On December 26, the Allies pulled back to Medjez el Bab.

The fighting on Christmas Day was futile, as it turned out. The day before, Allied commanders, meeting with Eisenhower at General Anderson's headquarters in the city of Constantine, Algeria, had decided to call off the attack on Tunis.

The first battle for Tunisia was over. The Axis had won.

7

Seizing the High Ground

Colonel Edson D. Raff was the kind of midlevel combat commander who saw what needed to be done and went ahead and did it without waiting for orders, the kind of innovative, aggressive commander any general would give a million dollars for—if he didn't have him court-martialed and shot.

The first combat operation of Raff's 503rd Parachute Battalion—the first American parachute operation ever—had, as we have seen, turned into a disaster with transport planes scattered from Spain to Algeria and the men who got that far set down in a muddy lake bed far from the action at Oran.

But Raff and his troops—by now a distinctly under-strength battalion of about 350 men—were back in action within days, this time with a successful and crucial contribution to the Allied war effort, the seizure of "the high ground." In this case, the high ground consisted of a series of airfields close enough to the front to begin to chip away at German control of the air over key mountain passes.

At 8:00 A.M. on November 15, just a week after the landings in North Africa, the battalion took off from the Maison Blanche airport in Algiers in 33 C-47 transport planes. Their goal was two airfields near the city of Tébessa, in Algeria near the Tunisian border. Raff's original orders were to seize the small airfield near the city. But in talking to a couple of Frenchmen familiar with the area, he learned that a larger and more important French airdrome was located at the nearby town of Youks-les-Bains. The only guide to their destination was an old French flying map marked with a small square indicating where Raff's informants thought the field was located.

Neither Raff nor anyone else knew what they were getting into. His cryptic orders to his men were: "Be loaded on your planes at dawn and follow me."

Despite the rudimentary nature of their map and the almost complete lack of intelligence about their target, the pilots managed to find the airdrome. They lined up and flew in steadily on course for the drop.

As the paratroops stepped out the cargo door of the first plane, they could see French troops with machine guns in trenches around the field. If the French opened fire while the 'chutists were in the air or as the planes paraded, unswerving, over the field, the whole operation would end in disaster. For the few moments it took the men to reach the ground, they were defenseless. And so were the planes as they held steady on course to make their drop.

The first plane discharged its paratroops, the second, the third. The French held their fire and so did the Americans. As the first men touched down, they found the French waiting to welcome them as friends. A short time later, Raff was able to report that the Youks-les-Bains airdrome and the smaller Tébessa airport were both in friendly hands. If the understrength parachute unit could hold these fields, they would not only deny them to the Germans but give the Allies their closest fields to the battlefront.

As soon as they had secured the fields near Tébessa, the paratroops moved on to take control of an even more important French airdrome near the small town of Thélepte in far western Tunisia. This would, for the next two months, be the most advanced Allied airfield in Tunisia—so far advanced, in fact, that there were few, if any, friendly forces between the airmen and the enemy; the sounds of tank engines in the night could be the Germans coming to overrun their outpost.

The reader will recall that the geography of Tunisia is dominated in its northern and central areas by mountains in the shape of an inverted "Y." The base of the "Y" is in the north. Stretching south from it are two mountain ranges known as the Eastern and Western Dorsals. While Tébessa and Youks-les-Bains were on the western side of the Western Dorsal, the airdrome at Thélepte was situated in the broad valley between the dorsals and thus closer to the action.

Security for the field was provided by French forces and some of Raff's men. But Raff was not content with seizing these vital forward airfields. For a few weeks, Raff became, in effect, the supreme Allied commander in a vast area of central Tunisia, fighting his own little lightning war while the bigger battle between the British First Army and the Germans was taking place in northern Tunisia.

Those who saw Raff at the time recall a stocky man who wore a carbine draped from his left shoulder, indoors as well as out. Somehow he acquired a small airplane and used it to flit about his domain, flying as low as he could because, as he explained, he liked to keep one foot on the ground.

Allied commanders back in Algiers were pouring almost everything they had into the big battle up north for Tunis and Bizerte. But they managed to scrape up a few meager reinforcements for Raff's battalion. Lt. Col. John Bowen showed up with the 3rd Battalion of the 26th Infantry, a part of the 1st Infantry Division, which was to play a major role in the later battles for Tunisia. Raff also had a company of the 701st Tank Destroyer Battalion, a small unit of the French Chasseur d'Afrique with motorcycles and armored cars and the services of four P-38 fighter planes.

Raff set up his headquarters in Feriana, a road junction a few miles south of Thélepte, and sent a platoon of paratroops down to the ancient city of Gafsa. They heard a report that the enemy was advancing on Gafsa. So they blew up 70,000 gallons of high-octane gasoline that belonged to the French. Even though the Allies would badly need fuel that did not have to be trucked in from hundreds of miles away, the paratroops decided it was best to make sure it did not fall into enemy hands. As soon as the sound of the explosion died down, the paratroopers pulled out of Gafsa.

There was no way this tiny handful of men could hold the town if the Germans and their Italian allies decided to take it.

But Raff was not content to let the Axis forces just walk in and take the city. On the morning of November 21, he received word from the French, who had intelligence agents stationed in every town and virtually every little hamlet, that an enemy force was advancing on Gafsa. Raff put together a Provisional Task Force of paratroops, infantry, tank destroyers, and the French Chasseurs, moved during the night, and by dawn the next morning, was in position in hills overlooking Gafsa. By that time, the Germans were already in the town.

At one minute before 7:00 A.M., Raff's four-plane air force strafed the enemy positions, providing cover for the tank destroyers and infantry as they moved across the open terrain toward the Axis defenses. With most of their machine guns and antitank weapons knocked out in the first few minutes of the onslaught, the Germans pulled out of Gafsa.

Gafsa, once an important link in the camel caravan route that connected settlements along the Mediterranean with Africa south of the Sahara, was then a pleasant little oasis of about 10,000 people—Berbers, Arabs, Jews who had lived there for nearly 2,000 years, and more recent arrivals from Europe. It had a 15th-century Arab-built citadel and a huge open-air swimming pool fed by warm sulfur water that soon became popular with the American soldiers.

But Raff's men had no time for such luxuries. They had barely arrived in the town when they received a report that an Italian tank column, moving in from the coast, had reached El Guettar, a dozen miles east of Gafsa, and was headed their way. Troops were immediately sent off to meet this new threat. By the time darkness settled over the battlefield, they had knocked out five of the enemy's medium tanks and forced the survivors to pull back to the east.

The exhausted men had just arrived back in Gafsa when they received word from the French that a German column had been spotted heading toward Thélepte. This was no vague rumor. The report was very specific: 15 tanks, six 88 mm guns towed by trucks, and motorized infantry. They had been seen approaching Sbeitla, which was 76 miles north of Gafsa and 42 miles north of Thélepte.

Raff, his forces already stretched impossibly thin, put together a new task force consisting of a platoon of paratroopers and a few tank destroyers and sent them north to try to head off the enemy column. The men got started out that night, shortly after the battle at El Guettar. They had been marching and fighting for two days, living on packaged K rations. Their vehicles had not been serviced since they left Algiers, hundreds of miles away. They reached the town of Feriana about 2:00 A.M., slept for a few hours, and then went looking for the enemy. They found that a German armored column had taken Sbeitla and then headed back toward Tunis, leaving an Italian unit to hold the town.

Early in the afternoon of November 24, with the sun nearly overhead, the American tank destroyers mounted a slight rise in the earth and bore down on the Italians. The paratroopers followed them down the hill toward the line, where the enemy had not yet finished their trenches. One tank destroyer was hit and stopped. But the crew continued to fire their gun, knocking out two enemy tanks. As the Americans approached the Italian lines, white flags appeared and the enemy soldiers began emerging from the ground, hands in the air. Several machine guns continued to fire, but they did little harm because the gunners were lying flat on the ground, holding one hand up to the trigger. They couldn't see where they were shooting, and most of the bullets arced off into the air.

The victory by the tiny American unit was gratifying in two ways: It resulted in the capture of about 100 prisoners and the destruction of a dozen light tanks. But even more important, it resulted in the capture of ammunition, new trucks, blankets, food, and wine.

The American unit pulled back to Feriana, where Raff had set up his headquarters, and turned defense of Sbeitla over to the French. With his attacks at two different places, more than 85 miles apart, within hours, Raff had given the enemy reason to believe he was opposed by a large American force spread all along the valley between the Eastern and

Western Dorsals. In fact, all Raff had was a tiny, fast-moving, hard-hitting mobile force that was not nearly large enough to form a defensive line through the whole long valley.

The false perception of a powerful force, which Raff had so skillfully created, seemed to be working on the minds of the German commanders. They stopped their probes toward Gafsa—for the time being—and began to fortify the Faïd Pass, one of the small number of crucial passes through the Eastern Dorsal, rather than repeating their probing attacks toward Sbeitla and Thélepte.

Raff and Bowen, the infantry commander, decided they didn't want the Germans at Faïd Pass either and decided to do something about it. Attacking from the west against the dug-in enemy positions would be not only costly but futile. Another pass, named Aï Rebaou, cut through the mountains about five miles south of Faïd Pass. It was little more than a rough camel track but good enough for the tank destroyers, which had rubber tires in front and tracks on the back. The only problem was that Aï Rebaou was heavily mined. Fortunately for the Americans, the Germans had neglected to station anyone in the pass to defend the minefield, perhaps because they, like the Americans, were trying to cover too much territory with too few men. But a minefield without antitank guns, artillery, and infantry to defend it is little more than a nuisance.

On the night of December 2, the tank destroyers, Bowen's infantry, and Raff's paratroops—plus a company of Algerian Tirailleurs, added at the last minute—cleared a path through the minefield and emerged on the eastern side of the Eastern Dorsal, behind the German positions. It was a perfect plan for a surprise attack—until it all fell apart. Slowed by the mines and having difficulty making their way in the dark, the attacking force was still some distance from the German lines when dawn broke. Surprise was lost.

The Germans used their artillery to keep the attackers at bay while they hastily rearranged their positions to face toward the east rather than the west. Instead of a quick surprise victory, the Allies found themselves bogged down in a slow, costly fight that went on for three days. But the enemy was running out of ammunition and supplies. In a desperate attempt to break through the Allied lines, a squadron of enemy bombers hammered the American positions while a column of supply trucks made a bold dash down the road toward the pass. The planes were driven off by machine gun fire and the column was turned back, but not before the American forces had suffered heavy damage from the bombing attack.

On the fourth day, the Allies brought in a French artillery force to fire on the German positions from the western side of the pass, now the rear of the German position. Bowen's infantry worked its way to within a quarter of a mile of the enemy. The paratroops took up a position to the east of the Germans while Algerian Tirailleurs moved in from the west. The infantrymen advanced under an intense artillery barrage that was not lifted until the Allied troops were within 50 yards of the enemy positions. Then the artillery ceased fire and the troops dashed forward with bayonets and grenades. Within a few minutes, the pass was in Allied hands.

The victory had not been cheap. The Americans and the French native troops fighting with them lost about a hundred men killed and wounded. About 200 enemy soldiers were captured.

In terms of the larger battles that were to come at this key pass through the mountains, this was a relatively minor confrontation. But, coupled with French seizure of two passes further north and the successful action by Raff's forces east of Gafsa, the Allies now had possession of all four of the crucial openings through the Eastern Dorsal.

For high commanders in their offices far to the rear, the bold action by Raff and Bowen was, of course, gratifying. Allied control of the passes would pose a fatal threat to Rommel as he ended his retreat across Africa and sought to join up with the German forces around Tunis and Bizerte. But possession of this high ground also posed a daunting challenge. Unless the commanders had the will and the troops to reinforce the poorly armed French soldiers holding the high ground, there was always the danger that the passes might be overrun, with heavy losses by the French. If the passes could not be held, it might be better not to have them at all.

But there was a very good reason to hold the passes, especially the one at Faïd. Having Faïd Pass, no matter how thinly held, in friendly hands added a measure of security as the 33rd Fighter Group set up shop at Thélepte at the Allies' most advanced airbase and plunged into the fight for control of the air.

8

Fight for the Air

Even before the pilots of the 33rd Group's 58th Squadron first touched down on the broad, grass-covered fields— the "foamy fields," as a passing journalist christened them— at Thélepte on December 11, 1942, the pressure had begun to build.

They could not have known it then, but the pressure on both the Americans and the Luftwaffe would increase continually until it reached a breaking point in the middle of January. The only question was who would break first—the Germans, as they watched their bombers take off and fail to return, or the Americans, battered by daily bombing and outclassed by the enemy pilots and their superior fighter planes.

Six pilots of the 58th Squadron flew their first combat mission on December 7—the first anniversary of the Japanese attack on Pearl Harbor—from the field in Algeria near the Tunisian border at Youks-les-Bains, seized a few days earlier by Colonel Raff's paratroops. The sweep, taking them over the nearby towns of Sidi Bou Zid and Faïd, then held by friendly French forces but soon to become the scenes of some of the toughest fighting of the campaign, was uneventful. But the news, when they returned to huddle in their makeshift shelters as cold winter rain squalls pelted the field, was depressing.

Another patrol, by the 33rd Fighter Group's 60th Squadron, had ventured further east to the coastal city of Gabès that same day. Lt. Perry F. Bowser, a 60th Squadron pilot flying a 58th Squadron plane, swooped down to strafe three transport planes parked at an enemy airfield. Caught by intense antiaircraft fire, he crashed and was killed—the first combat loss by the group. Only the day before, Lt. Rufus McLeod, also of the 60th Squadron, had been killed in a landing accident while escorting a flight of transport planes toward Tunisia.

Two days later, two German bombers approached the field at Youks through broken clouds. Lt. Charles B. Poillion, a pilot of the 58th Squadron, gunned his P-40 through the mud that covered the field and managed to get into the air. The enemy planes were still over the field. Ground crew members and other pilots stood in clusters and cheered as Poillion, guided by directions radioed from the ground, worked his way through the clouds and got into firing position. He fired long bursts at the two planes before breaking off to return and land. Neither plane was seen to fall.

He taxied off the field and then, as he prepared to park his plane, it slowly nosed over into the mud. It seemed an ignominious end to the squadron's first air-to-air combat until the next day, when word was received that ground troops had found the wreckage of one of the enemy planes on a nearby hillside—the first kill for the 58th Squadron.

Two days later, the pilots of the 58th Squadron flew on to Thélepte, the most advanced Allied airfield in that part of Tunisia. The 60th Squadron remained at Youks. Much to their dismay, the members of the group's third squadron, the 59th, had been ordered to turn their planes over to the French, as part of the deal that ended resistance to the invasion, so they were stuck on the ground back in Morocco.

As every soldier knows, while airmen may suffer terrible stresses in combat and, on any mission, may be shot down in flames and die, at least, if they survive, they fly back to a relatively safe airfield far behind the front lines where they will find hot food, a shot of whiskey, a warm room, and clean sheets. As the pilots of the 58th Fighter Squadron landed at Thélepte and moved into the French barracks on the field, they probably assumed that rule still held. They could not have been more wrong.

A welcoming attack by a German bomber quickly convinced them that anything rising above ground level was a target. The next morning, the pilots began to construct the first of a labyrinth of underground bunkers where they would live like soldiers in World War I trenches, listening constantly for the sound of aircraft engines, or perhaps even the deep rumble of tanks approaching over the hills from the east.

In those very first days, the pilots themselves maintained their planes, flew their missions, and dug their bunkers. This was all part of a logical army plan designed to move fighter units quickly and throw them into combat as fast as possible. Each squadron was divided into three echelons. First came the flight or advance echelon—the pilots themselves and their planes. Then came the air echelon—the mechanics and the most essential ground crews. Finally, the ground echelon arrived with the record keepers, the cooks, and all the rest of the nonflying personnel needed to keep the planes in the air.

The 58th Squadron was one of the three squadrons of the 33rd Fighter Group that had flown ashore at the Port-Lyautey airfield north of Casablanca during the initial invasion. A few days later, another squadron of P-40s made the flight from a British carrier, HMS *Archer.* This was the so-called Joker Squadron—as in the poker term, "the joker is wild"—headed by Maj. Philip Cochran. Made up of relatively inexperienced pilots, some of them just out of flight school, the Joker Squadron was there to make up any losses the other three squadrons might suffer during the invasion. Fortunately, losses were very light, so the pilots and planes of the Joker Squadron became available as replacements for future combat losses.

Cochran, then a 32-year-old veteran of the peacetime air corps, was in the process of gaining a kind of fame that, in this day of television and motion picture celebrity, seems almost quaint. He had become the fictional "star" of a newspaper cartoon strip. It happened this way: Cochran had gone

to school at Ohio State University with Milton Caniff, the
creator of a highly popular strip known as *Terry and the
Pirates*. As the United States entered the war, Caniff felt the
need to get his characters involved in the conflict. So he introduced a flamboyant air corps pilot he called Flip Corkin, pat-
terned closely after Cochran. Caniff's friend was a perfect
model for a cartoon strip filled with action and adventure—
a character with a certain disdain for egotistic brass hats.

Cochran told a revealing story in an Air Force oral history interview years later. Once during the conflict in Tunisia, he flew back to Algiers to get a new engine in his plane.
Sitting on a bench at the airfield waiting while the mechanics worked, he became aware of a commotion. General Patton
and an entourage were alighting from two C-47 transport
planes. But there were no cars to meet them, and Patton was
fuming. He strode up to Cochran, who stood and saluted.

"You get your ass out of here and get in there and get
me some cars," Patton demanded.

Cochran tried to explain he was just passing through.

"I don't care what establishment you belong to, you go
in there and get me some cars," Patton snarled.

Cochran thought to himself: "I'm a major in this guy's
air force, for heaven's sake. I'm no guy to be screamed at,
and furthermore, I have been up and gotten shot at, and I
got more combat experience than this guy is going to get in
the next four or five months. I kind of outranked him as far
as that went."

As he turned and started to walk toward the door, Patton shouted: "I said *run!*"

Cochran kept on walking. "I walked upstairs, and there
was a balcony on this thing. . . . So I went on the balcony
and sat up there and watched him fume some more and
watched him scream at people. Pretty soon the cars started
arriving and I got out of it."

Not one to be left out of a fight, Cochran left his Joker
Squadron at Rabat in Morocco and headed for the front. He
found a mixture of planes and pilots from the 58th and 60th
squadrons at Youks-les-Bains waiting, in effect, for someone
to tell them what to do next. Lt. Col. William "Spike" Mom-

yer, the group commander, had not yet arrived, so Cochran took charge. He moved with the 58th Squadron on over the hills to Tunisia, to the most advanced field at Thélepte, and left the 60th Squadron a little further back at Youks.

At this time, in early December, the first battle for Tunisia, in the hills surrounding Tunis and Bizerte, was still being fought and the outcome was uncertain. But the 58th Squadron, flying out of Thélepte, was too far south to play a direct part in that battle. Instead, it was involved in what would become the second battle for Tunisia, waged along the Eastern Dorsal. Both sides were making their major effort in the north and neither had significant ground forces available in this more southerly area. But, as in the north, the Axis held a significant edge in air power, with fighters and dive bombers flying from hard-surface runways at airfields along the coast and with heavier bombers coming in from Italy and Sicily.

The pilots of the 58th Squadron quickly sized up the enemy. Of most concern to the fighter pilots were the German Messerschmitt ME-109 and the newer Focke-Wulf FW-190, both single-engine fighters; the two-man JU-8 Stuka dive bomber, and the lumbering twin-engined JU-88 bomber. The obsolete Stuka and the bigger JU-88, carrying far fewer guns than the American B-17 Flying Fortress, proved to be relatively easy targets. But the fighters were another matter: they were able to fly higher and faster than the P-40s, enabling them to strike from above and then zoom up for another pass.

In an interview conducted by intelligence officers in June 1943, Cochran explained the difference between the performance of the German and American planes:

"People say the Germans use the sun more than we do, that they have more sense than we have, that they are better hunters. It is not true. They have an airplane that can get to the sun quicker than we can get to the sun. Therefore, who uses it? He does! When he comes down, he has a greater speed with which he can cut off the combat whenever he wishes, and go right on back up. I think that is the main point—the superior climbing rate of the German airplane."

The great advantage—really, the only advantage—of the American P-40 was its ability to turn, Cochran explained:

"We learned that the P-40 was quick in a turn and you couldn't find a guy on the field who wasn't ready to send a testimonial to, or kiss, the people at Curtiss Wright because of the quick turn of the P-40 that saved every one of their necks every time they turned around. I think I can count ten times when if the P-40 wouldn't turn I would have been gone long ago. The same with every kid there."

In the two months the 58th Squadron spent at Thélepte, violent death was to be an almost constant presence in the skies over central Tunisia and at Thélepte itself. As the death toll rose, so too did the psychological toll on the pilots and the ground crews as well.

Unlike most air force operations, where the air crews go off to face danger and possible death while the ground crews wait, and worry, in relative safety, the danger at Thélepte was almost as great on the ground as it was in the air. The attacks began as soon as the squadron arrived. At first a lone bomber would drop its bombs or a few fighters would sweep across the field, firing their machine guns.

In a typical attack, a JU-88 bomber would approach from the east at about 11,000 feet, then dive toward the field, dropping its bombs from about 4,000 feet. The attacks came with little or no warning because no radar had been installed along the Eastern Dorsal. The only warning was provided by a rudimentary system set up by the French in which lookouts would phone in reports of approaching planes.

"Any airplane was enemy to them," Cochran explained. "They were hard for them to distinguish. They had us running like mad—chasing our own planes some of the time."

Protecting their own airfield became the first priority for the Americans. In effect, this cut their combat effectiveness because planes assigned to patrol above the airfield were not available to assist in the ground war or to seek out other enemy targets. But these protective patrols paid off. The enemy soon learned that unescorted bombers were in grave danger.

"We sometimes could catch these people by taking off and catching them somewhere around in here [pointing 50 miles east of Thélepte] and discouraged them from doing this by getting three out of the first five we intercepted," Cochran said. "Then they started coming in with escort and you could just see the whole thing build up. They were building it up. It got so we had to have four and sometimes eight protecting our own airdrome."

Fortunately for the Americans, Thélepte was a difficult target. Set on a broad, level plain on the western side of the valley between the two mountain ranges, it was covered with almost white grass over a light sandy soil that quickly drained away water from the frequent winter rains. Most of the men built their dugouts in a ravine, digging through the lighter topsoil into the hard clay underneath. For many of them, the areas where they ate and slept were as much as a 45-minute walk from the area where the planes were repaired and readied for flight. Attacks aimed at the planes endangered only the men actually working around the planes. Attacks aimed at the men where they lived were likely to leave the planes unscathed.

Instead of a control tower, the controllers operated from a large pit in the ground that permitted them to see planes in the traffic pattern but also offered some protection from enemy bombers and strafers.

Business at Thélepte tended to center around two holes in the ground—the operations shack, known as Journey's End, and Hotel Leon, the home of Leon Caplan, a French lieutenant assigned as liaison to the American unit. The pilots, who usually flew two missions a day, spent much of their time at Journey's End, wearing all the clothes they owned and huddling in blankets, trying to keep warm. Cochran, who had a short, chunky build, looked even more chunky with one flight jacket worn over another.

Hotel Leon was often crowded during the day, serving as an unofficial office for the squadron. Two phones had been installed, one answered in English, the other in French. Two enlisted men sat at a shelf along one wall, typing up the unit records. The volume of records produced during the North African campaign, now carefully catalogued at the National Archives in College Park, Maryland, leads one to suspect that this modern army traveled with at least as many typewriters as machine guns and that at least at certain levels of the military bureaucracy, the typewriters were considered the more important weapon.

Cochran and Momyer tried to make educated guesses about when and in what strength the Germans would strike at Thélepte. But theirs was an inexact science and attacks could come with little or no warning. Simple precautions were soon instituted. Only a few men gathered in mess lines at any one time—and they lined up facing east so they would see the enemy fighters as they popped over the eastern hills, attacking out of the rising sun. Mechanics working on the planes dug foxholes within a few feet of where they worked so they could dive for shelter in the event of an attack.

While defending their own home base was a clear priority for the pilots of the 58th Squadron, that was obviously of very little contribution to the war effort if they couldn't carry the fight to the enemy. Unfortunately, there was a good deal of confusion about what to do and how it should be done.

The confusion went clear to the top of the chain of command. Maj. Gen. Carl "Tooey" Spaatz, whose 8th Air Force, based on the British Isles, was raided for planes to create the 12th Air Force in North Africa, complained that he could not understand "what, when and where" the 12th was supposed to do.

The confusion was compounded in the 33rd Fighter Group. Its original mission, while it was still called a *Pursuit* Group, had been focused on the air defense of the area between Philadelphia and Washington, D.C., even though it wasn't clear how enemy bombers could get across the Atlantic to attack the United States. In the spring of 1942, reports of large-scale ship movements by the Japanese renewed fears of an attack by carrier aircraft against the West Coast. This was a believable threat: the Japanese, unlike the Germans, had a fleet of aircraft carriers and had already used them for the devastating attack on Pearl Harbor. The 58th Squadron was sent to San Francisco and stationed at Mills Field, on the edge of the Bay at the Presidio. The 59th Squadron was assigned to protect Seattle. The ominous Japanese ship movements culminated in the Battle of Midway, in the mid-Pacific, rather than with attacks on the West Coast, and the two squadrons were sent back east again. During this entire period, the men of the group moved so often that they began to call themselves the Nomads. They found little time for thought or training in dealing with enemy fighter planes and how, or even whether, to provide close air support for troops on the ground.

The great emphasis in the air force was on building up the bomber fleet to carry the war to the European continent or to distant Japanese targets in the Pacific. The assumption was that American armies would not be fighting on the ground on the eastern side of the Atlantic for a couple of years, until the invasion of Europe. How to support ground troops was something that could be left on the back burner. And then came the decision to invade North Africa. Suddenly ground support was on the front burner, and the 33rd Group found itself thrust into a battle for which it was almost totally unprepared. Tactics for dealing with enemy fighters had been similarly neglected.

John Bent remembers an almost total lack of tactics. At 27 the oldest pilot in the squadron, Bent had enough experience in the world to do what he was ordered to do but also to question those orders in his own mind. The son of an Eastman Kodak executive, Bent had spent part of his youth in England, receiving a master's degree in chemical engineering from Cambridge University. He then spent almost a year studying in Berlin and improving his mastery of the German language. He spoke then—and still speaks—with a British accent. His friend Lt. Alton O. "Horse" Watkins nicknamed him Lord Bent.

Before the war, Bent received his first pilot's license in England, where he learned to fly an autogiro—a cross between a helicopter and an airplane—and, with some friends, later owned an airplane in the United States.

"We soon learned the 109s and 190s could out climb and outspeed us pretty much," he recalls. "So about all you did if you tangled with them, you turned like hell or dove. We had no particular tactics. We were outclassed. They'd send two or three of us out on a mission at once. That wasn't much fun. I think they just didn't do a very good job on that—the air force.

"I was on one mission with Horse Watkins. There were three of us. We went down to Gabès. We called it *Gay-bees*. It's *Gab-es*. We went down there and had to sit over the German airfield, which I thought was a lousy damn mission. There were three of us while there was a squadron down there. That's the way it was in Tunisia in those days."

On these two- or three-plane patrols, the planes just flew along together. If they were attacked, they did the best they could, which sometimes wasn't all that good.

One of the first rudimentary tactical orders issued by Cochran was how to react when attacked by German fighters diving down out of the sun. The natural instinct of an aggressive fighter pilot was to turn to face the attackers, climbing to meet them. But Cochran reasoned that by turning and climbing, the American pilots would lose both air speed and maneuverability. Instead, he advised taking evasive maneuvers and then trying to get on the tail of the attackers as they flashed past.

The wisdom of his advice was demonstrated right over the Thélepte airfield on January 15, 1943. A squadron of French pilots had just arrived, flying P-40s, newly painted on the tails with the red, white, and blue of the French flag, that they had received from the 59th Squadron. Their commander was Capt. Kostia Rozanoff, a blond Parisian whose great-grandfather had come from Russia. They called themselves the "Lafayette Escadrille"—the same name used by American volunteers who flew with the French in World War I. The history of the 58th Squadron describes the scene as the French pilots circled over the field in weaving, eccentric formations on that wintry morning of their first combat:

> It's hardly 0800 when the 58th men, going out to the line, hear the startling, but now familiar, gun rattle that chatters harshly. German Messerschmitt fighters are being intercepted by the Lafayette pilots in the first return air-bout for the Free French since the fall of France. But the battle goes poorly for the Tricolor planes. Attempting to climb up to fight individually with the Germans, against the Major Cochran precept for P-40 pilots to stay together and nipping the ME-109s as they dive, the Frenchmen offer valiant, but futile attack. A flying sergeant goes down in a long

trail of dirty black smoke over the ridge. Another crashes in, for a belly-landing, as the pilot is wounded, with his ship's cockpit badly shot up and blood-smeared. Another Frenchman, with his landing gear damaged, comes in for a forced landing. No German planes have been reached and, while they are kept from treating the field with an effective strafing, the Axis leaves as victors in this first flurry of the wild morning.

The arrival of the French pilots was part of a rapid build-up of air power at Thélepte. Although army records refer to *airfields*—in the plural—at Thélepte, those, like Bent, who were there remember it as one huge field, so broad that a number of planes could take off together in one long line. The pilots of the 58th Squadron were soon joined by the other two squadrons of the 33rd Fighter Group, the 59th and 60th, by a squadron of twin-engined A-20 light bombers from the 47th Bomb Group and by 25 P-39 fighter planes of the 92nd Fighter Squadron.

The pilots of the 58th Squadron found themselves involved in what Cochran called a "continued attack technique," chopping away to keep the Germans off balance. In a kind of air guerrilla warfare, the pilots might in the course of a single day strafe German airfields near the coast, escort the swift, low-flying A-20 bombers, and then protect the P-39 fighters, which carried a cannon in the nose, in low-level strikes at German tanks. All this in addition to guarding their own airfield.

This little-bit-of-everything technique didn't really satisfy anyone. The ground troops, suffering from German air superiority over the battlefields, clamored for more protection from the pilots. A single plane circling overhead, even if it didn't do anything else, was a big morale booster. Many of the pilots, of course, preferred to spend their time trying to shoot down enemy planes, seeking the magic five victories that marked an ace. Air commanders with a better feel for strategy—among them Cochran—argued that attempting to help troops on the ground by providing close air support by bombing or shooting up enemy guns and tanks in actual contact with friendly troops was a dangerous waste of time. Instead, they argued, their time was much better spent attacking troops and mechanized equipment moving toward the front or in repair depots behind the lines.

Cochran was very outspoken on what became a very contentious subject. Waiting to talk to a group of officers in June 1943, he heard a man behind him whisper, "He better be careful on that subject. He is liable to get in hot water." Cochran had his say anyway. He told how ground troops had asked them to attack two 105 mm guns that were causing them trouble. The fliers asked if the men on the ground could see the guns.

"No," they replied. "They're camouflaged. Every once in a while we can see the bursts."

"Here were people on the ground," Cochran continued, "*very, very close* and they couldn't see the things themselves and they expected the bombers to come over and, just like that, pick out those two 105 guns. . . . It ended up in an area bombing. It made us mad, because . . . right up the way ten miles we could see a whole enemy tank supply depot just sitting there. Perhaps it was guarded with antiaircraft, but there it was. You could hear the bombardiers coming back, saying 'J——! Did you see that target? Why didn't we take that?' That is what we thought was the important thing—to get the supplies behind the tanks and work on them and work on them. And I still think so."

Brig. Gen. James H. "Jimmy" Doolittle, the flier who led the raid on Tokyo in which B-25 bombers flew from the deck of an aircraft carrier in April 1942 and who now commanded the 12th Air Force in North Africa, illustrated the same argument with an anecdote.

He told how he had been asked to provide a fighter plane to protect a jeep sent out to repair a broken phone line. He refused. That same plane, he explained, was able to shoot down two enemy fighter planes.

The fighting on the ground in the area of central Tunisia covered by the planes from Thélepte began to develop in December and grew in intensity in January, after the Allies had given up, for the time being, their effort to take Tunis and Bizerte. Both sides built up their infantry and tank forces in the new battlefield in central Tunisia. There was action all along the Eastern Dorsal, from Fondouk Pass in the north down to Faïd Pass in the center, and on down to Gafsa, where two valleys stretched eastward toward the coast. Those battles will be described in detail in later chapters. The pilots of the 58th Squadron spent much of their time either attacking enemy forces on the ground, battling enemy planes over the battlefield, or striking at columns behind the lines bringing forward supplies and reinforcements.

On December 21, a four-plane formation strafed three truck-trailers near Kairouan. The violent explosions seemed proof that the trucks were loaded with munitions. More supply trucks were spotted by the afternoon patrol, which strafed a column of 100 trucks moving toward Faïd Pass, setting six trucks afire. Other planes struck at the truck column repeatedly until dark.

The following day, a flight led by Capt. Levi Chase, who was soon to be assigned as commander of the 60th Squadron, swooped down to strafe an enemy train, shooting up a locomotive and 10 cars. Climbing back up to altitude, they spotted three big German JU-88 planes bombing friendly ground forces. Chase had only one machine gun firing. The other five were either out of ammunition or jammed. Flying with him was Lt. Thomas A. Thomas, who had only 150 rounds left. The two fighters dove on the enemy bombers, shooting down two out of the three.

A few days later, Chase led a two-plane formation attacking a cluster of armored vehicles spotted in a dry creek bottom east of Gafsa. They reported the explosion of six of the vehicles. Four more fighters, called to the scene, strafed haystacks suspected of hiding enemy supplies. The "haystacks" exploded. Chase and the other pilots, flying low over the area, came under intense machine gun fire from the ground.

This experience led to a change in tactics. In the first few days on the front, when the pilots of the 58th Squadron spotted trucks carrying troops they would swoop down over the column without firing their weapons, giving the soldiers time to scramble to safety before the planes returned to fire on the trucks.

William W. "Spike" Momyer, who became an ace as commander of the 33rd Fighter Group in North Africa, is shown in a photo taken shortly before the war. (Source: National Archives)

But Chase's experience that day convinced him that such sportsmanship was too dangerous. As the squadron history reports: "Upon returning to Thélepte, Captain Chase expresses his intention of no longer buzzing convoys to give men warning as he goes after the vehicles—the machine gun fire from the ground gives him a new attitude towards the war."

Cochran had begun to get the 58th Squadron into shape and work out some basic tactics when "Spike" Momyer arrived and took over. Cochran became the group's operations officer.

Momyer, who was 26 years old, had dreamed of becoming a fighter pilot ever since, as a child, he had gone out to the local airport in Muskogee, Oklahoma, to see Charles Lindbergh passing through after his historic solo flight across the Atlantic in 1927. Before the United States got into the war, Momyer was sent to the Western Desert to help deliver the first P-40s to the British. As good hosts, the British took him along on several combat missions, being careful not to create an embarrassing incident by getting a pilot from a neutral country shot down. As a result of this experience, Momyer, alone among the pilots in the group, had some kind of a feel for what it was like to fly in combat against the Germans.

Most of the planes shot down by the Americans were the slower bombers. It was much more difficult to get one of the faster German fighters. But Momyer, escorting a raid by A-20 bombers on a truck park west of Gabés, succeeded in shooting down an ME-109 on January 5, 1943. He was flying high above the bombers when four German fighters dove on the bombers. Momyer, this time with the advantage of attacking from above, got on the tail of one of the enemy planes. The ME-109 went out of control, spiraling down into the ground. Already on his way to becoming an ace, Momyer had shot down a bomber the previous day.

There is no escaping the excitement still in Momyer's voice as he described his first shootdown in an oral history interview years later:

"I suppose it's the same with any other pilot who shoots down his first airplane, the excitement of it—your adrenaline runs so high. I often tell people that the damn rudder bar was going like that [he gestures to indicate the movement of the rudder bar, which controls the direction the plane is flying], and I had almost missed him. I was sliding back and forth. I was skidding too much in the first shot, so I took a wave-off target. Finally, I just took both feet off the rudder and put them back in and started to shoot. Boy! I was going to get him, no matter what! I think that most guys that have been in combat probably hold true to that."

That same afternoon, "Horse" Watkins was in a three-plane patrol escorting P-38 fighters attacking enemy armored vehicles in the area between Fondouk and Kairouan. This was on the eastern side of the Eastern Dorsal about 120 miles north of the area where Momyer had shot down the German plane. Watkins, a 25-year-old Texan with a blond beard, was a big, friendly man, a kind of best friend to everyone in the squadron. It was common knowledge that he was being groomed to command a squadron of his own.

As Watkins and his two companions watched helplessly from above, German FW-190 fighters dove on the P-38s, quickly knocking three of them out of the air. When he returned to Thélepte, visiting reporters gathered around Watkins to hear his account of the battle:

"We started down toward the FW-190s, but it takes a P-40 a long time to get anywhere and we couldn't help. Then, four more 190s dived from way up top and bounced us. I looped up behind one as he dived. My two wing men were right with me. I put a good burst into the sonofabitch and he started to burn, and I followed him down. I must have fired 125 rounds from each gun. It was more fun than a county fair. Lt. [James] Gray . . . put a lot of lead into another 190, and I doubt if it ever got home. The other two Jerries just kept on going."

Another pilot sought out by the visiting reporters was Lt. Walter Scholl. He was a member of the 59th Squadron, the group left back in Morocco after turning its planes over to the French. He and four other pilots arrived on the front lines in early January in damaged planes they had managed to patch together. On January 12, he scored the first victory for his squadron by shooting down an ME-109, which crashed near the field. The pilot was identified as Hans Herst, a 35-year-old German ace who had received the Iron Cross in 1939. But it was something that had happened more than a year before the United States entered the war that attracted the journalists' attention to Scholl.

On the afternoon of November 16, 1940, Scholl was playing for Cornell in a tense game with Dartmouth. With less than three seconds left to play, Cornell, which had gone 18 games without a defeat, was trailing 3–0. Scholl threw a game-winning touchdown pass for Cornell. What interested the reporters was that this was the then-famous "fifth-down pass." An official had made a mistake and permitted Cornell a fifth down instead of turning the ball over to Dartmouth after Cornell had used up its allotted four downs. After several days of controversy, it was finally agreed that Scholl should not have been permitted to throw the pass and that Dartmouth had won after all. In the winter of 1942–43, in the midst of battle in Tunisia, journalists, including some recently transformed from sportswriters into war correspondents, were still excited about what the usually staid *New York Times* had called "one of the most thrilling gridiron encounters that has ever been waged."

The growing pressure on the ground crews as well as the pilots at Thélepte was heightened by their sense of being in a dangerously exposed position, with enemy tank columns only a few miles away. There was no question about that: the pilots saw them every day. But then came rumors that there were German troops in the hills *behind* Thélepte. There were even those at Thélepte who claimed that they could hear the Germans working, tearing up roads and knocking down bridges.

This was not just nerves or paranoia, as German documents seized at the end of the campaign revealed. There actually were troops, delivered by gliders, a few miles to the west of Thélepte as part of what the Germans called Operation Riga. Despite the fears caused by the reports at Thélepte, however, the objective of the operation was not to knock out the air base. Instead, it was a bold effort to cut Allied supply lines at key points on a line stretching all the way from the Mediterranean coast on the north down almost to the Sahara Desert in the south.

The plans laid on by the Luftwaffe commander in Tunis called for 17 transport planes to carry supplies and paratroops and to tow eight gliders. The drop was made under a full moon on December 27–28, 1942. The troops were ordered to carry out their missions of destruction and then fight their way, if they had to, through Allied lines back to safety on the east side of the Eastern Dorsal. The raid, bold as it was, turned out to be a disappointment for the German commanders.

One group of paratroopers, assigned to knock out a bridge near the Allied supply base at Tébessa, was spotted by French troops. A patrol from the 168th Infantry Regiment took off after them on foot but couldn't catch up. They finally acquired a couple of mules, chased down the enemy troops, and forced them to surrender. Most of the other sabotage efforts were also thwarted or quickly repaired, and other enemy troops were hunted down and captured.

But the knowledge that there were enemy forces to the west as well as to the east of Thélepte added to the strain felt by everyone there, making the fight a war of not only bombs and bullets, but nerves as well. The pressure grew steadily more intense during the first two weeks of January as the Luftwaffe hammered away at Thélepte in larger and more frequent air raids. The obvious goal was to push the Allies back out of this forward base.

On January 11, as a number of the men, seated on empty gasoline cans, were finishing breakfast, four ME-109 fighters streaked over the eastern hills out of the rising sun to strafe the field.

Major John A. Woodworth, the group flight surgeon, had started before sunup on the long walk across the field from the hole in the earth where he slept to the headquarters dugout. He described what happened in a memoir written after the war:

> I had approached to within five hundred feet of the Group Hq area when there was an explosive roar behind me. I whirled around in time to glimpse the black cross insignia of the German Luftwaffe on the side of an ME-109 as it whizzed by me barely 50 feet away firing its machine guns and cannon. Caught in the open, I instinctively threw myself on the ground. A flight of three more German planes, flying wing tip to wing tip in tight formation, roared out of the sun and flew over me spraying the field with bullets, some of which threw up puffs of dirt a few feet ahead of me. Two P-40s that had been in the air since dawn, awaiting just such an attack, swooped down on the attacking Messerschmitts. Other P-40s took off in the midst of the attack to join in the fight. All hell broke loose as ack-ack artillery and machine guns joined their noise to the battle . . .
>
> I got up and ran to look for a foxhole. "Over here, major," someone called. A helmet appeared at the rim of a shallow bowl-shaped depression. I ran over and jumped in. Several men were lying in it, watching the dogfight. . . . Someone said Major [William] Roodenberg must have been hit badly, because he was lying on the ground about 50 feet away and hadn't moved. I ran out to him and found him lying in a large pool of blood. He had no pulse and was not breathing. I turned him over and opened his

shirt. There was an ugly, purplish hole in the left side of his chest. He had been killed instantly by a bullet through the heart. I got up and ran back to the men.

The pressure on both the Allied airmen at Thélepte and the attacking Germans can be said to have reached the breaking point on January 15, 1943, the day that started off badly with the defeat of the French pilots of the Lafayette Escadrille in their first fight since the fall of France.

Statistical records kept by the group tell part of the story. On December 2, just before it moved to the front lines, the group had 93 assigned aircraft, 71 of which were operational. On January 14, it had 54 assigned and 30 operational. In a month and a half, it had suffered attrition of 57 percent in effective aircraft.

At about 11:15 A.M. on January 15, two C-47 transport planes and their P-38 escorts were on the field being refueled when eight enemy fighters streaked across the field and zoomed upward again. Observers on the ground were amazed at the rate of climb of the German FW-190. At that moment, a four-plane early patrol, including Watkins and Bent, returned from a flight over the battlefield west of Gafsa. Unaware that an attack was under way, they lowered their wheels and lined up in the landing pattern.

Watkins was about to touch down when a German plane swooped in behind him and opened fire. Watkins, apparently not yet aware of what was happening, pulled up high enough to parachute. But as he touched down, he was unable to release his chute and was dragged along the ground, suffering a serious head injury.

Bent and the two other pilots managed to land safely. Bent, who had several bullet holes in his plane, explained what he thought had happened to Watkins:

"We used to leave our parachutes in the plane. You took off in any damn P-40 you got into, with a parachute in it. You didn't carry your own in those days. I think to start with you carried your own but we just left our parachutes in the plane. It was that much faster. But he was a big man, a huge chap and couldn't get out of the parachute he was in. It was a small one, for a small person. He was dragged on the ground. There was sort of a gale going when we landed."

Watkins was delayed reaching an army hospital because
the road was blocked by a truck, set ablaze by German strafing. He was carried around the wreckage and taken the rest
of the way on an armored personnel carrier but died on the
operating table. The squadron history says he died thinking
he had been hit by the field's antiaircraft, with his last words
being, "Those goddamned ack-ack."

Watkins's death points up the nature of wartime friend-
ships. Men can become close comrades and even be willing
to die for one another without knowing each other very well.
When the chaplain prepared a cross for Watkins's grave, he
marked it "Horace Watkins." And Liebling, the *New Yorker*
writer who had sought out Watkins for an interview, was so
impressed that he dedicated a book of his wartime writings
to Watkins. But he called him "H.S., Horse Watkins," rather
than Alton Watkins.

The attack which had led to Watkins's death had barely
ended when the field received reports of incoming bombers.
Nine JU-88 bombers appeared in the eastern sky, escorted
by four Italian Macchi 202 fighters. Two pilots of the Lafayette Escadrille and two members of the 59th Squadron were
in the air over the field.

The French pilots went for the Italian fighters and drove
them away. The two Americans already in the air went for
the bombers. Major Mark Hubbard, the 59th squadron
commander, caught two of them and shot them down. Lieutenant Carl Beggs caught another one. Two more 59th Squadron pilots who were on ground alert managed to get into the
air while the enemy bombs were falling. A bomb fragment
tore a large hole in the wing of Capt. Carmen "Dan'l"
Boone's plane as he took off, but he kept going. He caught
up with one bomber and opened fire. The plane swerved
into the path of another bomber, and they both went down
in flames. Boone continued his pursuit of the retreating
bombers, shooting down a third and then a fourth. Lieutenant R. H. Smith, who had also been on ground alert, got
one more. One bomber seemed to have gotten away but it
was later reported to have crashed, too.

That last bomber was probably the victim of antiaircraft
fire. But the story went around the field that it had been

shot down by one of the Italians, so there would be no one to tell how they had left the formation without protection.

The history of the 59th Squadron notes, "much rejoicing tonight." The victory was especially gratifying for the pilots who had been left behind in Morocco after turning their planes over to the French and were just now getting into the battle.

Despite the day's victory and the "rejoicing" that followed, Woodworth, the group flight surgeon, was becoming increasingly worried about the stress being felt by everyone, especially the pilots of the 58th Squadron, who had been fighting without letup for a month and a half.

His fears intensified the next day. Lt. Richard Cuthbert, a former member of the Joker Squadron, was flying a mission escorting bombers when a German fighter dove on him. Cuthbert, who was already at a low altitude, banked sharply to escape but his plane stalled out and he crashed and was killed, wedged between two olive trees.

That afternoon, Lt. Robert Okey, a friend of Cuthbert's, went out to the flight line and told the crew chief working on one of the P-40s that he wanted to take it up for a brief flight. The staff sergeant found the request a little strange but turned the plane over to Okey. He took off, flew away in the direction of the German lines, and was never seen again.

Woodworth spotted other signs of strain. He found several pilots showing evidence of combat fatigue. He grounded one of them because he appeared to be on the verge of hysteria. The stress was not limited to the pilots. Woodworth found two enlisted men who had been hiding in a ravine all day because they didn't dare walk across the field to work.

Strangely, flying combat missions seemed to offer some relief for the pilots. In an interview after the war, Cochran said he and the other pilots used to tell each other: "The best way to feel great is to get in the airplane and get over there and get in a fight, and you'll be amazed how good you feel, because your old heart will get going and your adrenaline will get going. . . . "

"We had been doing it so much I suppose our bodies got in that habit and then needed it. It needed that kind of hyping. . . . "

Cochran said he remembered urging General Doolittle to pull the entire squadron out of action, telling him: "Many of these guys, if you save them now, they'll be fighter pilots again somewhere else. They'll come back. But if you leave them in here much longer, they'll never fight again."

One of the worst problems, Woodworth found, was the stress on the pilots when they were on two-hour ground alert. They sat strapped in their planes, ready to take off in the event of attack. But until they got airborne, they were sitting ducks.

"The two-hour stint proved to be a spine-chilling torture because each one expected to be riddled at any moment by bullets from a strafing ME-109," Woodworth says.

Cochran used to urge his pilots to go into the nearby town of Feriana to drink some wine and relax a little. But the pilots didn't bother, partially because they feared that drinking would dull their performance in combat. Reed says that during the time he was at the field, he never even went into the closest little town, Thélepte.

As the ground fighting intensified, the pilots spent more and more of their time over the area east of Gafsa, an area where the 21st Panzer Division, part of Rommel's Afrika Korps, had been assigned after its retreat across Libya. The Germans were beginning to probe Allied positions in the two strategic valleys, running up against the 34th Division's 168th Infantry in a battle described in Chapter 10. It was here, on February 2, that the 59th Squadron suffered a morale-shattering defeat at the hands of the Luftwaffe in what the unit history candidly describes as "a truly disastrous day."

A six-plane formation took off from Thélepte that morning and headed southeast toward the scene of a developing tank battle near the town of Maknassy. The American pilots found themselves not only outclassed by the German fighters but vastly outnumbered. Observers estimated the Germans had 35 to 40 fighters and Stuka bombers over the battlefield in what, in World War I, would have been called a "flying circus."

Later in the day, a lone P-40 returned to Thélepte, the sole survivor of the patrol. Adding to the sense of loss felt by the squadron was the fact that both "Dan'l" Boone, who had downed four bombers on the day of the squadron's great victory on January 15, and R. H. Smith, who had accounted for one of the attackers, were among those shot down and killed.

The question of which side would break first was probably answered on January 15. After their devastating losses on that day, the German attacks on Thélepte dropped off dramatically. Attempting to knock out the most exposed Allied airbase had just proved too costly.

But the 33rd Group was, if not broken, at least badly bent by the constant combat and frequent bombing and strafing attacks. On February 10, eight days after the disastrous loss over Maknassy, the group was pulled off the front lines and sent back to a rest area. The group would return to fight again in a few weeks, but not before Thélepte itself would fall to a German onslaught on the ground.

PART TWO

MEETING THE FOX

9

Is Anyone in Charge Up There?

The order that General Robinett received on January 19, 1943, illustrates, in one brief paragraph, much of what was wrong with Allied leadership during the crucial month and a half between the unhappy end to the first battle for Tunisia and the opening of the third battle in mid-February.

Robinett, who had just taken over as commander of Combat Command B from General Oliver, was camped with his 3,400 men of the 1st Armored Division near Sbeitla when the order came by telephone from the behind-the-lines bunker of General Fredendall's II Corps headquarters. It said:

> Move your command, i.e., the walking boys, pop guns, Baker's outfit and the outfit which is the reverse of Baker's outfit and the big fellows to M, which is due north of where you are now, as soon as possible. Have your boys report to the French gentleman whose name begins with J at a place which begins with D which is five grid squares to the left of M. Further, CC/B will enter Corps Command net not later than 0900 hours, 20 January. CC/B will remain in contact with Satin Force at Tebessa.

Robinett, who was familiar with Fredendall's colorful choice of language, had little difficulty understanding that he

was to move his command north to a town named Maktar
and report to General Juin, the French general in charge in
that area. If the Germans had managed to intercept the message, it would have taken them only a few minutes longer to
translate the text, break Fredendall's simple code, and understand where Robinett was headed.

The reference to "Satin Force" was another matter.
Robinett could not have been expected to understand how
he was to move north to help repel a German offensive and
still play any role in Satin Force. His was a small part of the
general confusion then infecting the upper layers of the
Allied command structure.

Operation Satin was conceived about Christmastime of
1942. It was planned as a bold new stroke against the Axis
armies. The objective was to send an armored column smashing through from Gafsa, in central Tunisia, to the Mediterranean coast—to get in between von Arnim's Fifth Army in
the north and Rommel's German-Italian Army retreating
across Libya into southern Tunisia.

Whether Satin was to be just a large-scale raid or
whether the Allied force was to remain on the coast, blocking the two enemy armies from joining up, is not clear. Nor
was it clear in the minds of the Allied generals.

Orders to the 1st Armored Division, which would spearhead the operation, called for causing as much damage as
possible before pulling back to the west. But plans were also
made for supplies to be shipped by sea, on the assumption
that the raiders would seize one or two ports and settle
down to remain on the coast as a blocking force.

It was a bold and imaginative plan—and totally unrealistic, given the fact that many of the armored units that would
be required were only just then arriving in Tunisia after the
grueling trip over the snow-covered Atlas Mountains from
Oran and Algiers. It would take several more weeks, at best,
to put together the Operation Satin striking force.

The Germans didn't wait for the Allies to get their act
together, and that is why Robinett was sent hurriedly to the
north, rather than south to help spearhead Operation Satin.
On January 3, a German *Kampfgruppe,* or combat group—
somewhat larger than an American combat command—hit

the poorly armed French force holding the gap in the Eastern Dorsal at Fondouk el Aouareb and seized the gap. On
January 18, the Germans took two more passes and poured
through them down a long valley on the western, or Allied,
side of the Eastern Dorsal.

To some officers on the front lines, if not to those far to
the rear, it was obvious what the enemy strategy was. They
were attempting to pick off, one after the other, the passes
through the Eastern Dorsal. With these passes in their possession, they were in position to block any Satin-like attacks
on their crucial supply lines along the coast. They also posed
the constant threat of attacks on Allied supply lines and
bases to the west.

This German strategy also had another, perhaps unin-
tended, effect: It thwarted Eisenhower's hopes of concentrating the 1st Armored Division as a powerful striking force to
be used to take advantage of any apparent weakness on the
other side. Instead of concentrating the division, the Allied
leaders felt forced to split it up, sending Robinett north
while deploying other parts of the division, as they arrived,
further south.

Even worse—and through no fault of the enemy—the
Allied command structure was so confused that troops in
the field had trouble finding out who they were supposed to
take orders from and sometimes received conflicting orders
from two or more sources. They wondered, with considerable justification and not just in that normal soldier way, if
anyone was in charge up there. What happened to Robinett
and Combat Command B illustrates the degree of confusion
that prevailed during this second battle for Tunisia.

When he was camped at Sbeitla, Robinett was under the
command of Fredendall, who was busy digging a bombproof
bunker far behind the lines near Tébessa, in Algeria. The
GIs referred to the bunker behind the general's back as
"Shangri-la—a million miles from nowhere" and as "Lloyd's
very last resort." Fredendall was the commander of the new
II Corps, created as an American command to control Allied
operations in central Tunisia. But when Robinett moved
north, he was put under the command of the French General Juin, who assigned him to General Koeltz's French XIX

Corps. This left Robinett reporting to two separate commands of different nationalities, speaking different languages. Fortunately, Robinett, a graduate of the French cavalry school at Samur, spoke French. There was also the little matter of coordinating with the British, with their own command, who were also involved in the battle.

By the time Robinett arrived on the scene, the Germans, with Italian help, had achieved most of their objectives, seizing the high ground along the Eastern Dorsal and cutting off the French forces holding the passes. Their attention had then shifted to the Ousseltia Valley, running southwestward deep into Allied territory. It was here that Combat Command B went into action, counterattacking up the valley against stiff resistance. The Americans did not dislodge the Germans from the valley, but did succeed in pushing them back far enough that French troops who had been stranded on heights near the pass could escape back to Allied lines.

On the evening of January 21, Robinett was put under the command of another French general who, at 4:35 the next morning, ordered him to abandon his attack toward the east and instead to attack toward the north in an attempt to join up with a nearby British force.

By midafternoon, that attack was stopped by stiff resistance. Fredendall asked Robinett what reinforcements he needed to continue the attack. Robinett said he needed a strong force of infantry, artillery, and tank destroyers. Fredendall sent elements of the 1st Infantry Division to the scene as reinforcements with orders to operate in coordination with Robinett's force rather than under Robinett's command. Fredendall then ordered Robinett to call off his attack and go on the defense.

This order was directly opposite of what Robinett, who was still under French command, had been ordered to do by the French general. But Robinett couldn't follow those orders and continue the attack unless he had the reinforcements being sent by Fredendall. Robinett's report after the battle only hints at the frustration he must have felt: "As a result of conflicting orders, CC/B held present positions and continued active reconnaissance north. Message sent to II Corps giving situation and requesting clarification as to whose orders to act on and requesting coordination with French commander."

When the reinforcements finally arrived on January 24, the infantry, along with the armor of Combat Command B, made a successful attack up the Ousseltia Valley, but before they could seize control of the entire valley, they were abruptly told they were needed elsewhere and were pulled back out of the valley on the night of January 28–29. The passes through the Eastern Dorsal, which might have been seized before they were heavily fortified, were left in enemy hands.

Robinett, whose tendency to speak his mind did not endear him to his superiors, summarized the Ousseltia Valley campaign bluntly:

"This brief campaign, though successful, furnishes an excellent example of lack of coordination in the high command. The results could have been more decisive had command channels been simple and higher headquarters nearer the front. The clear head, energy, enthusiasm and presence at the front of General Koeltz saved what otherwise would have been a hopeless situation."

Koeltz, who commanded the military region at Algiers at the time of the landings, was seized by his colleagues who were cooperating with the Allies. When he was released, in the confusing period after the landings, he ordered his troops to resist the Americans. But as soon as the French laid down their arms, he took command of a French corps and became one of the most skilled commanders on the Allied side. General Bradley tells in his memoirs of a meeting in which Koeltz, who did not speak English, gave his briefing in French. A British general airily assured him everyone there spoke French. Bradley, who didn't, kept quiet and struggled to follow along.

Even before the American armor and infantry units pulled out of the Ousseltia Valley, Eisenhower had begun to entertain serious doubts about the feasibility of Operation Satin. To have any chance of success, the British forces that had pursued Rommel across Libya would have to be in position to keep him busy enough on the Mareth Line so he wouldn't interfere with the Satin forces. But by mid-January,

Montgomery's troops clearly would not be in position to keep Rommel pinned down. Eisenhower told Fredendall to cancel Satin.

Ominously for the Allies, Rommel had not only avoided the destruction of his German-Italian army, but, by falling back from one defensive position to another, had actually retreated faster than Montgomery's ponderous Eighth Army had been able to pursue. Rommel was thus moving into the old French Mareth line of fortifications, near the Libyan-Tunisian border, with time to prepare to fight Montgomery. By outrunning the British, Rommel had also put himself in a position, and allowed himself time, to take part in the fight for the passes on the Eastern Dorsal. The Desert Fox, though weakened and pursued by a powerful enemy, had again proved himself a formidable adversary.

On January 19–20, Rommel ordered the final stages of his withdrawal and sent a representative to the coastal city of Gabès to regulate the flow of traffic bringing supplies and reinforcements for his army. At the same time, he moved his 21st Panzer Division into reserve so it could receive new equipment and replacement troops. The division had suffered severely, but it would soon be sufficiently recovered to join the operations against the Allies, bringing a battle-hardened unit under command of the Desert Fox into contact with American forces for the first time.

Just as Rommel and Montgomery had been involved in a race across Africa, the two sides were in a race to build up manpower and supplies in Tunisia. On the Axis side, a vast air armada of 200 JU-52 aircraft and 15 huge six-engined ME-323 planes made twice-daily round trips from bases in Sicily and mainland Italy. They came in formations, called *pulks* by the Germans, of as many as 120 planes, flying at an altitude of 150 feet off the water. One flight left early in the morning, timing its arrival at fields at Tunis and Bizerte for about noon, when it was hoped that the Allied pilots had flown home for lunch. On the sea, the Axis relied on a fleet of small merchant ships, supplemented by 20 ferries—crude flat barges with a small pilot shack—plus a fleet of 14 submarines.

Both planes and ships suffered severely—and increasingly—from Allied attacks. Still, they managed to deliver a remarkable amount of men and matériel. From November 1942 through January 1943, they brought in 111,957 troops—81,222 of them German and 30,735 Italian—plus 100,594 tons of supplies.

The Allied supply line was much longer—across the Atlantic from the United States to ports in Algeria and then some 500 miles overland to the fighting front. Despite the distances involved on the Allied side, the Axis forces were clearly on the defensive, trying to hold their Tunisian bridgehead for as long as possible. Almost as soon as the Allies landed in November, Rommel summed up his gloomy forecast for the outcome of the war in North Africa:

> In the long run neither Libya nor Tunisia could be held, for . . . the African war was being decided by the battle of the Atlantic. From the moment that the overwhelming industrial capacity of the United States could make itself felt in any theater of war, there was no longer any chance of ultimate victory in that theater. Even if we had overrun the whole of the African continent, with the exception of a small strip of territory providing the enemy with good operational possibilities and permitting the Americans to bring their material, we were bound to lose in the end. Tactical skill could only postpone the collapse, it could not avert the ultimate fate of the theater.

Hitler and other Axis leaders, far removed from the scene and focused more on the loss of an entire army at Stalingrad, found Rommel far too pessimistic. Mussolini, still harboring the dream of creating a new Roman empire in North Africa, insisted on unrealistic efforts to retain control of Libya, his last African colony—and also insisted that the Italians should be in charge of the war in Africa. This all led to a strange command structure: Rommel remained in command but an Italian general was assigned to look over his shoulder and prevent any unauthorized retreats. Over the objections of the German generals, Hitler reluctantly agreed that the Italian high command in Rome—*Comando Supremo*—should be in charge of both German and Italian forces. And as soon as Rommel had finished retreating to Tunisia, his army would become the Italian-German Army, under an Italian general. To further confuse the command structure, the Axis forces already in Tunisia remained under the control of von Arnim, who insisted on fighting his own war with as little coordination with Rommel as possible.

Despite all these complications of coalition warfare, the Axis forces were able to carry out a remarkably coordinated and aggressive campaign for control of the Eastern Dorsal. Moreover, their attacks were cleverly focused on the weak points in the Allied defenses resulting from the Allies' own clumsy efforts at coalition warfare. Each of the January attacks was focused on the poorly armed French troops that provided the link between the British First Army in the north and the increasingly powerful American II Corps in central Tunisia. Each attack caused the British and the Americans to rush to the scene, usually too late to save the situation.

Robinett and his men had barely had time to set up their tents in their new camp near the big Allied supply base in Tébessa, Algeria, when they received word of still another German attack just to the north of the Ousseltia Valley, for which they had so recently fought. They hurried back north once more. By the time they arrived, on February 1, the enemy attack had been stopped by British troops and a battalion from the American 1st Infantry Division. Instead of heading back south once more, Robinett and his Combat Command B were ordered to set up camp near the town of Maktar. This put Robinett under the command of the British First Army rather than keeping him under the command of the American II Corps or his own 1st Armored Division.

Meanwhile, Roosevelt and Churchill arrived in Africa themselves for one of the most momentous strategy sessions of the war. In Casablanca they succeeded in arranging a public handshake between the famously arrogant General Charles de Gaulle, the leader of the Free French, and General Henri Giraud, a rival for control of French forces who had been spirited out of France in the mistaken understanding that he would take over the entire North African campaign. And they made some crucial decisions. They agreed that the next phase of the war would be a landing on Sicily, rather than on the neighboring island of Sardinia. Perhaps the most important—and controversial—outcome of the Casablanca Conference, which went on in secret from January 14 to 24, was the decision to fight until the Allies had achieved the "unconditional surrender" of the Axis powers.

No agreement had been reached on whether to make that goal public. But Roosevelt, to the surprise of Churchill, blurted out the phrase during a press conference ending the meeting. He later linked the choice of those words to a memorable moment in American history. On February 16, 1862, Ulysses Grant's Union Army forces surrounded the Confederate-held Fort Donelson, controlling traffic on the Tennessee River. When the Confederate commander asked what terms he would offer for surrender of the fort, Grant replied: "No terms except an immediate and unconditional surrender can be accepted." The surrender of some 15,000 Confederate troops and the capture of the fort caused a sensation in the North, and Grant was hailed as "Old Unconditional Surrender."

All this optimistic talk of "unconditional surrender" must have seemed very strange to the thin ranks of Americans trying to plug the holes in the Allied line running almost the entire length of Tunisia. The situation seemed to be slipping out of Eisenhower's control. After the Axis offensives in early January, he had reorganized his command, putting the British General Anderson in overall charge, with command over American and French troops as well as his own British First Army. But he gave Anderson orders that were overly ambitious, if not actually contradictory.

Anderson was ordered to "seize and hold" the eastern exits of the passes all along the Eastern Dorsal in central Tunisia—the passes the enemy had already taken or was busily gobbling up. But then Eisenhower added: "I deem it essential that you keep the bulk of the 1st Armored Division well concentrated, so as to be prepared to take advantage of any opportunity the enemy may offer to act aggressively as well as to counter strongly any enemy thrust that may develop."

General Fredendall, now subordinate to Anderson and subject to these same orders, decided that before concentrating the 1st Armored Division, he should give the portions of the division just then arriving in Tunisia the chance to test themselves in combat. In the process, he took over control of the division from its commander, General "Pinky" Ward, after ordering Ward to set up three new combat commands similar to Robinett's Combat Command B. This left Ward with a small division headquarters and technical responsibility for a division he did not really control.

The three new combat commands were Combat Command A, under Brig. Gen. Raymond E. McQuillin, Combat Command C, under Col. Robert I. Stack, and Combat Command D, under Col. Robert V. Maraist. All three commanders were drawn from the 1st Armored Division even though they would operate with infantry and artillery from the 1st and 34th Infantry Divisions under their control. In the next few weeks, all three of these new commands would get a far more harrowing test in combat than Fredendall or anyone else envisioned.

10

On-the-Job Training—
the Hard Way

C ombat Command C got its taste of war beginning early
in the morning of January 24, 1943. Colonel Stack led
his force of tanks, armored infantry, and field artillery on a
lightning strike from its camp at Gafsa to hit the enemy at
Sened Station, a crossroads 28 miles east of Gafsa.

By 6:00 that evening, they had cleaned out a small contingent of German and Italian soldiers and returned to
camp with two men wounded and two tanks lost, one by
gunfire, the other by a mine. With them, they brought 96
prisoners. Enemy dead and wounded amounted to nearly
100. The victorious Americans were elated.

Their joy was not shared by Ward, the division commander. He and the general commanding French forces in
that area had strongly urged Fredendall not to make the
raid. All it would do, they argued, was to stir up the enemy
and make it more difficult when they set out, a few days
later, to take their real objective, the more distant town of
Maknassy.

They were right.

The attack on Maknassy was scheduled for February 1.
It called for Stack and his Combat Command C not to return

to Sened Station, but instead to swing north from Gafsa, then strike toward the south on Maknassy. At the same time, Combat Command D, led by Colonel Maraist, would carry out the attack on Sened Station and then drive directly east to Maknassy.

As these plans were being developed, Fredendall's advisers were worried by the threat of an enemy attack on Faïd Pass—the pass closest to and in an almost direct line to the big Allied supply base at Tébessa and the crucial airfield at Thélepte. They urged him to reinforce the French unit that had kept a tenuous hold on Faïd Pass since it had been captured, with the help of the American paratroops, on December 3. But Fredendall reasoned that the strike at Maknassy would draw off enemy forces and actually help to protect Faïd Pass.

While the Americans and French debated, the 21st Panzer Division—the first batch of Rommel's desert veterans to arrive in Tunisia—hit Faïd Pass on January 30 along with Italian troops and German units from von Arnim's Fifth Army. They not only went after the French defenders in a two-pronged attack from the east, but also swung around to strike from the southwest in the rear of the French position.

The French, outgunned and outnumbered, fought fiercely while they called for, and waited for, the American armored cavalry to come to their aid. By the afternoon of the first day of the attack, they still held the pass but inside a cinching noose of enemies.

The closest Americans were members of General McQuillin's Combat Command A, 30 miles to the west in Sbeitla. McQuillin got one of those strange orders from Fredendall's headquarters: Counterattack to restore the French hold on Faïd Pass—but do it without reducing the covering force operating northeast of Sbeitla and without weakening the defense of Sbeitla.

McQuillin received the order about 9:30 A.M. on January 30. Half an hour later he had a company of tanks on its way to check out the situation. It was followed shortly afterward by a larger force, consisting of a company of tanks, a company of armored infantry, and an artillery battalion. But they came under such severe air attack that McQuillin decided to wait until the next morning, January 31, before continuing his counterattack.

Meanwhile, further south, Stack's Combat Command C had started out on its circuitous route to attack Maknassy from the north. Its path initially took it in the direction of Faïd Pass and the scene of the fighting there. Fredendall had to make a decision: Should he send Stack to help out the French and McQuillin, or let him continue on his way toward Maknassy? The French generals strongly urged that Stack be sent to help out at Faïd, and Fredendall initially agreed.

About the time that McQuillin decided to delay his attack, Stack, on his roundabout way toward Maknassy, received telephoned orders to head in the direction of Faïd to a small crossroads town known as Sidi Bou Zid. He was told to strike "in flank the force of enemy tanks and infantry thrusting at Sidi Bou Zid from the east, and also to strike any force moving from Maknassy to Sidi Bou Zid."

Stack camped about 30 miles southwest of Sidi Bou Zid that night. Although they were separated by only a few miles, Stack and McQuillin were not in communication with each other.

On the morning of January 31, Stack resumed his march toward Sidi Bou Zid. But about 4:00 P.M., he received radioed orders to "turn south and join in coordinated effort with Maraist on Maknassy." At the urging of a French general who thought Stack's force was urgently needed in the Faïd area, Stack checked with his division commander, Ward. But Ward, operating under strict orders from Fredendall, was helpless. All he could do was repeat the orders from the corps commander to break off his march toward the scene of the action and head south.

What had gone wrong? Apparently the corps staff, miles away in Algeria, had somehow gotten the impression that McQuillin had the situation at the Faïd Pass under control when in fact his force was in serious trouble.

McQuillin had begun his counterattack at 7:00 A.M. that morning. But the enemy had been working all night, emplacing antitank guns, heavy machine guns, and mortars in hidden positions in the foothills near Faïd Pass. Tanks, with their big guns, were concealed in gullies and behind undulations in the earth. A few small tanks ventured out onto the plain to lure the Americans into the trap. One company of American tanks took the bait and followed them right into the ambush. Nine tanks were knocked out in a few minutes.

Another arm of McQuillin's force, striking further south, also ran into trouble and was repelled. McQuillin reported his infantry retreating "in disorder."

The next morning, the French sent a strongly worded protest complaining about the failure of the Americans to hurry to the rescue of their forces at Faïd Pass and their failure, once they got there, to save the key pass and the surrounded French troops.

While all of this was going on, Maraist set out from Gafsa on January 31 for his planned attack through Sened Station and on to Maknassy. As part of his Combat Command D, he had not only tanks from his own 1st Armored Division but also two battalions of infantry from the 168th Infantry Regiment and the 175th Artillery Battalion, both part of the 34th Infantry Division.

The men of the 168th—the National Guardsmen from southwestern Iowa—had had a brief taste of combat against the French at Algiers, but this would be their first contact with the Axis forces. After the capture of Algiers, they had been assigned to guard against paratroop attacks behind the line in Algeria. The first of two battalions arrived near Gafsa by truck and was almost immediately ordered to move forward toward Sened Station. Their new commander, Colonel Drake, stopped briefly at Fredendall's II Corps headquarters near Tébessa, in Algeria, to receive orders for the attack toward Maknassy and then hurried to catch up with his troops near Gafsa.

Drake, who had just taken over from the popular Colonel "Iron Mike" O'Daniel, who had commanded the 168th in its landing at Algiers, was eager for a fight. He had waited a long time for this moment, biding his time during the long peacetime years, waiting for the chance to show his mettle in battle. A combat veteran of World War I, he knew that it was

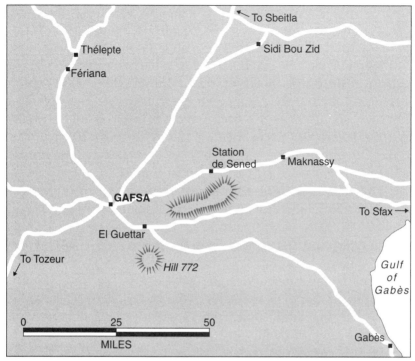

A series of battles was fought for the key communications junction at Gafsa, in south-central Tunisia, and along the highways leading from Gafsa to the Mediterranean coast.

only by shooting at the enemy and being shot at that his men could also become veterans.

After their all-night truck trip from Algiers, the men of the regiment's 1st Battalion unloaded their equipment, camouflaged it in a cactus patch, and then, after a brief rest, climbed back into the trucks and headed east. The drivers were supposed to allow 75 yards between each truck to make it harder for enemy planes to attack the column. But, tired and impatient, the drivers let the trucks bunch up.

The column had halted when Lt. Larry McBride heard the hum of the engines of planes approaching.

"I was standing on the running board of a 6×6 truck looking at the rear when the first silver-hued planes came over a rise, flying very low out of the sun. . . . " he later recalled. "The men were unloading and running to the flanks as the first three Messerschmitt 109s hit the column, one down the center, the outer two strafing the ditches and area up to one hundred yards to either flank. In all about twenty-three planes, ME-109s and JU-87Bs [Stuka dive bombers] took part in the raid. Casualties were not heavy except toward the head of the column where fifty-pound personnel bombs had made direct hits on a 1st Armored Division scout car and a 6×6 personnel carrier of Company A. The ME-109s, firing incendiaries with their 20 mm cannon, also got in some nasty work on the head of the column where 13 men were killed and 20 wounded."

The men, eyeing the bodies of those killed in the raid—some of them still burning—were reluctant to get back in the trucks. They were finally ordered to form up in columns to the right and left of the road and set off on a fast march to an olive grove about 2½ miles from Sened Station.

They were under attack the whole way.

Sergeant Popejoy moved up the valley with a group of tanks. He says the infantrymen called them "cannonball magnets—they draw all kinds of fire."

"Going down that valley was bad," Popejoy says. "Those Stukas just constantly went up and down, bombing. I saw tanks blown up, all burning. Soldiers halfway out of tanks, burned to death. One area there, I looked and there were five guys there. They were all dead. I could see no wounds on them. It was concussions from the bombs."

To add to the danger, an 88 mm gun was firing down the valley. The 88 is a direct-fire, high-velocity weapon that fires a shell 3½ inches in diameter. The sound of the muzzle blast and the sound of the shell passing are almost simultaneous. There is no time to duck.

Popejoy could feel fear grip him in the lower part of his back and start creeping up. But he resolved not to let it get hold of him. "Fear," he says, "will just eat you up."

But the bombs and the shells from the 88 mm gun had him scared. He says, "At Sened Station, I dug the longest slit trench that was ever dug in North Africa. Approximately three miles long. I swam up that valley with my shovel. I didn't want any part of that 88."

By the time the troops approached their target, it was dusk. They dug foxholes and settled down for the night.

During the afternoon, tanks probing the enemy defenses at Sened Station had been driven back by well-placed anti-tank guns. Much of the next day's work of cleaning out those obstacles would fall to the infantry, aided by artillery barrages.

During the night, reinforcements arrived on the scene after the long truck ride from Algeria. While it was still dark, the 2nd Battalion of the 168th Infantry moved up along the road from Gafsa, guided by a captain from the 1st Armored Division. At one point, he stopped to ask directions from a 1st Battalion sentry and then continued on toward Sened Station. He finally admitted he was lost. In the darkness, he had guided the battalion about a mile inside the enemy lines.

Still in the dark, the men began unloading their equipment and making camp. Staff Sgt. Wesley Miller, mess sergeant of Company F, hid his mess truck among the olive trees and then ordered his men to dig foxholes before preparing breakfast.

In the first light of dawn, the enemy troops became aware of the Americans setting up shop in their backyard. They fired flares into the air and began raking the area first with machine gun and machine pistol fire and then with mortars and artillery. The truck drivers sped away while the infantrymen dug in.

One shell hit Miller's mess truck, destroying the unit's stoves and kitchen equipment and all of Company F's records. Shrapnel killed both Miller and his first cook, Roy Shields.

Drake, preparing for the morning attack on February 1, went to the bivouac area where his reinforcements were supposed to have assembled. There was no sign of his lost battalion. His attack, scheduled for 7:30 A.M., would have to be carried out by only one battalion of infantry rather than two. At a commander's conference, held in the midst of a heavy bombing and strafing attack, Drake got a delay in the kickoff time to 9:30 A.M. to give him time to revise his plans.

Although Drake didn't realize it at the time, the enemy had responded to the earlier raid by Stack's force by pouring reinforcements into Sened Station—just as Ward, the division commander, and the French officers had feared. Drake not only had a smaller force than he had planned on, but he faced significantly more enemy soldiers than his intelligence reports had led him to expect.

Armored reconnaissance vehicles moved out ahead of the column, followed by infantry, tanks, and artillery.

McBride describes the attack:

> We left the edge of the olive grove well dispersed in a line of skirmishers. Before we had gone far, mortar fire started dropping among us. Men hit the ground and it took considerable organizing to get them moving again as this was the initial baptism of fire. The noncoms did a fine job of keeping the men moving through mortar and artillery fire even though they were also under fire for the first time. . . .
>
> About half the artillery was high-burst stuff. This was probably a good thing right at that time because it made the men realize that hitting the ground did not bring complete immunity to fire and that it was necessary to move through the artillery and knock out the enemy positions.

Tanks accompanying the infantry were forced to pull back because of fire from the enemy's 88 mm antitank guns.

"Then," McBride says, "we went on without tanks. Stuka dive bombers were over our positions constantly. The tanks on the left got the brunt of these attacks. Three of the planes were shot down that morning."

The Stukas, diving almost straight down with their sirens screaming, frightened the green troops. They also made them very angry. Whether the infantrymen shot down the Stukas or whether they were caught by American fighters is unclear. In any event, the men on the ground kept on firing as the German airmen drifted down in their parachutes.

"In all three instances the pilots took to the chute but only one reached the ground alive. The infantrymen did not like Jerry very much now," McBride recalls.

"That's the only time in the war I got mad," Popejoy says. "Combat soldiers don't really get mad, I don't think. I remember one group of Stukas came over and we shot down three of them with machine gun fire and rifles. We rifled them down. They swoop down real low. I was mad. I ripped the flesh off my hand trying to fire my semiautomatic rifle— my M-1. When a pilot hits the silk, he's automatically a prisoner. That's all well and good on the drawing boards, but it's not exactly the way it is when you see all of this. Those that came down, I couldn't shoot them fast enough. I was mad. I was crazy."

This instance of firing on men dangling in their parachutes seems to be an aberration. In most cases, troops refrained from firing on defenseless parachutists. In contrast, it was considered routine on both sides to fire on tankers attempting to escape after their tank had been struck and, in most cases, was burning. The difference between the two instances is probably based on the assumption that a flier whose plane has been shot down will become a prisoner and won't return to the battle. On the other hand, a tank crew that escapes might be back in action in another tank within hours.

The advance was finally stopped when a line of enemy tanks moved slowly forward, machine-gunning the infantry. The men scrambled back to an olive grove where they found Drake preparing for a renewed attack. McBride found morale still good and excitement high.

As the attack resumed, Lt. Col. John C. Petty, the commander of the 1st Battalion, led the way, firing his machine gun from a kneeling position. A machine gun burst caught him in the stomach, inflicting a wound from which he later died. Nearby, his second in command was hit in the head by the same machine gun and put out of action. The battalion was left without a leader.

Captain Bird, the young company commander who had played a key role in the capture of Algiers, took over as Drake rushed to the front to get the attack moving again.

Drake began firing his M-1 rifle at a nearby enemy tank. His men watched this futile act with bemusement. They figured that firing a rifle at a tank would, at best, go unnoticed by the tankers, and at worst make them mad. But, emboldened by Drake's example, the men began firing at the tank themselves. Suddenly, to their amazement, the tank turned and moved away.

Drake turned to Bird: "How about outflanking them from the right?"

Bird took three platoons and moved south and then east into an olive grove where he had his men fix bayonets. One platoon moved forward until it was stopped by a concentration of enemy fire. The men took cover and continued to shoot while a second platoon advanced on its right until it, too, was stopped. Bird then sent a third platoon, which he had held in reserve, swinging around to the right. Enemy fire dropped off noticeably as the first platoon rose up and charged into the town. As the infantrymen moved forward, they passed three American Sherman tanks that had been knocked out. The body of a tanker was draped over the hatch of one tank. Beside another, a lieutenant who had had part of his leg shot off was being treated by a sergeant who was himself badly burned.

As the infantrymen penetrated the enemy trenches, Drake sent his main force forward. At this point, they were joined by the men of the 2nd Battalion—the lost battalion—who had been pinned down in their foxholes all day. The battalion commander was wounded and Maj. Robert Moore, who had left the family drugstore in Vilisca, Iowa, to enter the service, took over command of the battalion.

By 5:00 P.M., the German and Italian defenders of the town began emerging from their trenches, hands over their heads. The Americans took 152 prisoners, including an Italian general. About that number were counted as dead or wounded. Captured equipment included three medium tanks, 12 new motorcycles, and a locomotive. The remaining enemy forces pulled back toward Maknassy.

The American infantry, artillery, and armor had tested themselves against the enemy and had emerged victorious. But Fredendall was impatient. "Use your tanks and shove," he ordered Maraist. "Too much time has been wasted already."

Under Fredendall's orders, the infantry was moved forward the next morning, February 2, to a line six miles east of the village they had just captured, to a ridge overlooking the rolling plain extending toward Maknassy, a dozen miles to the east. An armored force scouted forward toward Maknassy and reported they had seen only a few armored cars, doing the same kind of scouting job.

Another reconnaissance patrol spotted five enemy tanks moving into an olive grove in front of the infantry position about 11:30 A.M. A request for an air attack on this concentration was sent back to II Corps headquarters. About four hours later, a flight of American bombers passed overhead, circled the olive grove, and then headed back without dropping any bombs. As the planes passed over the American infantry, they unleashed their bombs. Fortunately, they caused little harm.

Drake sent an angry message to the air force: "Your outfit is a bunch of darn poor map readers. They just bombed my service train bivouac instead of the enemy concentration. Besides that, they are poor bombers as they missed that target by about 500 yards."

About 5:30 P.M., enemy planes bombed the 1st Battalion and reports of enemy tanks in the vicinity caused what Milo Green, the correspondent for the hometown newspapers back in Iowa, later described as "a completely disorganized retreat that turned into a headlong rout."

"Some jittery second lieutenant had put out a report that German tanks were breaking through just beyond the village," Green wrote later. Actually, 17 tanks had been seen in the distance but only three had approached close to the American position.

"In less than 15 minutes," Green reported, "hundreds of trucks, jeeps, tanks, halftracks and motorcycles were heading for the rear, six deep, at breakneck speed in a cloud of swirling dust and sand. I will long remember it for I was in that mad shambles sitting on top of a trailer behind a 6×6 truck bouncing up and down like a cork on the waves. Some coolheaded colonel finally managed to halt the stampede four miles to the rear and restored order. Flourishing his .45 automatic he ordered the mob to turn around and go back to where they had started from. Luckily there were no enemy tanks as reported and more luckily still no Jerry planes happened to see that long, bounding, defenseless column of vehicles. I later dubbed it the 'Gold Rush of '43,' for it looked exactly like a bunch of Forty-niners rushing to stake their claim."

While the force led by Maraist and Drake was making its slow advance toward Maknassy, Stack and Combat Command C had broken through a pass north of Maknassy on February 1 and were poised to join in the attack on the city. Chances for success, despite the delay at Sened Station, seemed good.

But then, on the night of February 1–2, Stack, by now beginning to feel like the yo-yo on the end of a string, received abrupt orders to break off and hurry far to the north to face a supposed enemy threat.

This left Drake's infantry and Maraist's tanks to carry out the advance on Maknassy by themselves. But while they were preparing for the attack, the generals, far back behind the lines, had other ideas. As early as February 1, before the battle for Sened Station, Eisenhower had ordered that if Maknassy were not taken by that evening, the attack should be called off and the 1st Armored Division brought back and concentrated for a later offensive even if that meant giving up efforts to hold positions along the Eastern Dorsal and abandoning Gafsa and the key airfield at Thélepte.

"If Maknassy is not taken by tonight, the whole division should be withdrawn into a central position and kept concentrated," Eisenhower ordered.

Whether subordinate officers failed to receive Eisenhower's orders or just ignored them is not clear. In any event, the attack toward Maknassy was allowed to go on until February 3, when it was finally called off. The withdrawal to Gafsa was carried out in a blinding sandstorm with Bird's company providing the rear guard, feeling their way along with their feet.

The attack through Sened had been costly. Casualties were 51 killed, 164 wounded, and 116 missing, with the heaviest losses in the 168th Infantry's 1st Battalion. Losses in equipment included four light tanks, nine half-tracks, and four artillery pieces.

The attack had also been futile. None of the terrain that had been seized was held. The enemy, undeterred by the threat to Maknassy, had gone right ahead and taken the crucial Faïd Pass. And the retreating troops had been forced to leave their buddies behind in poorly marked graves.

Almost immediately after their arrival back in Gafsa, the 168th Infantry was ordered north to a new position near Sidi Bou Zid. Drake received permission to take two of his three battalions on the new assignment and leave the 1st

Battalion, which had taken the brunt of the recent fighting, in reserve. He put Bird, who had been largely responsible for breaking the enemy resistance at Sened Station—and would later receive the Silver Star for his action there—in charge of the battalion.

Drake, whose personal example had helped to move his main force forward in the final assault at Sened Station, would also win a Silver Star for his performance. But as he led his two battalions north to Sidi Bou Zid, there were hints of a distinct note of hostility between Drake and at least some of his men.

The official record reports an order Drake issued shortly after the panicky retreat at Sened Station. Drake, it says, "issued instructions to all officers that no one would leave the line under fire. They would be ordered back to the line by an officer and if they disobeyed they were to be killed at once."

And Sergeant Green, in one of his "Brickbats," gave evidence of the hostility between Drake and some of his men. He tells of "the night on which a certain unpopular tyrannical colonel had the regimental adjutant going from sentry to sentry in the command post area smelling rifle barrels for powder fouling. The much-disliked colonel, for whom several men were laying, had discovered several bullet holes in his tent that were not the result of enemy fire."

Veterans now of a battle with the Axis forces in which they achieved a victory—meaningless as it turned out to be—the men of the 168th regiment and the 1st Armored Division moved north toward Faïd Pass, where they were soon to be engulfed in a battle from which they would be lucky to emerge at all, much less victorious.

As the scene shifted to the north, Colonel Darby and his Rangers, who had been involved in training and guard duty since the landing three months earlier, moved to Gafsa with orders to carry out three attacks on Axis forces in the area.

"We were to give the impression that Allied strength in central Tunisia was greater than was actually the case," Darby wrote later. "Night missions with fast movement, darting, pinprick raids, and heavy firing of weapons were to be our job. Secondly, we were to capture prisoners for identification of the steady flow of German and Italian troops then moving into Tunisia and Tripolitania. Throughout our operations, the 1st Ranger Battalion, though less than five hundred men, was also to inflict heavy casualties on the enemy. In effect, we could write our own ticket, as long as we did our job."

The first raid was aimed at an Italian artillery and anti-aircraft unit, part of the Italian Centauro Division and the 10th Bersaglieri Regiment, among the best Italian troops in North Africa.

Darby set out with half his battalion, nearly 250 men, on the night of February 11 toward the area of Sened Station. By that time, the Americans had pulled out and the enemy had moved back in. The Rangers rode about 20 miles by truck and then hiked another eight miles in the dark. Each man carried a C-ration, a canteen of water, and a shelter, half plus his weapons and ammunition. Before dawn, they erected their shelter halfs into pup tents, camouflaged them, and settled down for the day. As they rested in what they thought was a well-hidden position, several Berbers arrived and began swapping oranges for chewing gum, cigarettes, and candy. Not taking any chances that their visitors might wander on and tell the enemy what they had seen, the Rangers put their visitors under guard.

The men, wearing stocking caps instead of helmets, moved out in a long column about midnight, quietly making their way across the desert floor toward the Italian encampment. Sergeant Chuck Leighton was burdened with a big eight-pound Browning Automatic Rifle, or BAR, and 21 pounds of ammunition. When they got within about 600 yards, they spread out in a skirmish line. They moved on undetected to within about a city block of the Italian position. Then a sentry sensed their approach and a gun opened up, firing blue tracers. The Rangers, crawling on their bellies, crept forward under the enemy bullets, still not firing their own weapons to avoid giving the Italians something visible to shoot at.

"Someone in the squad on my left let out a yell and then all hell broke loose," Leighton recalled. "Captain Snyder [Max Schneider] called back for a BAR and I started to go faster up the hill. I had only moved a few feet when an explosion went off on my left and I was knocked over. I came to and still tried to find my way up the incline only to be pulled down by someone and told to stay down. When I finally got my senses together, I realized that I had been hurt. My left side seemed to burn and my left leg started to pain me. I stayed down."

The Rangers swept through the enemy camp firing rifles and tommy guns, throwing grenades, and using their bayonets and knives on the Italians, most of whom, startled from their sleep, were simply trying to get away. Six mortar crews laid a barrage on the enemy camp.

The battle went on for about 20 minutes, and then the firing stopped almost as abruptly as it had started. Darby called over his field radio for a report from his company commanders. Schneider reported he had two prisoners, but the transmission was garbled and Darby asked him to repeat his message. Two shots rang out. "Well, sir, I had two prisoners," Schneider replied and then explained that the men had tried to escape.

The raid exceeded all of Darby's expectations. The Rangers counted some 50 enemy dead and many wounded. Six men were taken captive.

The Rangers had lost only one man killed. But with 18 men wounded, they had a big problem. They were still deep in enemy territory, a dozen miles from the old French fort where trucks were supposed to meet them—and it was only a few hours until dawn. Darby divided the unit into a fast and a slow column. The fast column took off, marching at a brisk pace, while the slow column, including the wounded, the medical officer, aid men, and stretcher bearers, followed as fast as they could. The wounded knew they had to keep up or be left behind.

Darby had made the rules clear: "No member of the unit expected the battalion or the company to wait for him if badly wounded or to be carried to safety if it endangered the lives of other soldiers."

A medic examined Leighton's ankle and told him it was probably sprained. He wrapped a tight bandage around the ankle, over his boot.

"We took off at a very slow pace as most were in bad shape . . . ," Leighton recalled. "We still had nine or ten miles to go and wanted to get back to the fort before daylight. We were sitting ducks out in the open desert. My leg was almost numb now from pain, but determination and encouragement from the rest made me push on. After several hours of difficult walking and stumbling along, we arrived at the fort as daylight was showing over the hills on the east."

The fast column had arrived while it was still dark and had already loaded into trucks and gone on to the battalion camp near Gafsa. Leighton and the others in the slow column were taken out, a few at a time, by jeep so as not to attract enemy attention.

"While waiting for my turn to go back to Gafsa, I met an Italian who had helped his wounded buddy out and they had then become prisoners of war. He explained to me that we should have come over to them with the American flag and a white flag of truce and we could have captured all of them. They didn't want to fight for Hitler."

Leighton was eventually evacuated to a general hospital in Oran, where x-rays showed his lower left leg bone had a vertical split and the bone of his left ankle had been chipped. He was never able to rejoin his unit.

By the time the Rangers gathered at their bivouac near Gafsa, the Allies were in the process of evacuating the city and abandoning it to the enemy on the night of February 14–15. Confusion and apprehension among the city's population was heightened when six tons of ammunition, stored in the old French Kasba, or fort, was blown up, damaging nearby buildings and injuring a number of civilians. Darby was ordered to hold the town until the other Allied forces had gotten away.

Rumors of an enemy attack swept through the camp. They had some basis in fact. Elements of Rommel's Afrika Korps, plus Italian units, were within a few hours of the town.

Italian prisoners await the trip to a prisoner-of-war camp in the United States after the fighting near El Guettar. (Source: National Archives)

During the night, an outpost reported to Darby's command post that three columns of enemy troops could be heard moving in from the south. Darby sent a company out to investigate. He ordered them not to open fire without his personal approval. As the Rangers crept forward, the sounds, like those made by muffled engines, became more distinct. And then they got close enough to see what was making the noise: a herd of more than two hundred camels.

The Rangers, last to leave Gafsa, marched north past the then-abandoned airfield at Thélepte toward Kasserine Pass. But before they reached the pass, they were ordered to a position at Dernaïa Pass near the town of Bou Chebka, to the south of Kasserine, on the road that goes from Thélepte to Tébessa in Algeria.

By that time, the enemy, having taken control of the Eastern Dorsal and won the second battle for Tunisia, was swarming through those passes, and the crucial third battle for Tunisia was well under way.

11

A Spring Breeze
from the East

G eneral Eisenhower could not have picked a better time
to visit the Tunisian front than February 13–14, 1943.
His visit coincided with a brief pause in the conflict, but
everyone expected an enemy attack, with much hard fighting, in the days just ahead. You could almost smell it in the
air. The closer he came to the murky line between friendly
and enemy forces, the more ominous the situation seemed.

On the night of February 13, Eisenhower stopped at the
headquarters of General Ward, the 1st Armored Division
commander, near Sbeitla. General Robinett, whose Combat
Command B was stationed to the north of Sbeitla, happened to be there to confer with Ward.

Robinett, whom Eisenhower describes as "an old friend
of mine" from the peacetime army, had done more fighting
in Tunisia than any other American tank commander and
had spent a good deal of time driving up and down Tunisian
roads and back roads familiarizing himself with the terrain
and the military situation. While intelligence officers back in
Algeria expected the Germans to attack at Fondouk Pass,
near where Robinett's command was positioned, he told
Eisenhower he had patrolled that whole area and was con-

vinced that the expected enemy attack would come further south, at Faïd Pass. The Allied situation—attempting to hold a line 115 miles long with scattered, understrength units—was so perilous, he told Eisenhower, that the troops should be pulled back into better defensive positions "that very night."

Robinett's dire warning was only one of the many pieces of information Eisenhower picked up on his tour. Although Eisenhower was still listed as a lieutenant colonel in the regular army, he was wearing the four stars of a full general for the first time as a result of a promotion two days before. He had stopped first at the bunker occupied by the II Corps commander, General Fredendall, near Tébessa, earlier that Saturday afternoon. Although Fredendall was being criticized by the troops for locating his headquarters so far behind the front lines, Eisenhower concluded that given the area covered by the Corps and the poor condition of the roads, it was probably in a reasonable site. But he was amazed to find engineers tunneling into the sides of a ravine to build bombproof bunkers instead of providing protection for the front-line troops.

"It was the only time, during the war, that I ever saw a divisional or higher headquarters so concerned over its own safety that it dug itself underground shelters," he later wrote.

Eisenhower met with Fredendall and Fredendall's British superior, General Anderson, and found, despite the urgent bunker construction, an air of complacency at the Corps headquarters. That sense that there was time to get everything in order may, in his mind, have weighed against the urgent warning he received a short time later from Robinett. He made some notes of improvements he intended to discuss with Fredendall later and then continued on his tour.

Of particular concern was the way Ward's 1st Armored Division had been broken up and spread over much of central Tunisia, leaving Ward with only a few light tanks under his own command. The situation was so obvious, in fact, that newsmen accompanying Eisenhower questioned him pointedly on whether this was the result of a policy decision to split up the American army in Tunisia and subordinate it to British and French commanders. Eisenhower assured the correspondents he was eager to get the Americans working together in their own units—but not yet. He likened his situation to that of General John J. Pershing, the World War I commander of American forces in France, who agreed to throw his troops into combat wherever they were needed to stop an attack on Paris in March 1918.

In the briefings he received, Eisenhower could see how the American forces were spread out. In the north was Robinett and his Combat Command B, protecting the flank of the French in that area but under the control of a British general. Next came the somewhat weaker Combat Command C, the same outfit that had been called off a few days earlier when it was prepared to pounce on Maknassy. Then came General McQuillin's Combat Command A, the unit that had failed to prevent the Germans from overwhelming the French and taking Faïd Pass at the first of the month. They reported to an American—Fredendall, the II Corps commander—but Fredendall reported, in turn, to the British general.

If the Germans came through Faïd Pass, as Robinett had so confidently predicted, McQuillin's men would be right in their path. Eisenhower, accompanied by Ward and a small entourage of aides, headed for that hot spot, arriving late in the evening at McQuillin's headquarters in the little crossroads town of Sidi Bou Zid.

The briefing for the visitors was conducted by Col. Peter C. Hains III, commander of the 1st Armored Regiment. He described to Eisenhower how elements of the 1st Armored Division, under Lieutenant Colonel Waters, whose battalion had been involved in the heavy fighting in northern Tunisia in December, were situated on Djebel Lessouda, a 2,100-foot, freestanding mountain rising out of the rolling terrain eight miles north of Sidi Bou Zid. Also stationed on Djebel Lessouda were the infantry of the 2nd Battalion of the 168th Infantry Regiment.

Down on the plain near Sidi Bou Zid, Lt. Col. Louis Hightower had an armored force consisting of 51 tanks, 12 tank destroyers, and two artillery battalions.

The 3rd Battalion of the 168th Infantry was dug in on Djebel Ksaïra, eight miles southeast of Sidi Bou Zid and more than 11 miles from Djebel Lessouda. Djebel Ksaïra was the most advanced and most isolated American position— about three miles south of Faïd Pass and within two miles of enemy positions on the Eastern Dorsal. Drake, whose head-quarters was in a small olive grove about a mile and a half east of Sidi Bou Zid, was put in charge of the infantry but was told by McQuillin that any orders he gave to his 2nd Battalion, on Lessouda, would have to be passed through Waters.

Drake, under orders to defend his position to the last man, was deeply concerned about the situation he found himself in. He had some 1,600 men, only about 1,000 of them trained infantrymen. On the night of Friday, February 12, 200 replacements arrived at his headquarters, but the spectacle was not reassuring.

"These replacements arrived, part of them without arms of any kind and all carrying two heavy barracks bags of clothing," he later reported. "The roster that accompanied them did not have all of their names on it, but it did contain names of men who were not present. Upon questioning these men it was found that a great many had never fired a rifle in their life. That none of them had entrenching tools, nor bayonets and some were without rifles. Many of them were medical corps men, artillery men, tank destroyer men and everything except infantrymen."

That night, Drake's outfit also received six truckloads of *bazookas* and ammunition. The bazooka was a new, rather strange-looking, rocket-firing antitank weapon, powerful enough to knock out a tank if it hit in the right place. It was exactly what the infantrymen needed if enemy tanks came through Faïd Pass.

"Distribution of these guns and rockets were made Saturday," Drake wrote. "But due to lack of time for instruction they were useless. Every effort had been made to get just one bazooka for instructional purposes, but without success. They had been systematically forwarded to front line outfits where they were just as religiously thrown away."

On Saturday afternoon, observers on Djebel Ksaïra detected enemy activity, such as surveying artillery firing positions, to their east. As night came on, the sounds of the movement of large tank formations could be heard. Drake sent his heavy trucks back to a relatively safe position near Sbeitla.

At a few minutes before midnight, as Drake was finishing up his preparations for what he saw as an impending attack, he was summoned by telephone to McQuillin's headquarters. There, in a brief ceremony in a moonlit courtyard, Eisenhower pinned the Silver Star medal on Drake's chest for his performance two weeks earlier at the Battle of Sened Station.

The briefings Eisenhower had received during his busy day did not seem to alarm him. He had concluded, after talking with Fredendall and Anderson, that their arrangements for meeting the expected attack were "as good as could be made, pending the development of an actual attack and in view of the great value of holding the forward regions, if it could possibly be done."

His view that the preparations were "as good as could be made" was certainly not shared by those stationed out on those lonely djebels, although there is no evidence that anyone at the meeting in Sidi Bou Zid early on that Sunday morning put things as starkly as Robinett had a few hours earlier.

The disposition of the forces had been laid out in precise detail—down almost to the individual foxhole—in orders from Fredendall's headquarters. And although the men on the front line could not know it, those orders had been handed down from General Anderson's headquarters.

An aide had brought the orders to McQuillin's headquarters. Hains looked at them and saw that the forces stationed on Djebel Lessouda and Djebel Ksaïra could not maneuver and, to make matters worse, were too far apart to help each other out if they came under attack. He was so alarmed that he drove back to Ward's headquarters near Sbeitla to complain. Ward told him there was nothing he could do.

Waters, stationed up on Djebel Lessouda, got a visit from Ward, who passed on the orders from Fredendall's headquarters on where to put his troops. As Waters recalled later,

Ward said: "I've never seen anything like that in my life. I'm desperate. I don't know what to do. My division is taken away from me completely and I'm not in command of it."

During the day on Saturday, while Eisenhower was making his way forward, Waters and Hains drove up a back trail and tried to get a look at what the Germans were up to on the other side of the Eastern Dorsal. They were driven away by enemy aircraft before they could get a good look, but they remained suspicious. That evening, during a briefing at McQuillin's headquarters, Waters heard again the intelligence report that an attack, if it came, would be at Fondouk, not Faïd.

"General McQuillin, let me ask you a question, sir," Waters said. "Suppose tomorrow morning I wake up and I find that I'm being attacked by an armored division coming through Faïd Pass. What do I do about this?"

All Waters had under his command to face an enemy division was about 900 men. He later recalled he had "four tank destroyer guns, a company of medium tanks, a partial battalion of infantry up on the hill on foot, the artillery, and some spare parts and that was it."

McQuillin looked at Waters and told him: "Oh, Waters, don't suggest that!"

Waters left before Eisenhower arrived, thus missing the opportunity, if he had chosen to take it, to tell the commander in chief how worried he was. On his way back to Lessouda, Waters did not take the direct route because he had been warned the Germans might have patrols operating in that area. He took a road that swung back toward Sbeitla. On the way, he passed a column of cars carrying Eisenhower and his retinue up to McQuillin's headquarters.

During that tour, Eisenhower recalled in his memoirs, he was disturbed to come across an infantry commander who had been in a position for two days and had yet to put out mines to protect his unit.

"The commander explained, with an air of pride, that he had prepared a map for his mine defense and would start next day to put out the mines," Eisenhower wrote. "Our experience in north Tunisia had been that the enemy was able to prepare a strong defensive position ready to resist counterattack within two hours after his arrival on the spot."

Curiously, Eisenhower, having talked with everyone from the 1st Army and II Corps commanders down to officers on the front line and having observed the precarious position of that thin line of infantry, armor, and artillery, did nothing to change the situation. He says in his memoirs that he noted "the matters that I wanted to take up with General Fredendall," but by the time he got back to II Corps headquarters, "the German attack had already struck. It was too late to make changes in dispositions."

Basic to the problem faced by the Allies was that they simply did not know very much about what was going on on the other side of the Eastern Dorsal. McQuillin and his staff pleaded for aerial photographs of enemy dispositions, but never received them even though pilots from Thélepte were reporting verbally that they had seen large numbers of tanks gathering on the eastern side of Faïd Pass.

This paucity of accurate intelligence is puzzling. The Allies had managed to obtain one of the Germans' Enigma machines, used to transmit messages in supposedly unbreakable code. Unaware of the machine's loss, the Germans continued to use it. This permitted the Allies to listen in on the enemy's most secret communications. The information derived from this source permitted the Allies to wreak havoc on ships trying to supply the troops in Africa. It also helped Montgomery in his battles with Rommel. But if any of this secret information was shared with the commanders on the ground in Tunisia, General Anderson and his aides persisted in a fatal misunderstanding of enemy intentions.

In contrast to the situation on the Allied side, the Axis commanders seem to have had much superior intelligence. Each morning they sent over Photo Freddy—a spy plane flying so high it was out of reach of Allied fighters and anti-aircraft guns—to take pictures of whatever the Allies were up to. They also had very detailed knowledge of the Allied order of battle. Not only did they know that they were faced by the 1st Armored Division, but they knew that the division had been cut up into four combat commands, where the commands were, and what units they contained.

All this information was fed into the planning for Operation *Fruehlingswind* (Spring Breeze). Under those plans, elements of two panzer divisions had been assembled on, or just to the east of, the Eastern Dorsal by Thursday, February 11. Many of the units had used the cover of night to move into position, accounting for some of the confusion on the other side of the mountain about what was going on. The Axis commanders met on the afternoon of Saturday, February 13, at La Fauconnerie, about 40 miles to the east of Sidi Bou Zid, to put the finishing touches on their plan.

It called for the elements of the 10th Panzer Division and portions of Rommel's 21st Panzer Division to attack through Faïd Pass at dawn on Sunday, February 14. At the same time, the rest of the 21st Panzer Division would strike from the south. In all, there would be five columns headed toward Sidi Bou Zid.

At this point, Rommel himself was still occupied moving his army back out of Libya and consolidating its defensive positions on the Mareth Line in southern Tunisia. Command of Operation *Fruehlingswind* was given to Maj. Gen. Heinz Ziegler, deputy commander of von Arnim's Fifth Army.

On the surface, the Axis leaders appeared to have not only better intelligence, but also a much clearer concept of what they were doing and what they hoped to achieve than did the Allied commanders. But that impression is somewhat misleading. The plans for Operation *Fruelingswind* seem to taper off into indecision about what should come after the capture of Sidi Bou Zid and the hoped-for annihilation of the American forces assembled in that area.

"The mission of the Fifth Panzer Army is to weaken the Americans by destroying some of his elements and thereby confuse and delay his advance," the order for Operation *Fruehlingswind*, issued on February 8, said.

The limited nature of the attack was indicated by Rommel in his memoirs:

> . . . our first aim had to be to break up the American assembly areas in southwest Tunisia. Accordingly, the 21st Panzer with elements of the 10th Panzer Division was ordered to attack the Americans at Sidi Bou Zid and Sbeitla, with the object of breaking up and as far as possible

destroying their concentrations. At the same time, a combat group formed by my army was to dispose of the American garrison in Gafsa. *No further operational objectives were fixed for the moment.* (Italics added.)

Operation *Fruehlingswind* was thus conceived of primarily as a defensive measure, not as a major offensive. It was designed to throw the Allies off balance and prevent them from mounting their own offensive that would slash through to the coast and divide the Axis armies. But both von Arnim and Rommel—particularly Rommel—were thinking beyond this limited operation to a major offensive. The two commanders had quite different concepts, however, of what course this new offensive should take.

Von Arnim, worried primarily about the British forces in northern Tunisia, which still posed a threat to Bizerte and Tunis, favored a strike almost straight north through Tunisia to cut the British army's supply lines. Rommel, on the other hand, proposed an even bolder offensive that would strike west to capture the growing American supply base at Tébessa and then sweep north, deep into Algeria. Both sent their conflicting proposals to Comando Supremo in Rome and waited for a response.

Thus, as General Ziegler visited Faïd Pass on the evening of February 13 to make sure his forces were all in position for the morning's attack, his orders called for him to take Sidi Bou Zid and reconnoiter as far west as Sbeitla, but nothing more.

On the allied side, Waters ordered a patrol to go out the road toward Faïd Pass and set up an outpost. If that small unit saw or heard armored vehicles coming through the pass, it could give the warning and call for an artillery barrage. Waters, using a halftrack as his command post up on Djebel Lessouda, did not go out himself to make sure the outpost was in the right position.

If the intelligence estimates were correct, the Americans could look forward to a quiet Sunday morning—St. Valentine's Day. But Drake remained wary. He issued orders for breakfast at 4:00 A.M. and "stand to" at 5:00 A.M. Making sure his men were fed was not just an act of thoughtfulness on Drake's part. One of the more memorable legends of military lore is how Hannibal got his men up and fed them before attacking the Romans at the battle of Cannae in 216 B.C.E. The Romans, who entered the battle on empty stomachs, tired and collapsed in defeat.

During the night, the wind blew steadily from the northwest. The enemy's *Fruehlingswind*, more than a breeze and more than a month early for spring, filled the air with dust and masked the sound of the engines of hundreds of tanks as they moved up into Faïd Pass.

12

A Valentine's Day Surprise

When Col. Pete Hains, down on the flat land at Sidi Bou Zid, first heard the sounds of distant gunfire on the morning of February 14, 1943, he glanced at his watch. It was 6:35 A.M. He called John Waters, up on the side of Djebel Lessouda.

"What's going on over in your part of the world?" he asked. "We hear a lot of shooting in that direction."

Waters, who was monitoring the radio in his half-track, hidden in a wadi, said he hadn't heard or seen anything and had received no reports from troops stationed on the plain between him and Faïd Pass. He told Hains he would go up on a promontory above his half-track and take a look.

He adjusted the focus on his binoculars and peered toward the east into a reddish haze backlit by the rising sun. Urgent messages had been flowing back up the chain of command for months now, demanding better binoculars. But even if he had had a pair of the far superior German optics, Waters still would have been unable to see what was happening a few miles away through the haze. He hurried back down to his radio to report to Hains.

"I can hear some shooting far out there. There is a strong wind blowing, sand is blowing right toward me, a sand and dust storm. I can't see anything."

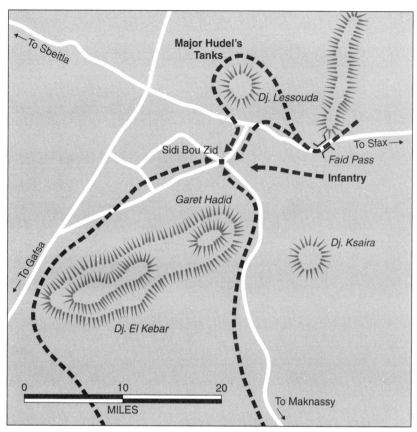

The American 1st Armored Division and 34th Infantry Division were badly mauled in the battle for Sidi Bou Zid on Valentine's Day, 1943. Dotted lines indicate how German columns converged on the Americans, cutting them off on isolated mountains.

Waters had stationed a small unit along the road toward Faïd Pass and had sent out a tank company before dawn. But he had heard from neither of them. It was only later that Waters learned what had happened to his early warning system.

The detachment that was supposed to be stationed close to Faïd Pass had mistakenly stopped four miles short of it. The tank company had gone out as scheduled, but Waters did not have radio contact with the company commander. Instead, he was linked to a major who was supposed to have gone with the company in his own tank. When Waters sent

The tiny village of Sidi Bou Zid was the site of a bitter defeat for the 34th Infantry Division and the 1st Armored Division in a battle that began on Valentine's Day 1943. In this view, looking to the north, Djebel Lessouda can be seen in the background. The roadway on the right runs toward the village of Porte de Lessouda. Faïd Pass, from which the enemy attack came, is off the photo to the right.
(Source: National Archives)

an aide to investigate, he found the major blithely asleep on his cot. The major hurried to catch up with the tank company, but almost as soon as he joined them, his tank was hit and his radio knocked out.

Up higher on Djebel Lessouda, Maj. Bob Moore, commanding the infantry battalion from the 168th Regiment, had a better picture of what was happening. He saw the onrushing German tanks overrun an artillery unit and a platoon of his infantry on the flat land in front of Djebel Lessouda.

"I tried to call Waters's command post but could not get an answer," he later recalled.

Down on the flat, the artillery unit Moore saw being overrun consisted of six self-propelled guns—105 mm howitzers mounted on halftracks—commanded by Capt. Bruce Pirnie.

"The desert between Faïd and Lessouda was just swarming with tanks, infantry and Lord knows what," Pirnie recalled. "We were just pouring out ammunition, using shorter and shorter range. I figured it was time to move out and I gave the word. It was a rat race, everybody for himself, tearing like crazy."

Pirnie had waited too long to give the order to pull out. Four of his guns were captured or destroyed, and 29 of his 100 men were captured.

Pirnie himself and four of his men piled into one of the halftracks and worked their way up onto the mountain. They got off a few shots until they were attacked by four German tanks. They dropped a thermal grenade down the barrel of their gun and scrambled up the hill on foot before they made contact with Moore's battalion.

In the fog of war, no one on the Allied side had a clear picture of what was happening or the size of the enemy force. But by 7:15 A.M., the situation was much clearer to Waters, and the news was alarming. He called Hains and told him he could see about 20 German Panzer IV tanks at the little town of Poste de Lessouda. This meant the Germans had already swung all the way around Djebel Lessouda from the north and were assembling to the south of the mountain, between it and the other American forces at Sidi Bou Zid and further away on Djebel Ksaïra. Moore, from his vantage point, saw not only those tanks which had passed to the north around Djebel Lessouda, but others swarming toward Poste de Lessouda from the east and southeast. Waters and Major Moore's battalion of infantry were surrounded—and the battle had barely begun.

Hains reassured Waters that Hightower, with two companies of Shermans and most of a company of tank destroyers—a total of some 50 armored vehicles—was on his way from Sidi Bou Zid toward the German concentration at Poste de Lessouda.

With the aid of the sandstorm and miscues on the Allied side, a massive German assault force of some 200 tanks and armored vehicles had achieved not only surprise but a big head start on a long day of battle.

※

The German tanks had begun moving up through Faïd Pass from the east at least as early as 4:30 A.M., feeling their way slowly through the sandstorm. Italian troops had been busy during the night removing mines and placing dim lights to guide the tanks through the pass and out onto the plain beyond.

Almost as soon as they began to emerge from the pass at about 6:30 A.M., American artillery, at the base of Djebel Lessouda, opened fire as the German tanks came into view. But by the time the artillerymen realized they were badly outnumbered and should pull back in the face of the attack by scores of tanks, it was too late. Their guns became mired in a swampy area, and they were surrounded and captured or killed before they could get away.

The German spearhead was led by a Major Hudel, a veteran of the fighting in December in northern Tunisia. His battalion of about 40 tanks of the 10th Panzer Division swept north of Djebel Lessouda and on around to the west side. When the tanks came across soldiers of the 168th infantry in foxholes at the base of the mountain, they pivoted with their treads to squash the men into the ground.

American guns based on the mountainside fired on the tanks. Hudel returned the fire as he passed at 30 miles an hour but made no attempt to clean out the guns. That was the job of the infantry, following up the tank attack. He moved down the west side of the mountain and then stopped near the Faïd-Sbeitla road, near Poste de Lessouda. It was this concentration of tanks that Waters reported to Hains. Hudel scanned the area to the east and south, looking for the other arms of the pincer that were supposed to close in on Sidi Bou Zid.

The German attack can be pictured, very roughly, as resembling a left hand, grasping like a giant claw for Sidi Bou Zid and the area surrounding it. Hudel is a long thumb reaching around Djebel Lessouda to the north. The index finger is a tank column speeding along the road from Faïd Pass to Poste de Lessouda. The middle finger is infantry

This is the view from Faïd Pass looking westward toward Djebel Lessouda and Sidi Bou Zid. (Source: National Archives)

heading directly for Sidi Bou Zid. The fourth finger is another column of tanks driving north toward Sidi Bou Zid, and the little finger is still another column of tanks and infantry heading toward the same target from the southwest.

Hudel thought those units coming from the south—portions of Rommel's 21st Panzer Division—might already be in Sidi Bou Zid, but he saw no sign of them.

So far, Hudel's part of the operation had gone perfectly. But Hudel was nervous. He could not believe they had caught the Americans completely by surprise. To him, Faïd was the only logical place for an attack, and the signs of a buildup must have been apparent to the Americans for several days. Perhaps he had blithely led his men into some nasty trap. He worried especially about the new American medium tank, the Sherman. Its 75 mm gun was capable of sending a shell crashing right through the frontal armor of his Panzer III and IV tanks at 1,500 meters. At that range, the shells from his 50 mm guns would bounce off the Shermans. If the

The wreckage of an American fighter lies on the battlefield near Sidi Bou Zid. In the background is Djebel Lessouda, where elements of two American divisions were trapped. (Source: National Archives)

Americans used their armor effectively, he could be in big trouble. But maybe the Americans, going into battle for the first time, weren't as skillful as he feared. One sign of that was a group of American tanks, in a distant cactus grove, opening fire on him while they were still far out of range, thus giving away their position.

This premature fire came from Hightower's tanks. Hightower drove his own tank onto a rise in the earth from where he was able to see Hudel's force at the base of Djebel Lessouda. More tanks and troop carriers were coming down the road from Faïd Pass. Hightower spotted the Panzer III and IV tanks about whose safety Hudel was worried. But he also saw several of the new Panzer VI Tiger tanks with their powerful 88 mm guns. He radioed McQuillin's headquarters that he was badly outnumbered and would be able to fight only a delaying action at best.

About the same time that Hightower was sizing up the situation, Hudel received new orders: "Advance of 21 Panzer Division from south has been delayed; Tank Battalion is to continue attack and to capture Sidi Bou Zid."

Hudel realized that a frontal attack into the face of the American guns would be suicidal. Instead, he ordered his tanks, concealed by clouds of dust, to spread out to the east and west and then converge on the Americans from all directions, thus splitting up the defensive fire. The American tanks remained close together, in effect using their guns as antitank weapons, instead of using their greater mobility to break up the Germans' encircling movement.

As Hudel began his advance, Axis planes, which had been striking at the Americans all day, made a concentrated attack on the Sidi Bou Zid area, apparently trying to pin down the Americans in the combat command headquarters there and prevent them from escaping to the west.

The German tactic of attacking the American tank formation from all directions was devastating. Sgt. Clarence Coley, Hightower's radio operator, saw a number of the American tanks hit. Sometimes two or three men got out. Sometimes none of the five crew members escaped.

Hightower ordered a withdrawal. His own tank zigzagged backward toward Sidi Bou Zid, keeping his frontal armor—and his gun—toward the enemy. He was the rear guard, trying to protect what was left of his force in its retreat.

It was not until 7:30 A.M., an hour after the first enemy tanks had emerged from Faïd Pass, that Drake, at his command post on the other side of Sidi Bou Zid, was alerted that the troops on Djebel Lessouda, including the 2nd Battalion of his 168th Infantry, were surrounded by enemy tanks. By that time the enemy was between him and Djebel Lessouda and might soon be in a position to cut him off from his 3rd Battalion on Djebel Ksaïra, about 4½ miles east of his command post.

From his vantage point, looking northwest, Drake could tell that a major engagement was under way, but he couldn't tell quite what was happening or who was winning. As he watched, he received a report of enemy, including tanks, approaching from behind him, from the southeast. Peering through his binoculars, Drake counted 83 enemy tanks, seeming to come from all directions.

A nearby artillery unit suddenly began what looked to Drake like a panicky retreat. He called McQuillin on the phone and told him what was happening. The withdrawal of the artillery unit had, in fact, been ordered, but in Drake's view it had gotten out of hand.

"You are on the spot," McQuillin told him. "You take charge and stop it."

"You mean for me to take command of all troops in the area?" Drake asked. Up to that point, he had been in command of only his own headquarters and the 3rd Battalion on Djebel Ksaïra. He was not even in direct control of his other battalion on Djebel Lessouda.

To Drake's question, McQuillin gave a one-word answer: "Yes."

Drake stopped the withdrawal, rounded up troops who were straggling back to the rear, and resumed his efforts to follow the course of the battle through his binoculars. His executive officer, Lt. Col. Gerald Line, remained at the regimental command post to keep in touch with McQuillin's headquarters.

About 11:00 A.M., Line was talking with McQuillin when he was abruptly told: "No more over the phone. We are leaving."

Line hurried out to find Drake and told him: "General McQuillin is on the telephone and said he is pulling out and for you to stay here."

What did this order mean? Drake's previous orders had been to hold his position to the last man. Did this mean McQuillin and the rest of Combat Command A were pulling out and leaving him alone?

Drake hustled back to his command post and grabbed the phone. The line was dead. Two men sent out to check the wires reported back a short time later: The telephone on the other end of the line was gone. Although Drake did not know where they had gone, McQuillin and his headquarters troops were in fact on their way to a village about ten miles to the west.

Plans had earlier been approved by McQuillin for the withdrawal of the 3rd Battalion from Djebel Ksaïra. But he and Drake had agreed that the men could not leave their outpost position during daylight. It was about noon when McQuillin and his headquarters moved out.

Drake's men asked him repeatedly if they shouldn't follow McQuillin in his withdrawal. By that time, in the early afternoon, it probably would have been impossible for the units Drake had with him down on the flat between Djebel Ksaïra and another mountain a short distance to the west, called Garet Hadid, to escape. They were pretty well surrounded, the Germans had almost absolute control of the air, and roads west of Sidi Bou Zid were already blocked by the enemy.

Drake's response to those who wanted to withdraw was, as he later put it: "He intended to attack; that it was his belief that an attack was his best defense, and that he was going to capture the high ground at Garet Hadid, about a mile to the front."

Actually, Garet Hadid was to the west of his position, away from Faïd Pass. But at that point in the battle, moving in almost any direction could properly be considered an attack.

It is some measure of the straits to which the infantry had been reduced that the troops Drake sent out as scouts, on each side of the road toward Garet Hadid, were members of the regimental band.

As the infantrymen moved toward Garet Hadid, they picked up reinforcements in the form of other units pulling back in the face of the German advance. A company of engineers from the 1st Armored Division showed up and offered whatever assistance they could provide. A platoon of light tanks reported in next. The lieutenant in charge said he had been ordered to pull back if faced with heavy German tanks. They joined the other units in a successful effort to seize Garet Hadid before the enemy could take control.

About 2:00 P.M., Drake scribbled a report of his situation on the only paper available—rough British toilet paper—and sent 1st Lt. Marvin E. Williams to try to reach Ward's head-quarters near Sbeitla with this message:

> Enemy surrounds 2nd Battalion (located on Mt. Lessouda) since 0730 hours this morning. Forty tanks known to be around them. Shelled, dive bombed and tank attack. All artillery pulled out at 1300 hours, still trying to locate them. McQuillin's headquarters pulled out at 1100 hours to southwest, did not notify except by message. Talked to McQuillin once by radio and he said help had been requested. Germans have absolute superiority, ground and air. Have stopped retreating TD [tank destroyer] unit and am attempting to hold my CP position. Unless help from air and armor comes immediately, infantry will lose immeasurably.

Williams skirted around Sidi Bou Zid, cut across country, and got to Ward's headquarters about 5:00 P.M. Ward told him a battalion of tanks was being sent on the following day to make contact with Drake and that he was being instructed to withdraw on the evening of the 15th. But Drake, back on Garet Hadid, knew nothing about the rescue attempt or the orders to withdraw.

Late in the afternoon, he took stock. He had about 900 men gathered for the defense of Garet Hadid. But about 300 of them—men from scattered tank, artillery, tank destroyer, and reconnaissance units—were not armed. As many weapons as possible were rounded up from shot-up tanks and half-tracks or where rifles could be found lying on the battlefield. Still, there were not enough to go around.

The Germans moved in cautiously around Garet Hadid. Drake feared an all-out assault while he was still preparing his defenses. If that had happened, the enemy would have gone right through the American position. Instead, the enemy surrounded the mountain on all sides and began a siege.

Just before noon, Waters called Hains by radio. He was operating out of his half-track, hidden in a ravine on Djebel Lessouda. Hains and Waters later recalled their conversation:

Waters told Hains that as far as he was concerned, the war was over.

"We'll sit here," he told him, "and do the best we can to report to you what's going on and try to keep in communications and be a source of information, but there isn't anything more that I can do. My infantry is up on the high ground . . . they are only foot infantry and they can't move. There is no infantry attacking them yet and there is no enemy at whom they can shoot. The tank destroyers are gone; the tanks are gone, the two antitank guns are gone, and the artillery is gone. So there we are."

As Hains recalled, Waters said: "Pete, I'm going to shut this thing off and go up on the O.P. They are all around here and looking at me now, but I don't think they have discovered this halftrack yet. If I keep on operating, they will. I will destroy it before they get too close. If I keep away, they won't find it as it is well hidden and I may be able to contact you again."

Hains told him to hold on until dark and then try to get his men out to a rallying point they had previously agreed upon.

"Never mind about me," Waters replied. "Just kill those bastards at the bottom of the hill."

Hains said he would do his best and signed off.

About 2:30 P.M. Waters checked in again, but Hains was out observing the tank battle and didn't attempt to call back until about 3:00 P.M. By that time there was no response, and there was no further contact with Waters.

Waters himself lost contact with Major Moore, the commander of the infantry unit further up the mountain. He sent his driver to work his way up to Moore with a message.

"On the way, I think our infantry shot him by mistake," Waters recalled. "He came back to me with a hole in his chest and died within several hours."

Waters was alone then with a captain who had been assigned to assist him. They moved their halftrack several times as they spotted German patrols nearby. About midafternoon, Waters was in one gulch, part of a dry riverbed, and the other officer was in a neighboring wadi about 50 or 100 yards away. The other officer was captured and then a German patrol, guided by some natives, came upon Waters.

"The Arabs moved back and forth as the battle went," Waters later explained. "They were always with the side that was winning because that gave them the opportunity to loot the dead. That was their reward . . . Those Arabs, in my mind, brought this patrol back to find me. I'm sure they did because they had been told that they would get a reward if they turned in any Americans."

Waters spent the rest of the war in German POW camps.

Further up on Djebel Lessouda, Moore, who had just taken over as commander of the 168th Infantry's 2nd Battalion during the fighting at Sened Station, put his men to work placing mines in ravines through which the enemy might approach his position. But he didn't open fire because from where he was, he couldn't tell friendly from enemy troops down below. Finally, about 9:00 A.M., a captain in charge of a mortar crew said he had identified an enemy artillery unit on the move within less than a mile of his position. Moore told him to open fire. More than 85 rounds of 82 mm mortar shells rained down on the German column. The effect, Moore reported, was devastating, with many soldiers killed or wounded and four vehicles set afire.

About an hour later, a lookout reported four small cars and a motorcycle approaching up a ravine. He couldn't tell whether they were friendly or hostile. When they got within about a city block, it was clear they were enemy, and Moore ordered his men to fire. Two officers and six noncommissioned officers—members of an artillery observation party—were captured.

During the day, German infantry made several seemingly halfhearted attempts to infiltrate the American position but were quickly driven back. About 4:00 P.M., the enemy had apparently located Moore's observation post. It was subjected to a heavy shelling by both artillery and 20 mm cannon fire. Moore moved his position and tried to contact Drake's headquarters by radio but couldn't get through.

Moore ordered his men to be alert for any attempt to infiltrate their positions during the hours of darkness and then settled down for the night.

About noon, Hightower broke contact with the Germans and pulled back into Sidi Bou Zid. He stopped his tank and climbed down to see if he could get an idea of the situation they were in. While he was gone, his crew, who had started out before breakfast that morning, heated up some cans of C-rations and had what seemed to them like a feast.

When Hightower returned, they headed out to the west. As they moved across the flat land away from Sidi Bou Zid, they could see other vehicles all spread out and heading in the same direction—away from the enemy. They hoped.

Of the armored vehicles with which Hightower had started out that morning, only a few remained. Out ahead of them were five tanks of Company H. Hightower was, in effect, bringing up the rear, moving along with his gun rotated back over the left rear fender. Seven German tanks were on their trail.

Sergeant Coley, who wasn't getting any response to his efforts to reach the other tanks by radio, went to work pulling shells out from their storage space under the turret and passing them up to the loader. He could hear Hightower, up in the turret, complimenting the gunner on hits on the German tanks. But the Germans, with their smaller guns, were also scoring hits on their tank. Coley could feel the tank rock and hear the loud sound as the projectiles hit and bounced off.

Suddenly a shell jammed in their gun. Their only hope now was to try to run for it. Hightower ordered the driver to head out as fast as he could. Just then, an enemy shell cracked through the armor on the left side of the tank, passing through the gas tank. Coley stared for a moment as the shell spun on one end like a top, sparks flying out the other end.

"Let's get the hell out of here!" Hightower shouted. He and the three other crew members bailed out of the burning tank. But Coley couldn't get his hatch open. He finally snaked his way across to the driver's hatch and dove out headfirst. He had run less than 50 yards when he heard an explosion and turned to see fire shooting out of their tank.

As soon as it went into combat, the gasoline-powered Sherman became notorious for burning when hit. Soldiers on both sides called it the "Ronson," after the flameproof cigarette lighter many of them carried. Actually, any tank, with its load of ammunition and fuel—whether gasoline or diesel—will explode and burn if hit in the right place.

Hightower and his crew took off across country, walking and running, until they found two half-tracks. One was broken down, and the men were wondering what to do. Hightower told them German tanks were right behind them and they'd better hurry up and do something. The men stripped the broken-down vehicle of its machine gun and ammunition, piled into the remaining vehicle, and sped off to the west.

When they reached friendly lines, Hightower found that of his original command, only seven tanks had managed to reach a rallying point away from the battlefield. He had lost 44 tanks, destroyed or captured, including four that had been under repairs and had to be abandoned at Sidi Bou Zid.

McQuillin and his key aides managed to make it to a small village about 10 miles to the west of Sidi Bou Zid, where they hoped to set up a new headquarters. But the enemy was so close behind that they kept on going all the way to Sbeitla, about 20 miles further west. Behind them they left not only Hightower's battered tank battalion but two artillery units and a reconnaissance battalion that had been virtually destroyed by enemy gunfire and almost continuous bombing and strafing attacks.

The retreat was also plagued by a mysterious problem with the fuel for their trucks, jeeps, and other gasoline-powered vehicles. The soldiers were forced to stop repeatedly to take off the sediment bowls from their fuel lines and empty out water that had collected there. Had their fuel become contaminated by accident, or was it sabotage? To add to the mystery, the tanks accompanying the retreating column did not have the same problem. In the confusion, the mystery was never solved.

By 3:30 P.M., with the Americans either knocked out of action, on the run, or marooned, General Ziegler, the Axis commander, concluded that he had accomplished his mission. He then made a major mistake. Instead of pounding after the fleeing Americans, he paused to regroup and decide what to do next. He was probably worried about leaving the elements of an American regiment in his rear, even though he had them surrounded. And part of the fault lies in the Axis hierarchy, which had sent Ziegler off without clear instructions on what he was to do after carrying out his initial attack on Sidi Bou Zid.

Rommel was not in command of the operation at that point, but it was his 21st Panzer Division, with its veterans of desert battles, that had been heavily involved in the fighting and the victory at Sidi Bou Zid.

"At this success," Rommel noted in his diary, "I urged the Fifth Army, which was in charge of the operation, to push straight on during the night, keep the enemy on the run and take Sbeitla. Tactical successes must be ruthlessly exploited. A routed enemy who, on the day of his flight, can be rounded up without much effort, may reappear on the morrow restored to his full fighting power. However, the 21st Panzer Division did not follow up the retreating Americans until the night of the 16th."

At the end of the first day of fighting, the Americans had not only suffered grievous losses but had left two infantry battalions and portions of an armored division isolated and surrounded on three widely separated mountains.

As reports of the day's traumatic events filtered into Ward's command post and then on up to Fredendall's and Anderson's even more remote headquarters, confusion about what was happening on the battlefield persisted. Eisenhower, on his way back to his headquarters in Algeria, was informed of the fighting but assumed it was a minor skirmish and went sightseeing. None of the top brass was yet willing to acknowledge that the 10th Panzer Division was involved at Sidi Bou Zid—even though that was the outfit Hightower had met that morning and one of the two German divisions the Americans had been fighting all day. The generals continued to fear that the 10th Panzer would suddenly swoop down through Fondouk Pass, further north.

Only reluctantly, late in the afternoon, did Fredendall and Anderson authorize the movement of several reserve units to gather for an attack on the morning of February 15 on the Germans at Sidi Bou Zid. The small Combat Command C, which was in reserve, and one battalion of Robinett's Combat Command B were ordered to move down toward Sidi Bou Zid. But Robinett and most of his experienced tankers were told to remain where they were, miles from the scene of the fighting.

Fredendall's orders to Ward made the next day's task seem simple: "As regards action in the Sidi Bou Zid area, concentrate tomorrow on cleaning up situation there and destroying the enemy. Thereafter collect strong mobile forces in Sbeitla area ready for action in any direction. . . ."

During the day on February 14, while the Germans were wreaking havoc on his colleagues in the 1st Armored Division at Sidi Bou Zid, Robinett found time to pen a letter to his brother, Dick, back in Springfield, Missouri, instructing him to send a check, under protest, to the Bureau of Internal Revenue, to cover an alleged underpayment of $32.41 on his income tax for 1941. When, a few months later, Robinett received his tax return for 1942, he returned it to the Collector of Internal Revenue with a brusque note saying he had been out of the country on overseas service since May 1942 and "I have neither the time, facilities, nor information necessary for the completion of the Return."

13

First Armored
to the Rescue

The armored unit that set out on its rescue mission on
February 15 had the look of a formidable force.

A battalion of 52 tanks, led by Lt. Col. J. D. Alger, was
flanked by tank destroyers and followed by artillery and
motorized infantry. From a kickoff point ten miles northwest
of Sidi Bou Zid, the column headed directly toward the
town. Its goal was to take Sidi Bou Zid and then set up a
screen so Drake could extricate his troops from Djebel
Ksaïra and Garet Hadid. Once these troops had been rescued, then Alger could turn his attention to what seemed
like the easier task of protecting the withdrawal of Moore's
infantry from Djebel Lessouda.

The assignment would appear straightforward, even simple. But as Alger and his 2nd Battalion of the 1st Armored
Regiment of the 1st Armored Division headed across the
plain, which looked from a distance as smooth as a billiard
table, they were heading almost literally into the unknown.

Alger had not arrived at the farmhouse where planning
for the operation was under way until almost midnight. He
was disturbed to find that no detailed maps or even sketches

of the area were available. When he asked what was known about the enemy he would face, he was told he might run into as many as 60 tanks, but no one knew what outfits they belonged to.

He probably didn't worry as much as he should have about the fact that his battalion, for which this battle would be its baptism of fire, was coming up against some of the most experienced, battle-hardened veterans in the German army. The 10th Panzer had helped spearhead the blitzkrieg into France in 1940 and had fought in Russia. The 21st Panzer was the first German division in Africa and had more experience in desert combat than any other unit on either side. Although it had been badly mauled in the long retreat across Africa, it still had a core of veterans able to draw on their experience in many battles.

To complicate his task, the "billiard table" approach to Sidi Bou Zid was cut by three deep wadis, what those familiar with cowboy movies would recognize as dry gulches. To cross those wadis, his tanks would have to line up single file, inviting sites for an ambush or aerial attack.

In fact, dive-bombing and strafing planes struck the infantry element of the column before it had even gotten under way, and caused a long delay in the beginning of the attack. So it was not until nearly 2:00 P.M. that the first company crossed the first wadi without opposition. A few minutes later, when the tanks emerged from the second wadi, they began to receive air-burst artillery.

The tank commanders reluctantly ducked down inside their tanks and fastened the hatches on their turrets. Shells that burst in the air cause relatively little damage to the tanks themselves. But the shrapnel raining down on the tanks forces the crews to "button up." The tank commander, who likes to ride with his head and shoulders exposed so he can see what is going on, is forced to peek through a tiny viewport or periscope to look for enemy tanks and guns and to guide his driver. It also slows down the column, from perhaps 30 miles an hour to three or four miles an hour.

As Alger had feared, the Germans had set up an ambush at the second wadi. But a platoon on his left flank spotted the enemy—four 88 mm guns flanked by two 47 mm antitank guns. The Americans moved fast. In a few minutes, they knocked out the enemy guns and overran the position, killing an estimated 50 soldiers.

As the Americans moved in close to Sidi Bou Zid, they hesitated, waiting for a promised attack by American planes. None came. About 3:00 P.M., one company rolled on into the town, destroyed a number of machine gun positions, and by 3:15 P.M. continued on east of the town in the direction of the infantry marooned on Djebel Ksaïra.

Alger had lost contact with some of the units under his command, but the reports he did receive indicated they would soon be in position to cover the withdrawal of Drake's men from Djebel Ksaïra and Garet Hadid.

Then, about 3:45 P.M., Alger received the first of a series of worrisome reports. A platoon commander reported enemy tanks—he couldn't tell how many—north of Sidi Bou Zid. Ten minutes later, a company commander reported enemy tanks coming from the south. He took them under fire, but they were moving off to flank him to the west.

At 4:30 P.M., Alger moved his tank to the north of Sidi Bou Zid to see what was happening there. When he was asked by radio for a report on his situation and what help, if any, he needed, he replied: "Still pretty busy. Situation in hand. No answer to second question. Further details later."

Suddenly his tank was hit by three shells, one after the other. They knocked off his radio antenna, destroyed his gun, and jammed the turret.

Fifteen minutes later, an armor-piercing round slammed into the engine compartment, setting off the automatic fire extinguishers. And then two more armor-piercing rounds hit the turret on the south side, killing the radio operator.

Alger and the rest of his crew bailed out and set off on foot to find the company operating north of town. At 5:30 P.M., Alger and two of his crew members were captured. Alger, like Waters on the previous afternoon, joined the growing list of Americans for whom the fighting part of the war was over. His promised "later" report on further details did not come until 1945—much later.

Between 5:30 and 6:00 P.M., the battered American tank battalion began pulling back out of the area, concerned now about its own safety rather than rescue of the stranded infantry. Most of the surviving tanks clustered near a hamlet two miles northwest of Sidi Bou Zid, where they were surrounded and destroyed by the German tanks. The armored infantry that had followed Alger's tanks barely escaped after nearly being cut off south of Sidi Bou Zid by enemy tanks.

General Ziegler and the other German commanders had been expecting a counterattack. That was one of the reasons he had not pursued the fleeing Americans on the previous afternoon. But when the attack came, it took the Germans a while to size up the attack and figure out how to react. They expected the American attack to be much more powerful, a major reason for their failure to react more quickly. They were reluctant to commit themselves to reacting to Alger's relatively puny force until they were sure where the *rest* of the Americans were.

When the German commanders finally convinced themselves that Alger's column was the entire American force, their reaction was swift and deadly.

Part of one regiment was sent down south of Sidi Bou Zid, along the base of Garet Hadid and an adjoining mountain, to take up a position on the flank of the approaching Americans. It was already in position before its presence was detected.

Another tank unit was held east of Djebel Lessouda, waiting for the appropriate time to strike. Artillery and antitank units were positioned throughout the area, hidden in olive groves. This all amounted to a massive ambush, with scores of tanks, including the formidable Panzer VI Tigers, lying in wait.

The Americans were even permitted to cross the second wadi without serious opposition before the air-burst artillery opened up and the tanks moved in from north and south to crush the American column.

Lt. Kurt E. Wolff, commanding a German tank company in the force that had moved in south of the approaching Americans, wrote an account of the battle that was published in a German magazine a short time later. While it is difficult to tell exactly how his actions fit into the overall battle, his account gives a feel for what was going through the minds of those on the German side.

He was about to have coffee with his company commander when a lookout spotted the approaching American tanks. Wolff was ordered to try to hold up the American column until another unit could maneuver around onto the enemy's flank.

Wolff rolled up onto a flat hill covered with cactus and watched nervously as the Sherman tanks passed in review before him. All they had to do, he thought, was to turn quickly, overrun his small force, and then turn to face the regiment in the distance. The Americans stopped, focused on the German tanks to their front. They seemed not to know what to do.

Suddenly Wolff received the order: "Fourth Company attack!" He hesitated for a moment, wondering if his commander realized how badly outnumbered he was. Then he sent one platoon to the left. His right platoon made a headlong dash toward the Americans. The center platoon waited three minutes and then followed the right platoon. They were still out of range, so their guns were silent.

"We got to within about 2,000 meters of the enemy," Wolff recalled. "It was simply incomprehensible to us, but he was staring straight ahead at the tank regiment far to the right of us which apparently was also in motion, and not one of the enemy tanks turned its turret toward us.

"Just at this moment our artillery began to lay its fire down on the approaching enemy. It did the very thing we needed. The enemy became uneasy. We were able to improve our positions. Everything was moving along as if on the training field."

Wolff was ordered not to fire under any circumstances. He was too far away for his company's fire to be effective, and the other company was not yet in position.

"We had to wait. My men kept estimating the distance to the white steel bodies of the enemy and asking excitedly when they could begin to fire. The shells were already in the firing chambers."

The two companies continued to move toward the American column, still undetected. Then came the order: "Fourth Company open fire. . . . " Then: "Fourth Company continue to advance."

"Victory was between these orders," Wolff wrote,

> for scarcely had the first shells left our guns than the first three enemy tanks were on fire. They were burning. The flames were red and the first billows of smoke over the field of battle were dark gray and black. Anyone who has ever been in a tank battle knows how the heart beats when the attack starts rolling. There is nothing happening, only the noise of the motors is there—and the waiting enemy. But when the first shells have found their mark and the first red fire is seen on the horizon, then the heart is relieved and the feeling of danger, of not being able to weather the storm, has disappeared. . . .
>
> There were at least 15 burning tanks ahead of us and the most advanced of our tanks were already making their way between the destroyed American tanks in the rear.
>
> The adjoining regiment on the right had also come up during this time and had knocked out the foremost enemy tanks which, in the beginning, had driven past us on our right. The remaining enemy tanks had retreated, and had passed us in such a favorable position that the platoon on the right had a special battle of its own.

As the firing tapered off, the Germans stared in awe at the scene before them, the burning American tanks almost seeming to have been lined up to have their picture taken. Wolff recalled how his battalion commander, "laughing like a boy, went from company to company asking us and him-self too: 'Did you ever see anything like it? Did you ever see anything like it?' "

Wolff, whose company had not suffered a single death, was elated, the day's victory pushing out of his mind the long, humiliating retreat across Africa with Rommel's army.

"I can still see the long line of fires in front of which our tanks cruised up and down, their engines humming, calm yet proud after a good day's work," he recalled.

❊

Only a handful of Alger's tanks managed to make it back out of the German trap. Of the 52 tanks that started out that morning, 46 were left on the battlefield, burning or abandoned. But reports of the day's fighting were so fragmentary and conflicting that even hours after the shooting had died down, Allied commanders didn't know what had happened.

At 10:30 that night, Ward sent a message to Fredendall: "We might have walloped them or they might have walloped us."

It took a while for the truth to sink in to Ward, Fredendall, Anderson, and others in the Allied chain of command that they had lost two armored battalions, plus artillery and other units, on two successive days. Observers on a mountain to the west of the battlefield could see scores of tanks burning late into the night.

And at the end of the second day of the Battle for Sidi Bou Zid, the infantrymen of the 168th Infantry were still stranded on their three lonely outcroppings of rock.

During the day on February 15, the Germans seemed content to harass the American infantry on Djebel Lessouda with an artillery bombardment about every two hours. Major Moore's men scanned the western horizon for signs of American tanks coming to their rescue.

About 10:00 A.M., with still no sign of a rescue attempt, a medic came to Moore's command post and told him one of the German officers they had captured the day before wanted to talk to him. Moore accompanied the medic back to where the wounded German was being treated.

"This officer said that we were entirely surrounded and that he knew his comrades would come in and rescue him and wanted me to surrender," Moore later recalled. "I did not even answer him but immediately went back to my CP."

One of the armored officers was in contact with McQuillin's headquarters by radio. He was told to hold on, that help was coming.

Looking down from their vantage point, however, the Americans could see that the German officer was right: They were indeed surrounded by enemy infantry and tanks. And then, in midafternoon, they spotted the dust raised by Alger's battalion moving across the plain from the west. Help was on the way.

The men trapped on the hill watched in dismay as their rescuers, caught in the German ambush, were destroyed in a two-hour battle. At dusk, as a cloud of smoke rose from the burning tanks, a lone P-40 swooped down over Djebel Lessouda and dropped a message ordering Moore to withdraw from the mountain, beginning at 10:00 that night, and "bring everything you can."

Moore called his company commanders together and outlined his plan for the escape attempt.

"The order," he later recalled, "was for all men to walk in two files about one yard apart from front to rear and at least 30 yards between columns, but to make no effort to try to sneak through, that our best chance of getting out was to simply march right through their positions, as far as we could, before they realize who we are.

"In case we were encountered by the enemy, we were not to fire, but to disperse and proceed individually or in small groups of twos or threes to a designated rendezvous."

All of the prisoners, including the walking wounded and even the litter cases, were told that they were prisoners of war and were coming with the Americans.

"They were . . . instructed that if they made one false move or noise of any kind to attract attention, that they would be bayoneted on the spot," Moore recalled.

The men spent the early hours of the evening taking apart the weapons they couldn't carry and burying the parts. Their vehicles were all disabled.

And then, about 10:30 P.M., the men began quietly picking their way through the dark down to the southwestern edge of the mountain before setting off across the plain toward the west, paralleling the road toward Sbeitla.

One might suppose that this attempt to march right through enemy lines would be the most traumatic thing that had ever happened to Bob Moore, far different from life back in Villisca, Iowa, where he had worked in his father's corner drugstore before his National Guard unit was called to active duty.

But never far from Moore's thoughts was the memory of a terrible thing that had happened on June 10, 1912, when he was seven years old. On that night, someone entered the home of his uncle and, with an axe, killed his uncle, his aunt, four cousins, and two visiting children. A suspect was arrested and Moore, although a child, attended one of the three trials. But no one was ever convicted, and the murder of the eight persons remains an unsolved crime. It left a scar deep in Moore's psyche that would today be recognized as post-traumatic stress syndrome.

"As the head of the column reached the western edge of the mountain, we encountered a German 88 mm gun in position," Moore recalled. "We were so close to it that we could have easily reached out and touched it as we passed by. One of the gun crew got up and said something to us in German, then looked back at the column. I did not answer, nor did anyone else, and he must have thought we were part of his own men."

The Americans continued on down off the mountain for about a mile until they reached the point where a unit of American soldiers was supposed to provide protection for their withdrawal. They heard voices coming from a clump of trees. Moore walked toward the trees to tell them his column was passing through. He could see someone walking toward him, about 30 yards away. As Moore approached, the man called out to him—in German. Moore did not answer, but circled back to his own men, about 100 yards away. The German shouted again. When he received no answer, the enemy opened up on the column with their machine guns.

"I gave the order for all men to scatter and to run like hell," Moore recalled. In the darkness, the Germans were apparently not sure what they were firing at. Their initial rounds were high and passed over the Americans. Mortar rounds soon began to fall on the head of the column and then on the troops in the middle. As the fire shifted from one part of the column to another, the companies that were not under fire moved off into the darkness.

Several of the men were hit and a few surrendered, but the bulk of the column got away and kept moving until about 5:00 A.M. on February 16, when they came upon guides who had been sent out to meet them. With Moore were 230 members of his battalion and remnants of Waters's armored unit. Later in the day, a few more men also made it to safety.

While the Germans seemed content to harass Moore's men on Djebel Lessouda with sporadic artillery fire, they were much more aggressive in trying to dislodge Drake's hodge-podge unit on Garet Hadid.

With the several pieces of artillery he had managed to assemble, Drake was able to keep the enemy tanks at bay during the 14th and 15th. But German infantry made repeated attacks, three times penetrating as far as Drake's command post before being driven back. Several enemy snipers worked their way up into the mountain and caused a number of casualties before they were rooted out.

On the afternoon of February 15, Drake and his men saw a column of tanks in the plain down below and radioed a warning to Alger. But the American tankers assumed that Drake had seen them, rather than Germans, and sent back the reassuring message: "Get ready to ride on the bandwagon!"

But there would be no bandwagon. Drake's men had not received any food for two days, and they were just about out of water. And the relentless enemy attacks continued.

At one point, the enemy pushed in Drake's right flank. He sent two platoons to drive the enemy back. But then danger threatened from his rear, where a tall cone of rock stood as a silent sentinel. Six men—all that he could spare— were assigned to protect this key defensive position. The enemy managed to kill three of the men and seize the cone. The three survivors reported back to Drake. He then sent a lieutenant and six members of the regimental band to retake the position. The seven band members held the pinnacle for several hours, until they were all killed. "They did retake it and their efforts saved the entire position from being penetrated," Drake reported.

Drake was in radio contact with division headquarters. He sent increasingly urgent requests during the day on the

15th for food, ammunition, and air and artillery strikes on the enemy. None came. At night, the radio link faded out and there was no further communication with the outside world until morning. Drake thus did not know that Moore's battalion, on Djebel Lessouda, was pulling out that night.

On the morning of February 16, the situation was critical.

"At this hour," Drake later wrote, "the situation was thus: The rear of the position was driven in; the right flank was in process of being driven in; ammunition was running low; the center had been penetrated three times by tanks and the lack of water was becoming increasingly grave. The men having not eaten or had a drink of water for three days, along with the hot weather and nervous exertion, reduced many to a pitiful state."

At about 2:30 P.M. on the 16th, Drake received a radioed message from General Ward. As he recalled, it said something like, "We can do no more for you. The decision is yours. I will try to have supplies dropped to you."

Drake was puzzled. What did Ward mean, "The decision is yours?" Did it mean he was no longer under orders to hold his position? Did it mean it was up to him whether to surrender, continue to defend the position, or withdraw?

As Drake and a few close aides pondered the message, they received another about 3:00 P.M.: "Look for dropped message at 1700 hours [5:00 P.M.]." Drake assumed he was going to be ordered to try to withdraw and began making plans to get off the mountain. Stephen W. Kane, the chaplain, stood out in the open, raised his arms in supplication, and prayed for guidance in their withdrawal.

At 5:00 P.M., three American planes flew low over Garet Hadid and continued on to drop a message at Djebel Ksaïra, 4½ miles away. It was not until 8:00 P.M. that the message was decoded and transmitted back to Drake. Fortunately, it was the order he had expected: Withdraw that night.

After dark, Drake's men busied themselves slashing the tires of all their vehicles, burying magnetos and radio parts, and hiding machine gun bolts so nothing would be usable—and doing all of this as quietly as possible so as not to alert the Germans to their imminent departure.

At 10:00 P.M., the Americans began working their way down off the mountain they had held for two desperate days and walking to the west toward friendly lines.

Drake's third battalion, on Djebel Ksaïra, under the command of Lt. Col. John H. Van Vliet, Jr., was farther to the east than Drake's unit, but it was more fortunate in one sense. First Lt. Harry P. Hoffman, commander of the regiment's Company K, found a well in the rear of his position, so his men at least had water to drink, although his men, like Drake's, had received no food since the evening of February 13.

Van Vliet's troops were hammered almost constantly with artillery. The enemy set up its six-inch howitzers in the open between Djebel Ksaïra and Garet Hadid and fired bursts of three shells. The Americans had nothing with the range to shoot back, so they just had to sit there and take it. Still, even after word got around that they were surrounded, Hoffman found morale was still good and the men seemed not to be worried.

About three o'clock on the afternoon of February 16, Van Vliet called a meeting of his company commanders. One after the other, the officers reported hand-to-hand fighting, continued shelling, and a mounting toll of men killed and wounded.

They began drawing up plans for a withdrawal across the plain to the west. Some of the officers argued for a withdrawal right away, in daylight. But Van Vliet insisted the attempt be made in the darkness.

After Drake received the order to withdraw, passed on from Van Vliet, he ordered the withdrawal of the Third Battalion from Ksaïra to begin half an hour before his men began to leave Garet Hadid. Theoretically, that would give Van Vliet's men time to catch up with Drake and form a single long column.

Actually, by the time Van Vliet's men finished hiding and destroying as much equipment as they could, it was almost midnight when they formed up and began their trek toward friendly lines. There were thus two columns of Americans strung out across the plain, marching along under a cloudy sky. From time to time, a bright moon broke through the clouds and shone down like a spotlight.

Van Vliet's men had barely made it down off the mountain when they were challenged by Germans in a scout car. One of the Americans tossed a grenade into the car and set it afire. Fortunately, the explosion and fire did not alert other nearby Germans, and the Americans continued their march.

Their route took them over broken ground with a number of dry wadis to be crossed. The men, weak from lack of food, began to straggle and throw away equipment, including the machine guns and heavier weapons they would need to fight their way through if the enemy tried to stop them. Hoffman and other officers tried without much success to keep the men from doing this.

Drake led his men right through a German tank park and bivouac area without being detected. By dawn, they were within sight of their goal, a mountain named Djebel Hamra. They had covered more than 22 miles during the night, with only a brief rest about midnight.

Following up behind, Van Vliet's men also saw the mountain, seemingly only a short distance away, its base covered in mist. But Van Vliet and his officers were worried. Their column was spread out over a wide area, and they didn't know where portions of it were.

About 7:00 A.M., Hoffman saw a long column of vehicles half a mile away. Van Vliet looked through his glasses. German soldiers were moving toward them. Soon tanks and machine guns opened fire on the Americans. The infantry surrounded them but stayed carefully back out of range.

As Hoffman later recounted what happened, Van Vliet ordered him to go back and look for the rest of their column. He left Van Vliet in a cactus patch about 11:00 A.M. and wandered across the plain until about 4:00 P.M. without finding the rest of the battalion. He could hear firing still going on back where he had left Van Vliet, so he waited until about 7:00 P.M. and, using his compass, began walking cross-country toward Sbeitla. Van Vliet and most of the rest of his battalion were either killed or captured that afternoon.

Drake, who had with him about 400 men—only half of whom were armed—got within about a mile of their goal when he and his men encountered a German motorized patrol. The enemy soldiers surrounded them at a distance while several tanks with yellow tigers painted on their sides circled the Americans.

Drake spotted German infantry running to surround them from the rear. He asked for volunteers to try to head them off. First Lt. William Rogers, a 1st Armored Division artillery officer, led a dozen men to a knoll in the rear of their position. They managed to hold off the enemy for just about an hour before they were all killed.

The surrounded Americans fought for about 3½ hours. Then, as they ran out of ammunition, firing tapered off. As it did so, a German armored car flying a white flag dashed into the midst of the Americans. Drake told his men to wave it away. When it didn't leave, they opened fire. German tanks followed the armored car into the circle, cutting the American unit into small groups. Those who did not surrender were killed.

One tank approached Drake. An officer pointed a rifle at him and shouted: "Colonel, you surrender!" Drake, by his account, turned his back on the tank and walked away. Two soldiers with rifles followed him until an English-speaking major picked him up in his car and took him to the German regimental headquarters. Drake later described the scene, referring to himself in the third person:

> The German general immediately came forward to see him, drew up at attention, saluted and said: "I want to compliment your command for the splendid fight they put up. It was a hopeless thing from the start but they fought like real soldiers."
> The German commander promised Colonel Drake that all the American wounded would be cared for and that he could leave American medical personnel to properly look after them, but immediately upon Colonel Drake leaving the field, the American medical personnel were carried off as prisoners and the American dead and wounded left to the ravages of the Arabs who proceeded to immediately strip the dead and wounded and to beat insensi-

ble those wounded who protested to the stripping of their clothes. The American prisoners were assembled in a group and under guard marched back that afternoon and night along the road to Dj[ebel] Lessouda. Those Americans who were slightly wounded or who became ill because of fatigue, lack of food and water and could not keep up with the column were ruthlessly bayoneted or shot. Many were walking barefooted because the Arabs had taken their shoes from them under the supervision of the German soldiers.

The men were marched all day without water, despite Drake's pleas to the German commander. That night, they were herded into a circle on the open desert and nearly froze. The next morning, they were packed in trucks and eventually ended up in POW camps in Germany and Poland.

One of the few Americans to escape, of all those trapped on Ksaïra and Garet Hadid, was Lt. Colonel Line, Drake's executive officer, who managed to hide himself when the Americans were surrounded and eventually worked his way back to friendly lines.

In addition to the losses among the tank and artillery units in the earlier phases of the Battle of Sidi Bou Zid, the Americans had now lost another battalion of infantry.

News of the calamity that had befallen the 168th Infantry was reported by the newspapers almost immediately. But it was several more anxious days before members of the families of the National Guardsmen from the little towns of southwestern Iowa received official word of what had happened to their sons, husbands, brothers, and, in some cases, boyfriends.

Word that telegrams were coming spread in the little town of Red Oak on March 6, and the families gathered in the Johnson Hotel next door to the Western Union station. And then, during the evening, 27 telegrams were delivered informing family members their soldiers were missing in action.

Harold Jenkins, a farm boy who lived near Red Oak, and Eleanor Thomas, who lived across the road, were sweethearts, but they decided not to marry when his National Guard unit was called up. He was one of the soldiers captured trying to escape from Djebel Ksaïra. A short time after the battle, Eleanor's father heard a rumor in town and told her, "They say that Company M has all been wiped out." She refused to believe it until the telegrams came in. That night she went to Harold's home, and she and his parents sat quietly in the dark for a long time.

Other telegrams—a total of some 200—were delivered in nearby Villisca, Council Bluffs, Glenwood, Shenandoah, Clarinda, Neola, Atlantic, and Audubon. No other such cluster of small American towns suffered such a severe loss during the war. *The Saturday Evening Post* calculated that if New York City had suffered losses in the same proportion to its population as Red Oak, population 5,600, the toll would have been 70,000.

For many of the families it was another year or more before they knew whether their men had been killed in action or whether, like Jenkins, they were in the majority who had survived and were interned in German POW camps.

Not all of them would make it home, but Jenkins did, married Eleanor, and settled on a farm near Red Oak.

14

"Men Just Running—
It Was Panic!"

The message to Paul Robinett from II Corps headquarters was vintage Fredendall: "Move the big elephants to Sbeitla, move fast and come shooting!"

Finally, after elements of the 1st Armored Division and the 168th Infantry had been battered for two days, Robinett's Combat Command B—as close as the United States then had to a veteran armored unit—was finally called south to confront the rampaging Germans after sitting out the earlier fighting.

By the afternoon of February 15, the second day of the Battle of Sidi Bou Zid, the whole situation had changed. At 5:00 that afternoon, about the same time Alger's armored battalion was in the process of being destroyed, General Anderson, the First Army commander, finally requested and received permission from Eisenhower to shift the Allied defensive line back to the chain of mountains known as the Western Dorsal.

This was the move that Robinett had urgently advised Eisenhower to make when the two men met near Sbeitla a few hours before the panzers came surging out of Faïd Pass

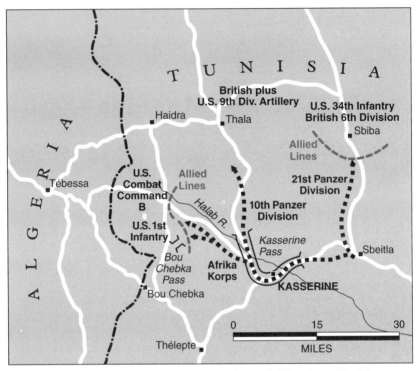

After the Battle of Sidi Bou Zid, Americans fell back to Sbeitla
and then through the Kasserine Pass. Germans and Italians, under
Rommel, attacked toward Sbiba, Thala, and Tébessa and almost
scored a breakthrough before being driven back. This was the high
point of the Axis effort in Tunisia.

on Valentine's Day. It was the move that Eisenhower had
himself considered earlier but had not been able to bring
himself to execute until it was almost too late.

Now this repositioning of an army had to be done in a
great hurry, with tired, hungry, scared troops, under pressure from the enemy. For this maneuver to work, it was
essential that the Allies hold the line at Sbeitla for a time,
although the commanders couldn't agree on just how long it
had to be held.

At Sbeitla, a deep river channel forms a natural line of
defense. The city had been a major center of trade and defense for thousands of years. As the Americans passed through
the city, they saw the well-preserved remains of a Roman
metropolis. Behind Sbeitla lay the broad, rugged Kasserine

Brig. Gen. Paul McD. Robinett, center, commander of the 1st Armored Division's Combat Command B, confers with staff officers at his forward command post in the Maknassy Valley. (Source: George C. Marshall Archives)

Pass. To its north lay Sbiba Gap and to the south lay the town of Feriana, with a road leading westward into Algeria.

The longer the Americans held Sbeitla, the more time they would have to secure the key passes through the Western Dorsal. But once the Germans took Sbeitla, they would be free to try to press through one or more of the passes. If they succeeded, this would put them in a position to attack the big American supply base at Tébessa, Algeria, or to swing north, cutting off the line of supplies to the British units facing toward Tunis and Bizerte.

By the time Anderson's order was passed down the chain of command, the American army was in panicky, headlong flight, leaving scores of tanks burning on the battlefield.

First Lt. A. Robert Moore, executive officer of a company in Alger's battalion, had been left behind in reserve on February 15 at the unit's jump-off point with his own tank, a wrecking crew, and the kitchen crew. (This Robert Moore, a tanker, is not to be confused with Maj. Robert Moore, the infantryman.)

"When the radio traffic ceased, we couldn't contact anybody," he recalls. "So I started out to see if I could pull anybody out. Me, one lone tank. I didn't have to go very far before I saw everything burning. I used a little discretion. No sense walking into that!"

Moore joined up with Hightower, the commander of the battalion destroyed on the first day, and other survivors of the two days of battle and tried to organize a rearguard action between Sidi Bou Zid and Sbeitla about 15 miles east of Sbeitla. Moore set up his position on one side of the road, with another officer on the other.

The Germans, who had intercepted a message indicating the Americans planned to abandon Sbeitla, advanced cautiously, running into a surprisingly tough defense, during the day on February 16.

That night, the Germans fired their artillery generally in the direction of the American lines, what the military call reconnaissance by fire: If the Americans fired back, they would know where they were.

The reaction was much more dramatic than the Germans might have imagined. Some of the shells fell in an olive grove where a group of Americans were resting. They were weary after days of fighting and retreat and increasingly convinced that their leaders didn't know what they were doing. Moreover, they had no experience fighting at night. As the first shells fell among the Americans, vehicles began pulling out onto the road and heading west. In a few minutes, the road was jammed with tanks, trucks, half-tracks, and jeeps, all trying to get away. Soon, advancing Germans were mixed in with the fleeing Americans in the dark.

Moore, still trying to hold the line, recalls the scene:

"If we saw a shadow, we fired at it. There were several occasions when men went by, no guns, just running. It was panic. Anybody who calls it anything else just doesn't know what panic is. Of course the Germans encouraged that. You'd have a column of vehicles going along and there would be a German vehicle. They would ride along and then they would open up. We knew they were Germans because they had white tracers. They would mix right in with the column and that created even more panic."

One of those caught up in the fleeing column was Pirnie, the armored division artillery officer who had joined up with Major Moore's infantry on Djebel Lessouda and then escaped with them. When the infantry got the order to leave the mountain, Pirnie and a few of the survivors of his unit took off across the plain in a half-track. When dawn came, they hunkered down in a wadi and waited for dark, hoping the passing Arabs wouldn't betray them.

"We took off that night toward Sbeitla and got into the damnedest rat race you ever saw," he says. "The Germans were streaming down the road. The Americans were streaming down the road ahead of them. We got onto the road and we found ourselves in a German convoy. It was kind of spooky, but we were not caught. We were able to get out of the convoy off the road and go over the desert. That night . . . I found what was left of my battalion, which wasn't much."

Pirnie, asked if the American withdrawal really was a panic, responded: "It was. It was a rat race. The Americans were just running away and the Germans were just running after them."

How did he feel to be involved in such a headlong retreat?

"When you're doing things like that, you're trying to save your neck," he says. "We were just looking for a way to stay away from the krauts and get back to friendly troops. Which we did."

It was this mess into which Robinett and his men descended early on February 16 to take up their positions to the southeast of Sbeitla. He later recalled "arriving in time to see the rest of the division streaming back across the broad plain to the east." Their assignment was to hold the line southeast of Sbeitla long enough for the rest of the American army to retreat back into the Western Dorsal and set up defenses in Kasserine Pass, the passageway through the mountains west of Sbeitla. Hightower, with units he had been able to cobble together into a blocking force, set up his position to the north of Robinett.

They were just getting into position when American engineers blew up the ammunition stored in Sbeitla. The sound of the explosion convinced many of the fleeing troops that the Germans were shelling the city or were already behind them. The flight intensified.

At one point, Lieutenant Moore, with the crew of his lone tank, held off an overwhelming German force until they ran out of ammunition.

"We lost the track in going around a little djebel," Moore recalls. "The track must have been loose because it bunched up under the tank. We were going to try to put it back on. I was the maintenance officer, so I had all the tools. But crawling up to the top of the hill, we could count roughly seventy or eighty German tanks moving very slowly toward Sbeitla.

"Hightower got word to me to delay them as long as you can. Well, I lay there on my belly with a pair of field glasses and we dumped a whole load—we had about 90 rounds assorted HE [high explosive], armor-piercing and smoke rounds—just by yelling back to the gunner, move to the right, move it up. We dropped a couple of smoke shells as near the center of those tanks as we could. Then we just fired the rest, just HE and armor piercing. It was all just indirect fire. Just let it go. I could see them break their formation to get away from it. They thought an artillery unit had them under fire. We emptied the ammo and decided to get out. We took the breech block with us and the radio.

"I tried to burn the tank. This is a laugh. I had a thermite grenade. I dropped it in the gas tank and nothing happened. We opened the engine compartment, put a hand grenade between the cylinders, pulled the pin and we ran."

Robinett and his men organized their defense as well as they could during the day on February 16 and on into the night. Tanks were hidden in wadis and depressions in the earth. Behind them, the artillery was arrayed, prepared to fire over the tanks at the oncoming Germans. Out in front of the main line of defense, a battalion of tank destroyers formed an outpost line.

North of the Faïd–Sbeitla road, the remnants of General McQuillin's Combat Command A—the unit involved in the fighting on the first day at Sidi Bou Zid—set up its own defense line. McQuillin himself shifted his command center to the west of Sbeitla and was out of touch with the division headquarters and with Robinett. Colonel Hains, McQuillin's second in command, remained at the unit's old command post east of the city and did his best to organize his dispirited troops into a defense line. Hightower and others stayed their ground, but much of Combat Command A joined the stampede to the rear.

The Americans expected the Germans to attack at dawn on February 17. But the enemy leaders were being cautious. They checked out the terrain where Combat Command A was arrayed and found it was not suitable for a large-scale tank attack. They thus decided to strike south of the Faïd-Sbeitla road against Robinett's Combat Command B, where the terrain was more favorable but the defense was much more formidable than it was north of the road. They also decided to wait for additional reinforcements coming up from Sidi Bou Zid, so the attack didn't come until just before noon.

The German tanks first encountered the outpost line of tank destroyers and hit them in three successive waves. The tank destroyers fought for about half an hour, shifting positions and using smoke. But then, as they moved back to a rallying point, they found the enemy fire so intense that they kept on going back toward Sbeitla. Officers at Robinett's command post stopped some of them and turned them around, but the rest continued on into the city. At least some of them apparently intended to swing back into the line of resistance, but once they became enmeshed in the traffic heading west, they were pulled along away from the fighting.

As the Germans swept past the outpost line, the artillery units backing up the main line of resistance were in the process of changing positions. The result, Robinett later wrote, was that "the artillery support was woefully inadequate."

Pushing on against the American line, the Germans came upon a tank battalion commanded by Lt. Col. Henry E. Gardiner, in civilian life a lawyer for the Anaconda Wire and Cable Company in Chicago. It is hard to hide a Sherman tank because it has a high turret and the upper portion of the tank must be exposed for its gun to be aimed effectively.

But Gardiner had managed to hide his tanks well enough so that the Germans were almost among them before they realized they were in a trap.

"Just about noon I counted 35 enemy tanks coming rolling over a rise in the ground almost to our direct front, a distance of about three miles away. There were others but I didn't have time to count them," Gardiner later recalled.

"We held our fire until sure it would be effective and then let the tanks that were in view have it in what amounted to almost a volley. It stopped the attack cold and the enemy was obviously very much surprised to find that they had run into such organized resistance."

When Gardiner gave the order to open fire, his tankers knocked out or damaged some 15 enemy tanks. The surprised Germans backed off. So far, Gardiner had not lost a single tank.

As the Germans prepared to resume their attack, the artillery, finally in position, got the range and caused further damage to the attacking force.

It was not until an hour later, at about 2:15 P.M., that the Germans attacked again, this time on Gardiner's southern flank.

Shortly after the Germans renewed their attack, Robinett received the order to withdraw to the west. Gardiner realized he was in serious trouble and asked for permission to withdraw. He was told to hold his position until a nearby infantry unit had had a chance to pull back.

When Gardiner was finally given permission to move back, ten of his tanks, including his own, were hit. He later gave this account of his narrow escape from the advancing enemy:

> As we entered a wadi just beyond the left flank of our front and turned away from the direction in which the enemy was advancing, I spotted a German tank at about 300 yards, My gunner rapidly got off a round at this tank. It fired an instant later, the shell breaking our right track and bringing us to a halt. We were hit immediately a second time and our tank burst into flames. Three of us bailed out through the turret and started to run but came under machine gun fire from the enemy.
>
> As we started to crawl over to secure the protection of our tank, I heard a cry from the assistant driver who had gotten out through the escape hatch [under the tank.] He

was wounded in a leg and unable to walk. The driver had been killed. Using our burning tank as a shield, I worked back to him and got him on his feet. Using me as a crutch, we made it around a turn in the wadi and were momentarily out of danger . . .

I climbed out of the wadi to look around. As I came up on the level, I found myself looking into the eyes of a commander of a German tank which was about 10 yards distant. I ducked back into the wadi and told the tank sergeant that there was an enemy tank just above him. I directed that he make a run for it but to swing his turret around, elevate his gun, and be prepared to fire the moment the German tank came into view. The enemy tank could of course hear ours and it got off the first round which tore away one of the turret hatches. A second shell hit it in the engine compartment, bringing it to a standstill. The crew jumped out and scattered.

Things were happening awfully fast and I knew that if the rest of us were going to escape being killed or captured we could not remain where we were.

The wadi we were in had many small gullies leading into it. We started to move up the main wadi when a German tank came into view behind us and opened up with its machine gun. We scattered and I ran up one of the draws leading into the wadi. It was a shallow one and I had only gone a short distance when I came up on the level of the surrounding countryside. I couldn't go back because the German tanks were rumbling up the wadi and I couldn't go any further forward because I would have been completely in the open.

Gardiner dropped down behind a tiny sagebrush-like bush and buried his face in the sand as three tanks rumbled by him no more than 20 yards away. He finally managed to work his way to the rear and catch up with the remnants of his battalion.

"This battalion and its commander were in large measure responsible for the successful defense of Sbeitla," Robinett later wrote.

Robinett's command succeeded in breaking contact with the enemy about 5:30 P.M. They refueled at a gasoline dump near the town of Kasserine before moving back through the pass to an assembly area on the road that leads north toward the hilltop town of Thala.

Meanwhile, other elements of the 1st Armored Division moved north of Sbeitla to join with the 34th Infantry Division in the defense of the pass at Sbiba.

To the south, another portion of the division retreated out of the town of Feriana and continued up into the mountains west of Thélepte.

One of the most serious consequences of the decision to move back to the Western Dorsal was that it meant giving up the forward airbase at Thélepte. All of the planes that were flyable were removed before the Germans reached the field, but 34 planes that could not be flown out were destroyed.

Lt. Col. Fred M. Dean was the commander of the fighter group that had moved into Thélepte to replace the 33rd Fighter Group when it pulled out in early February.

"We had to leave much of our equipment, including airplanes that were temporarily disabled," Dean later recalled. "It was a really bad show. . . . Our engineers came in, and they were destroying our airplanes. I actually saw them put incendiary little bomblets into some of the airplanes that we left, and they were on fire as I was leaving. . . .

"I was leading the last squadron out, and my airplane wouldn't start. Most of the ground forces had already left by truck. The Germans were within minutes of us, and my airplane wouldn't start. . . . The enlisted line chief of my old squadron was still there because he was going to be *the* last man out. He drug over an auxiliary starting unit, and I got started and went on my merry way, and the Germans came in immediately afterward. He [the line chief] saved himself a jeep, and he got out."

Dean later heard there was considerable discussion in the headquarters about whether he should receive a medal for the evacuation of the field or be court-martialed for leaving so much equipment behind. He was finally awarded the Silver Star.

15

Rommel Takes Over

F ield Marshal Rommel has gone down in legend as the Desert Fox because of his often brilliant maneuvers in his back-and-forth battles with the British across Egypt and Libya. But the situation he confronted in central Tunisia in the late winter of 1943 was more like what he had faced as a young officer fighting in the Alps in World War I.

The Allies had already been defeated in the Battle of Sidi Bou Zid when Rommel completed his retreat into Tunisia on February 15. He turned his attention to this new battleground and immediately saw the possibilities for a great Axis victory—and a chance to restore some luster to his own image, tarnished by his long flight after his defeat at El Alamein.

Looking at his maps, Rommel could see the Americans retreating from their series of defeats in the desert-like plain into the mountains of the Western Dorsal, where rugged peaks rose in some places to 6,000 feet and the passes required a climb to 2,000 feet or more.

On the afternoon of February 18, Rommel talked on the phone with von Arnim, the commander of the Fifth Army, based in Tunis. The two generals did not like each other very much to begin with, and they fell into a sharp disagreement over what their armies should do next. Von Arnim wanted to strike at the British still menacing Tunis and Bizerte.

Field Marshal Erwin Rommel confers with his staff shortly after
arriving in Tunisia at the end of his long retreat across Libya.
(Source: National Archives)

Rommel wanted to hit the Americans while they were still
reeling from the defeat at Sidi Bou Zid and before they could
bring in more men and equipment. Field Marshal Kesselring, the Axis commander in the entire Mediterranean area,
thought Rommel a "gallant soldier," but he also considered
both Rommel and von Arnim guilty of "pigheadedness."

After talking with von Arnim, Rommel sent a message to
Kesselring and to Comando Supremo in Rome, which was
still calling the shots in Tunisia. He asked that both the 10th
and 21st Panzer Divisions be assigned to him for an immediate strike at the great American supply and headquarters
concentration at Tébessa, a short distance from the Tunisian
border in Algeria.

Kesselring, who was meeting with Hitler at his headquarters on the eastern front, responded favorably but said
he wanted to talk with Mussolini before giving his approval.
With the night slipping away, Rommel sent another urgent
message asking that the two divisions be rushed to him.

Finally, just before midnight, Comando Supremo came
through with the order giving Rommel the two divisions he

had asked for and command of the upcoming battle against the Americans.

The order said:

> In view of the ascertained inferior combat value of the enemy, a unique opportunity is now offered to force a decisive victory in Tunisia. To that effect all means must be employed to exploit former successes. . . . The objective of this operation will be to threaten the rear of the British First Army by a broad thrust to the north and if possible isolate it, or at least to force the enemy at the Tunisian front to withdraw.
>
> With this in view the following is ordered: F.M. Rommel with all available mobile troops of the German-Italian Army and the newly attached 10th and 21st Pz. Dias., and with greater concentration of forces and stronger screening of the west flank, will attack over the general line Sbeitla-Tébessa, Maktar, Tadjerouine, next on Le Kef. . . .

Rommel was deeply disappointed by the order. As he read it, his instructions were to strike north toward the Tunisian town of Le Kef rather than eastward toward Tébessa. This was more like the more timid and limited plan von Arnim had in mind than the sweep to victory that Rommel envisioned. He wanted to smash the Americans at Tébessa and then charge north through Algeria to the Mediterranean, far behind the British menacing Tunis.

"This was an appalling and unbelievable piece of shortsightedness, which did, in fact, ultimately cause the whole plan to go awry," Rommel wrote in his memoirs. "A thrust along that line was far too close to the front and was bound to bring us up against the strong enemy reserves.

"At other times, our higher authorities were so wildly overoptimistic that they hardly knew what to demand of us next; now, however, when a little boldness really was required, they lacked the guts to give a wholehearted decision. But there was no time for argument, otherwise no effective operation, capable of breaking up the American assembly areas, would materialize at all."

Actually, it may have been Rommel who also lacked boldness at this point. The orders from Comando Supremo were sufficiently ambiguous that he probably had the freedom to

carry out his bold stroke through Tébessa and then to the
north if he had just gone ahead and done it. Kesselring seems
to have thought that was what Rommel was going to do.
Instead, Rommel took the more cautious approach of aiming
his attack north toward Le Kef. Ironically, the British, who
had long been reluctant pupils of Rommel, expected him to
take the quick, tactical route—toward Le Kef—rather than
the longer strategic route through Tébessa. Thus, while reluctantly obeying his orders, Rommel went the way his enemy
expected him to go.

Rommel arrived at the southeastern entrance to Kasserine Pass about noon on February 19. What he found could
not have pleased him. The troops now under his command
were spread out over scores of miles, in effect waiting for
someone to tell them what to do.

His own Afrika Korps had sent some 35 to 40 truckloads
of infantry to begin probing into Kasserine Pass earlier in
the morning. The 21st Panzer Division was on its way north
toward Sbiba, the pass through the Western Dorsal about 25
miles north of Sbeitla. And the 10th Panzer Division, which
had played such a key role in the victory at Sidi Bou Zid,
had, incredibly, already left the field of battle and moved
clear back on the other side of the Eastern Dorsal to Kairouan under orders from von Arnim.

Rommel also had under his control the Italian Centauro
Division and the Bersaglieri Regiment. The Centauro and
part of the German 21st Panzer were concentrated south of
Sbeitla near Feriana and the old Allied air base at Thélepte.

After looking over the situation at Kasserine, Rommel
drove north toward Sbiba. He was convinced, from what he
had seen so far, that his main avenue of attack should be
northward through Sbiba, the shortest and most direct route
toward Le Kef—the city he had been ordered to capture—
rather than through the Kasserine Pass toward Tébessa, his
own preferred target.

On the Allied side, the delay and confusion among the Axis
commanders, plus the time bought in the defense of Sbeitla,

had provided the opportunity to prepare defenses, hurried and imperfect as they were, and to bring in men and weapons from far back in Algeria.

At eight o'clock on the night of February 18, Fredendall phoned Col. Alexander N. Stark Jr., commander of a regiment in the 1st Infantry Division. Stark was with his troops at a bivouac south of Tébessa, some 35 miles over rough, muddy back roads from Kasserine Pass.

"I want you to go to Kasserine right away and pull a Stonewall Jackson," Fredendall told him. "Take over up there."

"You mean tonight, General?" Stark asked.

"Yes, immediately; stop in my CP on the way up."

By 7:30 the next morning, Stark had set up his command post about three miles inside the pass from the western side. Under his command he had not only his own infantry regiment but also a small contingent of tanks from the 1st Armored Division and a combat engineer unit that had been at work since the previous day preparing defenses in the pass.

Stark immediately set about establishing defensive positions on the two towering djebels on each side of the pass—the military's favored high ground. The engineers worked at establishing a minefield to stop, or at least slow down, any attempt to drive tanks right through the pass. The mine-laying did not go well, however.

During the night while Stark was moving toward the pass, an engineering officer was ordered to lay mines in front of an infantry unit on the north side of the pass. He loaded a truck and drove up to where he expected the infantry to provide men to do the actual work. When he got there, no one knew he was coming. Finally, a mine-laying detail was rounded up and sent up the road. But no one knew exactly where the mines were supposed to be laid, and the men had only their small entrenching tools to work with. They ended up scattering the mines across the road on the surface.

On the western side of the pass, two powerful tank units were held in reserve. To the north toward Thala was the British 26th Armored Brigade. To the southeast was Robinett's Combat Command B.

About noon on February 19, French observers reported that the German infantry who had been seen earlier getting out of their trucks at the entrance to the pass were scaling the mountains on each side. Stark concluded that a full-scale attack on the pass was under way. The question then became whether his relatively small force could hold off the enemy long enough for reinforcements to rush to their aid.

At the Sbiba Pass north of Sbeitla, British and French troops were joined by General McQuillin's Combat Command A, the unit that had been mauled at Sidi Bou Zid. Much of the responsibility for the defense of the pass fell to the 34th Infantry Division, commanded by General Ryder. He had been in charge during the landing at Algiers, but most of his division was freshly arrived in North Africa. For these men, Sbiba would be their first taste of combat. Survivors of the two 34th Division battalions that had been stranded during the Battle of Sidi Bou Zid added their experience to the defense at Sbiba.

The allies also set up a defensive position at Dernaïa Pass, also sometimes called by the name of the nearby town of Bou Chebka, on the hill line west of Thélepte. This third possible avenue of attack by the Axis was relatively lightly held by a part of Darby's Rangers, French troops, and American infantry. Neither the attackers nor the defenders seemed to think the main battle would take place here even though an attack at this point could move swiftly on Tébessa.

After being the last Americans to leave Gafsa on the night of February 14, the Rangers found time for a brief period of training. Carl Lehmann particularly remembers being introduced to the "sticky bomb."

"We had a sticky bomb—a British wonder weapon," Lehmann recalls. "It wasn't worth a shit. The outer thing was just a shell. You pull the pin and the shell would fall off. Then you're supposed to stick it on the goddamn tank. Darby made this speech and he says, 'Breathes there among you with a soul so dead he doesn't know you have to pull two pins on this damn thing?' He says, 'We're going out there with these tanks wandering around fancy free and you're going to have these sticky bombs. And if you see any tanks, God help the tanks.' Anyway, we didn't see any tanks."

After the Battle of Sidi Bou Zid, as the scene shifted to the Eastern Dorsal, one of Darby's companies was sent to join the 1st Infantry Division near Kasserine after General Allen, the division commander, asked Darby to, in Lehmann's words, "send me a company and a commander who has some balls." The rest of the Ranger battalion remained at Dernaïa Pass.

Lehmann, with his M-1 rifle, was stationed as a sentry on the road leading up into the mountains.

"This was really my first action, where I fired on the enemy," Lehmann recalls. "I was on guard when these Italians came down the road. They were wearing red fezzes. The French artillery supporting us wore red fezzes, so I thought they were French."

Lehmann was on a bluff overlooking the road. Another guard was down on the road and he walked out toward the truck as it approached, holding his rifle across his chest at port arms.

"He thought they were French, too," Lehmann says. "He went up and they had this conversation. Then they snatched his gun away from him. They turned the truck around. There was a 20 mm gun in the back of the truck.

"I said, 'French or not, they ain't going to shoot at us.' So I dropped down. I was within a hundred yards. I just kept shooting people who tried to get behind that 20 mm.

"I was elevated, one hundred feet above the road. They saw me looking through glasses at them. They came out and pointed and they hit the ditch with their guns and they were going to take me as a target. But I dropped down and I could see the truck but they couldn't see me."

For a while, Lehmann was all by himself and there was just the *pop, pop, pop* of rifle fire. And then other Rangers rushed to his aid and "all of a sudden it was full of machine gun fire."

The Americans quickly killed or captured all of the Italians. Both Lehmann and the guard who had initially stopped the truck emerged from the little battle unscathed.

During the night, the bulk of the 1st Infantry Division, which had been in the Ousseltia Valley northeast of Kasserine, was shifted to the Bou Chebka area, where it could help to block any attack on the pass or to move north to help in the defense of the Kasserine Pass.

During his visit to the 21st Panzer Division at Sbiba Pass, Rommel quickly changed his mind about trying to force his way through Sbiba toward Le Kef. The division, slowed by muddy roads, managed to work its way through a narrow minefield but then ran into a deeper, more difficult one. When Rommel arrived, the division commander was in the process of trying to outflank the allied line while preparing to attack on a broad front.

Rommel urged a more concentrated attempt to break through up the middle, but the Allies, who had concentrated their artillery in support of their tanks and infantry, had carefully plotted the positions where their shells would fall. When the Germans tried to advance, they were stopped cold. They were not even able to advance far enough to commit their infantry.

For the 34th Division, the successful defense of the line at Sbiba was an encouraging introduction to combat. These green American troops had managed to stop a veteran German panzer division and force the vaunted field marshal to change his plans.

Rommel had planned to bring the 10th Panzer Division, just now returning from its detour to Kairouan, to back up the attack through Sbiba. He now decided to send the division into the Kasserine Pass to reinforce his Afrika Korps and the Italian units engaged there, making the attack through Kasserine Pass his main effort.

While Rommel was on his visit to the Sbiba front, things had not been going well for his troops at the Kasserine Pass. Although what Colonel Stark and his observers saw earlier in the day looked like a major attack to take the pass, it was in fact a short-sighted attempt to send a column of tanks smashing right through the allied positions. Despite the reports Stark had received of German infantry climbing the hills on each side of the pass, the enemy did not succeed in seizing the high ground.

As Rommel described the situation: "The trouble was that they had gone the wrong way about it. After fighting for so long in the desert, the officers had suddenly found themselves confronted with a terrain not unlike the European Alps. The hills on either side of the pass ran up to some 5,000 feet and were held by American troops accompanied by artillery observers. [The German commander] had unfortunately confined his attack to the combined hill and valley tactics and should have taken possession of the hills on either side of the pass in order to eliminate the enemy artillery observers and get through to the enemy's rear."

When the day's fighting ended on the evening of February 19, the Allies were still in possession of the western end of the pass and the German attempt to take the pass in a quick-and-easy, one-day attack had failed.

But Stark was in trouble. He knew it, and British officers who visited the pass knew it. British Brigadier Charles A. L. Dunphie, who commanded an armored brigade stationed northwest of the pass, visited Stark and was disturbed by what he saw. He found Stark without any reserves to meet a renewed attack on the next day.

At about 8:30 P.M., Stark asked Fredendall for reinforcements: tanks, tank destroyers, more infantry, and artillery and air support. Dunphie recommended to his superiors that he move his brigade down into the pass to beef up its defense. But the British generals, still worried about the threat at Sbiba, refused to let him move from his position, where he could go either way—to Kasserine or Sbiba.

The only help Stark got was a very limited one. Dunphie was permitted to send a detachment of 11 tanks, a company of motorized infantry, plus some artillery and antitank guns under the command of a British officer, Lt. Col. A. C. Gore, who was ordered to move to the northwest end of the pass at 4:40 A.M. on February 20.

During the night, the Germans made a number of attempts to infiltrate the American lines and did succeed in getting between some of Stark's troops and his headquarters, which he had been forced to move back to avoid having his communications lines repeatedly cut by enemy artillery.

At 7:30 A.M. on February 20, Rommel showed up in Kasserine. He was not happy with what he found.

The previous day's attack had been resumed, but only half of the 10th Panzer Division, which he had counted on to help push through the pass, had arrived. As Rommel put it, von Arnim had "held back part of it for his own purposes." Even more irritating, von Arnim had also held onto 11 of the new 56-ton Panzer VI Tiger tanks.

"Now 10th Panzer Division's motorcycle battalion was to join in the battle," Rommel wrote. "Unfortunately, we heard and saw nothing of it for almost the whole of the morning. When I inquired from [General Fritz] von Broich [commander of the 10th Panzer Division] what all the delay was, he told me that he had detailed a different unit for the assault, as he wanted to reserve the motorcycle battalion for the pursuit. The assault unit was still on its way up to the front.

"Once again, valuable time was being squandered. I was extremely angry and ordered the commanders to take themselves closer to the front where they could get a proper view of the situation. I had the motorcyclists brought forward immediately, for the Americans were growing stronger every hour and our position consequently more difficult. From midday onwards the attack was resumed in fierce hand-to-hand fighting."

It was in this crucial phase of the battle that the Germans introduced their *nebelwerfer* into the North African fighting for the first time. This was a terrifying artillery weapon consisting of six tubes, each containing an 80-pound rocket bomb. When the electrical trigger was pressed, all six rockets screamed skyward, spewing flame, before arcing over and smashing into a target as much as four miles away with a huge simultaneous explosion. Although the Germans felt they were dealing with stiff resistance, the American line began to crumble. After a little more experience, the Americans realized the *nebelwerfer* was notoriously inaccurate. But in this first use, it had the desired effect. Some units panicked and ran. Others were simply overrun.

As the Germans neared the western exit from the pass, the road branched. One branch ran to the west, toward Tébessa. The other ran to the north, toward Thala and on to Le Kef.

Colonel Gore, with his small British armored force, tried to block the road toward Thala. He fought until his 11 tanks had all been knocked out of action and then pulled back after suffering heavy casualties. A platoon of tankers from the 1st Armored Division also fought until they, too, were overwhelmed.

By dusk, the western exits to the Kasserine Pass were in German hands and the Americans had suffered another bitter defeat, this time at the hands of the Desert Fox himself. As Rommel came forward to admire the tanks and other equipment left behind by the Americans, he saw truckloads of prisoners beginning their long journey to camps in Germany and Poland.

While the battle was raging in the pass, Robinett received orders to move his Combat Command B from its bivouac south of Tébessa on a roundabout route to the Kasserine Pass. He was ordered to go north to the little town of Haïdra, then east to Thala and finally south toward the pass, where he was expected to reinforce Stark's force.

Strangely, Fredendall's order to Robinett instructed him to move his "division." Robinett noted the use of the word but didn't ask Fredendall whether this was a simple mistake or whether he had come to believe that Robinett, whose

A tank with its cupola shattered and its tracks blown off lies beside
the road through the Kasserine Pass. (Source: National Archives)

command had been operating independently for months,
really commanded a division and not just about one-third of
a division.

Robinett, along with two aides, went ahead of the column and met Fredendall on the road south of Thala. While
Fredendall was often pictured as hiding away in his bunker
far behind the lines, he was in fact out on the roads checking the situation. But he apparently never went as far toward
the front nor became as personally involved in the battle as
his adversary, the Desert Fox.

When Fredendall and Robinett met, Fredendall had
heard enough to know that Stark's force was in serious trouble. "There's no use going down there, Robbie," he told
Robinett. "They have broken through and you can't stop
them now."

"Well, goddamnit, General, we'll go down and try," Robinett replied.

Actually, Fredendall was right, to an extent. Robinett and
his tankers never did get in a position to help out Stark. But

Fredendall also failed to understand how badly the situation at the pass had deteriorated. He expected Robinett and Brigadier Dunphie's British troops to be in a position on the following day to launch a counterattack to drive the Germans back out of the Kasserine Pass. The scattered British and American forces were all supposed to come under the control of British Brigadier Cameron Nicholson in what was called "Nickforce."

About 2:00 A.M. on February 21, Robinett and Dunphie met at the post office in Thala with Brigadier C. V. McNabb, chief of staff of the British First Army. Nicholson was on his way to Thala over muddy roads but had not yet arrived. McNabb, who probably had a better overall grasp of the situation than anyone else, told the other two officers that the situation was desperately critical. Together, he told them, Robinett and Dunphie had all the tanks available between Rommel and Le Kef. As Robinett recalls the conversation, McNabb emphasized the importance of preserving their tanks.

The three men tossed around ideas. Finally, Robinett proposed a plan: Instead of an immediate counterattack, he would place his force on the south side of the Hatab River, which runs in a deep gorge from an area north of Tébessa down through the Kasserine Pass. Dunphie would place his troops on the north side of the Hatab in a position to defend Thala. Then, Robinett suggested, they would remain on the defensive until the Germans had struck and become disorganized. Only then would the Allies strike back.

Dunphie and McNabb agreed to put the plan in action, even though Nicholson had not yet arrived, and left to join their troops.

Robinett's Combat Command B continued to move during the foggy night. But instead of continuing on to Thala, as originally planned, they moved from Haïdra down to the south to take up their position along the south side of the Hatab River, protecting the road from the Kasserine Pass to Tébessa. Robinett set up a line to intercept soldiers retreating before the German onslaught. He even rounded up some survivors of the fighting at Sidi Bou Zid who had walked all the way through or around the enemy lines. Robinett, who

The Hatab River cuts a deep channel through the Kasserine Pass.
(Source: National Archives)

intended to fight the forthcoming battle with infantry and
artillery as much as possible, in order to conserve his tanks,
organized them into makeshift companies and deployed
them for the defense of the valley.

One of these survivors was Captain Harry Hoffman, commander of Company K of the 168th Regiment's third battalion. He was one of the few members of that battalion to
make good his escape from Djebel Ksaïra during the Battle
of Sidi Bou Zid. After becoming separated from the rest of
the battalion, Hoffman, using his compass, headed cross-
country toward Sbeitla. Along the way, he was joined by two
soldiers from the second battalion, which had been on Djebel Lessouda. About eight o'clock on the morning of February 18, they arrived in the hills overlooking Sbeitla, where
they had hoped to find friendly troops. Instead, they saw
German tanks going into the town.

Hoffman set a compass course toward Tébessa, on the
other side of the mountains looming to the west of Sbeitla.
Along the way, they were joined by two more soldiers. They
walked all day and all night through the mountains, hungry,

tired, and footsore. They finally found an Arab who, for 1,500 francs, guided them around a German-controlled area to a point where they secured a ride to Tébessa on the morning of February 20. Hoffman and his companions had covered more than 100 miles through enemy lines in two and a half days of almost constant walking.

While Robinett was organizing his defensive line, Dunphie set up part of his 26th Armored Brigade in a blocking position south of Thala on the road leading up from the Kasserine Pass.

Whether because they feared a counterattack or just because of weariness from the previous day's fighting, the Germans did not renew their offensive until midday on February 21. It was time they could ill afford to waste.

Rommel sent the 10th Panzer Division up the road toward Thala. The Afrika Korps took the road toward Tébessa. The 21st Division remained in its position south of Sbiba—remained there, in fact, even after the Allies had moved back.

In splitting up his forces, Rommel consciously violated the basic rule that calls for a military commander to mass his troops for an attack. "By deploying troops at several danger spots I hoped to split the enemy forces far more than our own," Rommel wrote.

The German column striking toward Thala was a formidable force of 30 tanks, 20 self-propelled guns, and 35 halftracks. As it approached, Dunphie was in a precarious position. His light tanks were outclassed by the German tanks in both the range of their guns and the strength of their armor. Despite McNabb's worries about preserving tanks, Dunphie decided his only course was to fight a delaying action, hiding his tanks as best he could, shooting as the Germans approached, and then pulling back. He knew he would lose some, perhaps all, of his tanks. But he also knew he was due to be issued new Shermans in a few days anyway. He decided to "spend" his tanks as he backed toward Thala, making the Germans pay as heavily as possible for them.

Dunphie's strategy did slow the German advance. About noon, Rommel came up to the front lines to see what was going on and was unhappy with what he saw.

"The division was not getting forward fast enough and I had to be continually at them to keep the speed up; they did not seem to realize that they were in a race with the allied reserves," Rommel recalled. By 1:00, with his encouragement, the division "was advancing in great strides toward Thala."

The road toward Thala runs across a series of ridges. Dunphie fought at each of the ridges before moving back. At the last ridge before Thala, the British had set up their main line of defense. Using smoke to mask his movements, Dunphie, who had already lost 15 tanks, moved the remnants of his force through a gap in the defense line to supposed safety, like escaping into the fortress in the nick of time. But the Germans were too close on his heels. Before the British could close the line after Dunphie's command car rolled through, the German tanks were inside the line, firing from the rear at the infantry and antitank guns that were supposed to have kept them out.

For three hours, until about 8:00 P.M., the battle raged in a seething mixture of smoke, flares, exploding artillery shells, and the crackle of rifle and machine gun fire. At one point, the Germans succeeded in penetrating up the hill into Thala itself. Finally they pulled back, taking 571 prisoners with them. They had destroyed 38 tanks, 12 antitank guns, a number of other weapons and motor vehicles, and two airplanes.

The British had won the battle in the sense that the Germans had pulled back. But they had suffered so severely they had little left to prevent the enemy from rolling right on through Thala to Le Kef on the following morning.

Rommel remained at the front, at one point coming under fire himself, until late afternoon. He reported seeing the bodies of several British soldiers lying beside their antitank guns.

"Arabs had plundered the bodies and robbed them of their clothing. There was nothing to be seen of these ghouls, which was fortunate for them, for they would otherwise have had something to remember us by," Rommel wrote.

Late in the afternoon, Rommel drove back down toward Kasserine. Off to the right he could see and hear a heavy artillery duel on the road that branches off to Tébessa, where his Afrika Korps was battling with Robinett's Combat Command B.

✳

South of the Hatab River, the attacking force consisted of the Afrika Korps and parts of the Italian Centauro Division. Robinett and his combat command had struggled along over a muddy road during the night and had arrived at their assigned positions in time to set up artillery and antitank guns on the road leading toward Tébessa.

When the attack came, the Germans and Italians soon found themselves under heavy fire from three sides by artillery, antitank, and tank destroyer guns. It was this battle that Rommel became aware of on his way south from Thala. He quickly realized that his forces were not making much headway.

Enemy planes bombed and strafed the American artillery. But new automatic antiaircraft weapons knocked down two planes and damaged or drove others away. The Americans were beginning to realize that the screaming Stuka dive bomber, which they had feared so much at first, was extremely vulnerable to antiaircraft fire because the plane presented itself as an easy target during its long, straight bombing dive.

At the end of the day, the Axis forces were four miles short of their goal for the day.

During the night, both Robinett and General Terry Allen, commander of the 1st Infantry Division, began thinking of a counterattack on the following day, February 22.

Allen had the bulk of his division in the area of the Dernaïa Pass, southwest of the Kasserine Pass. Robinett's forces were to the northwest. If they could coordinate their actions, they might drive the enemy back into the Kasserine Pass. But communication was difficult. Enemy bombing attacks had knocked out some key telephone and radio links. Robinett was not in touch with Nicholson, the commander of Nickforce, who was supposedly in charge of the whole operation. He was also cut off from Dunphie and Allen and had only intermittent contact with II Corps headquarters. As a result, Allen sent one battalion on a long, circuitous march during the night to position it for the next day's fighting. When they approached their goal in battle formation, they found Robinett's men had already been there for a full day.

Things on the Axis side were almost as confused. One unit of tanks, artillery, and infantry marched all night and was surprised to find itself in General Allen's territory, seven miles out of position. The enemy infantry recovered from their surprise and managed to overrun an American artillery position, capturing five howitzers, three antiaircraft guns, and 30 vehicles. But then the German soldiers realized they were cut off from their own artillery and tanks and trapped under heavy American artillery fire.

The fighting was confused by the fact that some of the German soldiers were wearing French and American uniforms. American officers later concluded that the Germans were not wearing the uniforms to be deceptive but because they were cold. This was especially true of the Afrika Korps troops, who had been sent into the mountains in the winter in the same clothing they had worn in the desert.

A mixed force of German and Italian units attacked Robinett on the morning of February 22, again trying to break through on the road to Tébessa.

For a while, the situation facing both Allen and Robinett seemed to be touch-and-go. Allen even received orders to prepare for a general withdrawal. By the time those orders arrived, both Allen and Robinett were preparing to go on the offensive.

Allen began his counterattack with his 16th Infantry Regiment at 3:30 P.M. They quickly reclaimed the guns the Germans had captured earlier in the day and overran the enemy position.

"As the lines of our infantry reached their positions, the Germans broke and ran," Allen wrote in his report on the battle. "Some 400 surrendered to a group of 13th Armored Regiment tanks on reaching the valley. Our attack was followed by a counterattack by Combat Command B . . . from the northeast side of the valley."

Infantrymen of the 16th Regiment of the 1st Infantry Division patrol between Feriana and Kasserine on February 25, 1943, following the retreating Germans after the Battle of Kasserine Pass. (Source: National Archives)

The order to prepare for a general withdrawal was probably triggered by the much more perilous situation at Thala. There, the Germans had installed themselves on the ridge that had been the British line of defense on the previous day. If General von Broich, the commander of the 10th Panzer Division, had known how thin the line was standing between him and Thala and Le Kef, he might have cracked right on through within a few minutes. But he didn't know. In fact, aerial reconnaissance reports confused him. Instead of attacking, he waited for the enemy to attack him.

Actually, there had been a dramatic change on the Allied side of the line—not enough in itself to resist a determined German attack, but enough to mislead von Broich and add considerably to Allied morale.

Five days earlier, when the enemy was in the process of taking Sbeitla and advancing into the Kasserine Pass, Allied commanders began a desperate search for any units that could be rushed to the front to stop the German advance.

Their attention focused on the 9th Infantry Division. But most of the division was scattered in several locations far back in Algeria. The division artillery, stationed in Tlemcen, Algeria, might be able to get there in time to help out. But it was more than 700 miles from the battlefield, and most of the division's infantry was even further away.

Brigadier General S. LeRoy Irwin, the artillery commander, received an order on the morning of February 17 to move to the battle area. By 4:00 P.M., his force was on its way. It consisted of 12 155 mm guns, 24 105 mm's, 12 mounted 75 mm guns, and several platoons of 37 mm anti-tank weapons. The column contained 411 vehicles and 2,170 officers and men and stretched more than 10 miles long.

Leading the way, because they were the heaviest and slowest, was the 155 mm battalion commanded by Lt. Col. William C. Westmoreland, who, as a four-star general, later commanded American forces in Vietnam.

The route led over narrow, icy roads through 3,000-foot-high passes. Only brief stops were allowed, for gas and food. After each stop, the sergeants had the difficult task of rousing the tired drivers and getting them on the road again.

After covering 735 miles in 100 hours, Irwin's artillery rolled into Thala during the night of February 21 and immediately moved into positions already surveyed for them by British officers.

Irwin took his place in the forward British observation post and quickly decided to use some of his 105 mm howitzers as antitank guns. Normally, the howitzer fires its shell into the air, and it follows a curving path up and down to the target. But Irwin knew the gunners of one battalion had practiced bore-sighting their weapons so they could be fired directly at a target. He moved them up onto the front line in a position to fire directly at the enemy tanks. Two of the guns were knocked out, but not before they had destroyed two German tanks and several other lighter vehicles.

At dawn, the Allies did two things. The British commander sent a small detachment of tanks out to attack the German line. And at the same time, Irwin's artillery began a furious barrage that continued through the day.

The Allies were, of course, attacking von Broich's division. But, more significantly, they were working on his mind. He quickly brushed off the tank attack. But it made him think the enemy was prepared to follow up with a bigger attack. The big explosions caused by Westmoreland's 155 mm shells also helped to convince von Broich that all of that heavy artillery that had arrived during the night must be part of an infantry division.

He was wrong on both counts: the Allies didn't have the strength for a bigger attack, and the rest of the 9th Division infantry was hundreds of miles away. But instead of attacking himself, von Broich hesitated.

What had happened on the Allied side also worked on Rommel's mind.

"I drove up to Thala again, where I was forced to the conclusion that the enemy had grown too strong for our attack to be maintained," Rommel wrote in his memoirs. "Later, at about 1300 hours [1:00 P.M.] I met with Field Marshal Kesselring, who arrived at my H.Q. . . . We agreed that a continuation of the attack towards Le Kef held no prospect of success and decided to break off the offensive by stages."

Rommel and Kesselring had differing views of their meeting.

"Field Marshal Kesselring, his undoubted merits aside, had no conception of the tactical and operational conditions in the African theater," Rommel noted. "He saw everything through rose-colored glasses and had now been further strengthened in his self-delusion by our successes over the Americans. He thought that many more such opportunities would occur and that the fighting value of the Americans was low.

"Although it was true that the American troops could not yet be compared with the veteran troops of the Eighth Army, yet they made up for their lack of experience by their far better and more plentiful equipment and their tactically more flexible command. In fact, their armament in antitank weapons and armored vehicles was so enormous that we could look forward with but small hope of success to the coming mobile battles. The tactical conduct of the enemy's defense had been first class. They had recovered very quickly after the first shock and had soon succeeded in damming up our advance by grouping their reserves to defend the passes and other suitable points."

Kesselring, in his memoirs, recalled a long talk with Rommel at his headquarters near Kasserine. He found him "in a very dispirited mood."

"His heart was not in his task and he approached it with little confidence. I was particularly struck by his ill-concealed impatience to get back as quickly and with as much unimpaired strength as possible to the southern defence line. . . . His apathy betrayed his reluctance or inability to grasp the significance of the operation which was then in progress toward Tébessa."

Interestingly, Kesselring, in his recollections, seems to have it in his mind that Rommel was still pursuing his original proposal of attacking Tébessa rather than following Comando Supremo's orders to strike toward Le Kef.

As he headed back to Europe, Kesselring ordered von Arnim to meet him at the airport in Tunis. He found that meeting even less satisfactory than his session with Rommel. "It was very one-sided and finally led to my calling off the attack on Tébessa," he says.

16

Changing of the Guard

For Maj. Gen. Ernie Harmon, the 100-mile nighttime ride from Constantine to Tébessa was almost a nightmare.

"It was the first—and only—time I had ever seen an American army in rout," he wrote later. "Jeeps, trucks, wheeled vehicles of every imaginable sort streamed up the road toward us, sometimes jammed two and even three abreast. It was obvious there was one thing only in the minds of the panic-stricken drivers: to get away from the front, to escape to some place where there was no shooting."

Several times, Harmon and his aide were forced off the road into a ditch, and he began to fear that they would be wrecked, perhaps even killed, by the oncoming mob.

This harrowing ride through the Algerian night understandably seared itself into Harmon's mind as confirmation of the fragmentary reports of a great military disaster in the Kasserine Pass that he had heard at Eisenhower's headquarters in Algiers and at his advanced headquarters in Constantine.

Harmon was the commander of the 2nd Armored Division. He had led his troops in the successful landing at Safi, south of Casablanca, on November 8. But since then, while portions, and then the entire 1st Armored Division, were heavily involved in Tunisia, Harmon and his men had remained back in French Morocco, on guard against an attack from Spanish Morocco that never came.

On February 20, Harmon received a telegram ordering him to report to Algiers "for limited field duty." He flew to Algiers and met with Eisenhower that afternoon. He found Eisenhower worried by reports of the serious military set-back in Tunisia and perturbed about friction between Fredendall, the II Corps commander, and Ward, the 1st Armored Division commander. Eisenhower had just received a report from Fredendall complaining about Ward's handling of his division and asking for his immediate replacement. He had also received reports that Fredendall had lost the confidence of the men under his command.

Eisenhower told Harmon he wanted him to hurry to Tunisia and either take over command of the Corps from Fredendall or the division from Ward, whichever he thought was necessary. Harmon gave this report of his reaction:

> In my astonishment, I blurted out: "Well, make up your mind, Ike, I can't do both."
>
> "That's right," he replied. "But right now I don't know what is to be done down there. I'm going to send you as deputy corps commander. Your first job is to do the best you can to help Fredendall restore the situation. Then you will report direct to me whether you should relieve Ward or Fredendall."

Harmon finally arrived at what he later described as Fredendall's "curious headquarters . . . dug into the walls of a ravine outside Tébessa," about two o'clock on the morning of February 23. He found Fredendall sitting near a stove working with his operations officer. His first words startled Harmon: "We have been waiting for you to arrive. Shall we move the command post?"

Having found his way there in the dark, Harmon had only the vaguest idea where the command post was in rela-tion to the battlefront. But he decided to be decisive in spite of his ignorance. "No, sir," he replied, "we will let it stay right here."

Fredendall told his operations officer that settled it: the command post would stay where it was. He handed Harmon a paper putting him in command of the British 6th Armored Division and the American 1st Armored Division. Then followed a cryptic account of the situation Harmon would find when dawn broke in a few hours: the British were holding the line at Thala, the 1st Armored was blocking the road to Tébessa, and Fredendall expected the Germans to deliver what he termed their "Sunday punch" at daylight.

Harmon set off about 3:00 A.M. in a radio-equipped half-track to visit the two division commanders now under his control. His staff consisted of his aide, a driver, a signal officer, and a lieutenant colonel. On the way, Harmon made up his mind what needed to be done. He later admitted his plan seemed a bit simpleminded. He described it this way:

"We were confronted with a situation in which our troops were running away. First, those in authority must order the men to stop running and turn around. Then we must try to win back the ground that had been lost. I adopted a little motto for the day: We are going to hold today and counterattack tomorrow. Nobody goes back from here."

As Harmon visited Ward at his divisional headquarters at Haïdra and drove on toward Thala, he understandably felt, from what he had seen on the road toward Tébessa and all of the reports he had heard that the responsibility for turning around a desperate situation rested on his shoulders.

What he did not realize was that, despite all that he had seen and heard, by the time he arrived at Thala early on the morning of February 23, the decisive battle had been fought on the previous day and it had been won by the British, with the help of Irwin's 9th Infantry Division artillery, at Thala, by Robinett's Combat Command B on the road toward Tébessa, and by Terry Allen's 1st Infantry Division on the southwestern approaches to the Kasserine Pass. In fact, Allen's infantry had already gone on the offensive the previous afternoon, sending the enemy streaming back in disarray.

When the enemy failed to follow through with the expected Sunday punch, Harmon began working up plans for a counterattack. But by the time the plan was ready, the Germans had, as Harmon later acknowledged, "made a clean getaway."

During the night of February 22, the Axis forces packed up and hurried back down through the Kasserine Pass, scattering mines as they went. Rommel's last great offensive of the African campaign had run out of steam far short of its goals.

It was then that the Allied commanders made the same mistake that General Ziegler had made after his victory at Sidi Bou Zid a week before: They didn't pursue the retreating enemy. *McClellan*

Robinett, with the benefit of hindsight, said later that he should have moved his Combat Command B through the Bou Chebka Pass and caught the fleeing Germans from behind as they emerged from the Kasserine Pass. But without orders from above, he didn't.

As he later wrote: "A major decision was required but no one with authority to make it was at hand. The fleeting opportunity, the golden chance, was soon gone forever. . . ."

As Harmon headed back to Algiers to report to Eisenhower, he had the perhaps understandable, but mistaken, impression that the actions he had taken after arriving at the front had saved the day. As he put it: ". . . it must be remembered that when I took command 24 hours earlier the Allied troops were running away. In one day they were turned around and on the attack."

Actually, as Robinett later noted, it was Fredendall who had put Combat Command B and the 1st Infantry Division in the right place at the right time so they could not only protect Tébessa but pose a threat on Rommel's flank as he pressed north toward Thala. And this, of course, was done while Harmon was still hundreds of miles from the scene.

The Allied success in stopping Rommel also owed a good deal to the failure of the Desert Fox to use his forces most effectively. During the crucial fighting on February 22, the 21st Panzer Division sat placidly on the road south of Sbiba. If that division, roughly a third of Rommel's entire force, had pressed vigorously against the American 34th Infantry Division, or moved the short distance westward to help in the assault on Thala, Rommel might well have been able to break through toward Le Kef and even on to the Mediterranean.

But Harmon was not concerned with Rommel's short-comings. His focus was on the American command structure, and he had a decidedly negative impression of Fredendall. This is what he reported when he arrived back at Eisenhower's jubilant headquarters in Algiers:

"Well, what do you think of Fredendall?" Eisenhower asked.

"He's no damned good," Harmon responded. "You ought to get rid of him."

Fredendall was one of those officers, of whom there were a number in both the army and navy, whose peacetime skills—caution and patient time-serving—did not suit them for battlefield command. And when things went wrong at Sidi Bou Zid and the Kasserine Pass, Fredendall took the blame even though he had only limited control over the troops supposedly under his command.

In contrast to his opinion of Fredendall, Harmon told Eisenhower that Ward "was doing well." But he said Ward had been badly handled by Fredendall, explaining how Fredendall had bypassed Ward, giving orders directly to Combat Command B.

Harmon was tempted when Eisenhower asked if he would like to command II Corps, replacing Fredendall. But he hesitated only a moment before telling Eisenhower it would be unethical to take over from a man whose replacement he had recommended. Instead, he suggested that George Patton, who had also been cooling his heels back in Morocco since the invasion, be called forward to command the corps.

Eisenhower was getting the same sort of reports about Fredendall from a number of other officers. A short time later, he summoned Patton to take over from Fredendall. But Fredendall was not sent home in disgrace—far from it. Eisenhower had promised him a promotion, so he pinned on the third star of a lieutenant general and returned to the States to a hero's welcome and command of a training army.

This was only one of a series of top-level command changes that, if not resulting from the debacles at Sidi Bou Zid and Kasserine, at least coincided with those setbacks.

On February 20, while the Battle of Kasserine Pass was under way, Gen. Sir Harold R. L. G. Alexander was named to command of a new 18 Army Group, following up on a decision made by Roosevelt and Churchill at the Casablanca Conference. The numeral 18 was a combination of the designations of the British 1st Army, operating in Tunisia, and Montgomery's 8th Army, just then crossing into Tunisia. Alexander, who had commanded the last British units remaining ashore during the evacuation of Dunkirk in 1940 and later fought in Burma, had, until assignment to his new job, been stationed in Cairo as British Commander in Chief, Middle East.

General Bradley, writing after the war, was lavish in his praise for Alexander:

> A patient, wise, and fair-minded soldier, it was Alexander who, more than anyone else, helped the American field command mature and eventually come of age in the Tunisian campaign . . . [A]mong all the British officers I was to know, none possessed these qualities in greater abundance than did Alexander.

Alexander's arrival put this experienced officer in command of both Anderson's and Montgomery's armies. Alexander did not replace Anderson, who, in the opinion of many American officers, had botched things by micromanaging Fredendall and his American corps. But as Anderson's superior, he was placed in a position to vastly improve relations between the British and Americans.

Before formally taking over command, Alexander toured the battlefront on February 18 and found things in such disarray that he decided to take charge immediately. He, like Harmon, came away with a distinctly negative impression of Fredendall and the American command structure. But, again like Harmon, it is unlikely that anything he did in the few days between his taking charge and Rommel's decision to break off his offensive made any real difference in the outcome of the battle. What did make a difference was that he permitted Patton, when he took over a short time later, to command all of the American forces even though Patton's II Corps continued, to a frustrating degree, to wag like the tail of the British dog.

Patton, a much more flamboyant and forceful commander than Fredendall, arrived at II Corps headquarters in a

Allied commander Gen. Dwight D. Eisenhower, center, and
Lt. Gen. George Patton, right, met on March 17, 1943, in Feriana
with Gen. Sir Harold R. L. G. Alexander, after the British officer
took command of the new 18 Army Group. (Source: National Archives)

siren-blaring parade of armored scout cars and halftracks
bristling with machine guns, with their radio antennae whip-
ping in the air. Patton stood in the lead vehicle, his helmet
and the bumper of his command car emblazoned with the
two-star insignia of a major general.

Without even a brief courtesy call on his predecessor,
he promptly issued orders designed to instill discipline but,
even more, to let everyone know that a new man was in
charge and that big changes were under way. From now on,
Patton decreed, all soldiers would wear their helmets and
neckties and be clean-shaven at all times. Nurses in the hos-
pitals and mechanics in their motor pools were not exempt
from wearing helmets. Frontline soldiers were expected to
wear neckties. Violators were fined $50 for officers and $25
for enlisted men, and Patton himself made a point of rounding up and turning in those who ran afoul of his order. The
only recorded incident where he backed off was when he
spotted a man who appeared to be one of Darby's Rangers
wearing a knit beanie instead of his helmet. Darby explained

that the man was actually a British chaplain attached to his outfit and Patton, roaring with laughter, relented.

The helmets-and-neckties order was not calculated to win the hearts of the GIs, but it certainly got their attention—and that's what Patton wanted to do.

Fredendall and Ward had not gotten along. And for some reason, Patton distrusted Ward. It may have been the reports Patton had heard of the battering suffered by elements of Ward's division at Sidi Bou Zid—when, of course, Ward's division was fragmented and he was not really in command, even of the fragments—or it may have been some long-simmering feud left over from the small, closed community of the peacetime army. But Patton did not replace Ward—not yet.

As Patton took over II Corps, General Bradley arrived at the front with orders from Eisenhower to move around and keep him informed of what was going on. Patton was perceptive enough to recognize that this third wheel from headquarters was there not so much to help him as to keep an eye on II Corps as a "spy" for Eisenhower. He quickly arranged to have Bradley assigned as his deputy, thus placing Bradley under his command. This did not, however, prevent Bradley from continuing his reports back to Eisenhower.

Public attention focused on Fredendall's replacement by Patton and Alexander's arrival at his top-level command position. But a change that was at least as important received far less notice. Air Marshal Sir Arthur Coningham, a New Zealander who had been in charge of the highly effective British air arm working with Montgomery in his pursuit of Rommel, was placed in charge of all the tactical air forces—those whose responsibility it was to support the ground forces.

In the three months since the November landings, ground commanders and their troops had complained often and bitterly about the lack of air support for their operations. On some occasions, the lack of coordination was so bad and the level of frustration on the part of the ground troops was so high that they fired on anything that flew—friendly as well as enemy. Part of the problem, of course, was the unfavorable battlefield situation. All too often, enemy air bases were just over the next hills while the nearest Allied airfields were hundreds of miles to the rear. When Allied planes showed up, the Germans simply landed and waited for ten minutes or so until the Spitfires and the Warhawks had to return home for fuel.

But a big part of the problem was doctrinal. The ground commanders thought it was they, not some distant air force bureaucrat, who should control the tactical aircraft flying in support of their troops. When they needed a fighter to drive off the Stukas or a fighter-bomber to attack enemy tanks, they wanted to be able to call for help on their own authority and get it, right now.

The air commanders, on the other hand, pointed out that what the ground commanders wanted would not only require more fighters than they had but would also require the fighters to sit on the ground, waiting to be called into action. They feared they would fritter away their air power if the ground commanders were permitted to use their planes as, in effect, a supplement to their artillery. Much better, they argued, was to use their aircraft to gain control of the air by hitting enemy airfields and battling the Axis pilots before they got to the battlefield. It would also be much better, they said, to strike at concentrations of enemy troops or tanks moving toward the battlefield—bombing or strafing a column of troop-carrying trucks or fuel tankers—rather than trying to knock out enemy soldiers in their foxholes or seeking out enemy tanks after they had spread out on the battlefield.

Coningham stepped boldly into this bitter dispute and came down solidly on the side of the airmen. In Coningham's favor was the fact that the policy he put in place had worked brilliantly when he was in charge of the Desert Air Force under Montgomery. When Allied ground commanders in Tunisia objected, he could call on Montgomery as a witness in his behalf. His policy was gradually accepted and was to serve as the pattern for air–ground cooperation when the scene of action turned to Europe later in the war.

Curiously, while all these changes were taking place, there were no heads rolling on the Axis side, which had, after its initial successes at Sidi Bou Zid and the Kasserine Pass, bungled its great offensive and retreated back to the Eastern Dorsal. Rommel was rewarded with promotion to command of an army group.

Even as Rommel's troops were fleeing from Kasserine, von Arnim was permitted to launch an offensive against the British in the north—an attack that quickly turned into another disaster. When the operation was called off, von Arnim had lost 90 percent of the tanks he had committed, and the British were still in position in the mountains west of Tunis.

If that offensive had been conducted at all, it should, under the orders from Comando Supremo, have been coordinated with Rommel's attack toward Le Kef. Such a coordinated attack could have caused real problems for the Allies. But it was also probably impractical to do both things at once because both Rommel and von Arnim were counting on using the same troops—the 10th Panzer Division.

As von Arnim's belated attack petered out, the initiative shifted firmly and finally to the Allies. From early March on, the Axis were fighting not to win, but to stave off defeat as long as possible—to delay Allied landings in Sicily, mainland Italy, or southern France and perhaps to save as many troops and as much equipment as possible in a withdrawal reminiscent of the British evacuation of Dunkirk in 1940. But the Axis were far from defeated as the Allies prepared for their spring offensive. Much hard fighting lay ahead.

17

The Battle of El Guettar

F or George Patton, who liked to think of himself as the reincarnation of famous but long-dead warriors, few places could have been more conducive to reveries about battlefield glories of the past than Tunisia, where Numidians, Phoenicians, Carthaginians, and Romans, to say nothing of the more recent French, had lived and fought for countless centuries.

As he took over as II Corps commander and moved his headquarters forward to Feriana, Patton had under his command three American infantry divisions—the 1st, 9th, and 34th—and the 1st Armored Division, plus a field artillery brigade and seven battalions of tank destroyers, a total of 88,287 men. It was the first time in this Tunisian campaign that the American divisions had all been brought together as divisions under an American commander. But Patton was still held on a short leash by Alexander, the 18 Army Group commander, who had formed a quick and unfavorable impression of the American army's fighting ability and its leadership during his tour of the front in the latter stages of the Kasserine and Thala battles.

During the month of March, he issued no less than five sets of orders to Patton. In some details, one differed markedly from the next. But they all had a common theme: The

259

major role of Patton's forces was to support an impending offensive by Montgomery's 8th Army. Montgomery, who was noted for his careful preparation for battle, now had his forces arrayed in southern Tunisia, facing the Axis army in defensive positions along the Mareth Line, which had been built by the French as a defense against the Italians next door in Libya. He was about ready to launch his offensive. Any action by the Americans, even of a limited nature, would draw off Axis forces and make Montgomery's job easier. Alexander's secondary goal was to give the Americans limited objectives that would provide them with experience in battle and the chance to score some morale-boosting victories.

All of this, of course, was a great frustration to Patton, who hungered for the opportunity to crash through to the coast, catching Rommel's army between his forces and Montgomery's. Patton may also have pictured a confrontation in which he would defeat the legendary Rommel. But this was not to be.

On March 6—the same day that Patton took command of II Corps—Rommel's forces launched a spoiling offensive against Montgomery. But the battle plan had been dictated by the Italian Field Marshal Giovanni Messe, over Rommel's strong objections. In much of the fighting in the desert, Rommel had successfully used a right hook, swinging around to hit the enemy on the flank, or even from the rear. This time, he proposed a different approach—a pincer attack using two divisions to strike from the north, near the coast, with two more divisions working their way around to hit the British strongpoint at Médenine from the rear. After a stormy meeting of the German and Italian generals, the vote went against Rommel, and Messe's plan for the customary right hook was adopted. The attack failed, as Rommel had predicted it would, with the loss of 50 of the 145 tanks involved in the attack. The failure was not due to a faulty plan on the part of the Axis generals, but instead was the result of the British success in breaking the Germans' secret codes. Montgomery had the enemy's entire battle plan before the first shot was fired. With the failure of the spoiling attack, the Axis forces braced themselves for Montgomery's own drive to the north.

Although eager to push through to the sea, Patton understood Alexander's orders for a more restrained stance and searched successfully for a historical precedent. He found it in the Civil War's Second Battle of Bull Run (or, as he phrased it, using the Southern terminology, the Second Battle of Manassas). There, on August 29 and 30, 1862, Stonewall Jackson, with 25,000 men, held the attention of an entire Union army while General Robert E. Lee maneuvered his Confederate forces into position to hit the Federal troops on the flank, inflicting a disastrous defeat.

In keeping with this plan, Patton's forces were divided into three areas of operations. The 34th Division was assigned to join with the British in an attack against the German troops holding the gap in the Eastern Dorsal at Fondouk el Aouareb. This action, which was separate from the fighting further south in the valleys to the east of Gafsa, will be treated in detail in Chapter 18. The two other infantry divisions—the 1st and the 9th—and the 1st Armored were deployed in the Gafsa area. Throughout the fighting during this period, the 33rd Fighter Group was heavily involved. The air war will be treated in detail in Chapter 19.

In the south, the first goal was the seizure of Gafsa itself. Gafsa had been taken by the Americans in the early days of the Tunisian fighting, then abandoned to the advancing Axis forces, and now it was up to Patton to seize the oasis once again for the Allies. This would provide a point from which to supply Montgomery after he had broken through the Axis forces at the Mareth Line.

In those days, long before the concept of political correctness, the plan was given the designation of Operation Wop. Patton's planners used the slang word for Italians because Gafsa and some of the positions immediately to the east were then held by Italians rather than Germans. The fighting in this area is designated in Army history by the more delicate title of the Battle of El Guettar, although almost all of the fighting took place in the area to the east of that little town.

It was obvious to the Americans, from the ruins all around them, that this area had a long history, stretching back a couple of thousand years into Roman times. But they could not see the much deeper layers of history that lay beneath their feet. Scientists have found sites in the area where prehistoric people lived more than 8,000 years ago.

On a recent scientific visit to the area, Dr. Christopher Swezey, a geologist with the U.S. Geological Survey, was surprised to find, in the sands of southern Tunisia, .50 caliber and 20 mm machine gun bullets fired during World War II lying alongside arrows fired by other warriors perhaps two or more millennia before, brought together in the shifting sands.

Ancient history provided a perfect model for the American seizure of Gafsa, called Capsa by the Numidians. Marius, a Roman general, marched his troops down from the north by night for a surprise attack, slaying the men, selling the women and children into slavery, and destroying the city. Because of its location along the north–south trade routes, the city quickly grew up again as a Roman outpost.

Following in Marius's footsteps, Terry Allen brought his 1st Infantry Division rolling down from Kasserine, past the airfields at Thélepte, to Feriana. Then, on the night of March 16–17, they raced the 45 miles down the road for an attack on Gafsa on the morning of March 17, timed to correspond with Montgomery's offensive against the Mareth Line.

Following the approach used by Marius centuries ago, Allen's forces struck Gafsa from the east, west, and northwest. Overrunning a few outposts, they worked their way through minefields, looking out for booby traps, into the town. But the Italians had already departed.

Moving back into Gafsa along with the troops were a madame and eight girls from the city's *maison de plaisir*, riding in the back of a truck atop a load of ammunition. During the Allied retreat from Gafsa, they had taken a similar ride to Tébessa, where they set up shop in that city's bordello, with the Tébessa madame at one entranceway and the Gafsa madame at the other.

As their truck arrived back in Gafsa, the American colonel designated as the town mayor barred their way, exclaiming: "You can't send those blankety-blank girls back into Gafsa. I don't want any such thing as that down here in this town."

Col. Samuel L. Myers, who had found himself a kind of guardian of what he called "the Gafsa Girls," argued. The mayor finally agreed the girls could return to Gafsa if they set up washtubs and did the soldiers' laundry rather than providing the kind of services they had earlier.

Myers, who went on to become a lieutenant general, later recalled visiting the new laundry. He found girls bent over washtubs set up on benches. Clotheslines filled the house's courtyard. Everything was exactly as the mayor had ordered. But then the madame motioned Myers to follow her to the back of the garden. Myers recalled what he saw next:

"There had been a wall built there out of mud bricks, and there was a little doorway through that wall, through which we went; and there was a whole row of nice, newly built, mud houses. In those mud houses, the girls who were not busy washing were busily engaged carrying on their profession, just as routinely as it had always been done."

The stuffy officer who wanted to keep the girls out of Gafsa may have had a clearer appreciation of the situation than Myers. Before the invasion, medical officers had worried most about two threats to the health of the American soldiers: typhus and malaria. There was, in fact, a severe typhus epidemic in North Africa at the time of the landings. Before the invasion, troops were given a new typhus vaccine even though there had not been time for tests to make sure the vaccine would work. Fortunately, it provided almost perfect protection. Only 11 soldiers contracted typhus and none died. Malaria, too, turned out to be a non-problem because it was not malaria season during the winter and early spring.

What did become a major health problem was venereal disease, even though every soldier who ventured into certain areas of the cities was required to submit to a prophylatic treatment at one of a series of "pro stations," whether or not he had had intercourse. The problem became so severe in his division that General Harmon, at the urging of his medical staff, set up an army bordello where the women were regularly inspected for signs of disease.

As the Americans moved back into Gafsa, Darby's Rangers went a few miles further southeast to capture the village of

El Guettar. With Gafsa in his hands, this is the geographical and tactical situation that confronted Patton:

Gafsa is linked to the sea by two roads. The more northerly road runs generally east through the crossroads at Sened Station and the village of Maknassy to the Mediterranean at Sfax. To the south of a rugged mountain range, another road runs to the southeast through the village of El Guettar to the Mediterranean at Gabès. A few miles beyond El Guettar, a side road branches off to the left and parallels the main road before rejoining it a few miles further on. Because of the eucalyptus trees along this route, the GIs nicknamed it the Gumtree Road.

The two infantry divisions were assigned to the more southerly route through El Guettar toward Gabès. The task of the 1st Infantry Division was to seize the high ground to the north of the Gafsa–Gabès road and along the Gumtree Road. The job of the 9th Infantry Division, somewhat later, was similar: to take the hills south of the Gafsa-Gabès road. When the high ground was secure, then the tanks could be sent down the road to the east.

Patton assigned Ward's 1st Armored Division to take Sened Station and then move east to Maknassy. Using maneuver, rather than a direct assault, Ward took Sened Station on the night of March 20–21. This put the Americans right back where they were after the heavy fighting at the end of January and beginning of February, before the order to withdraw to Gafsa and then to give up Gafsa itself.

From Sened Station, Ward's forces moved on the night of March 21–22 the 20 miles to Maknassy and prepared for an attack. But then they discovered that the enemy troops had already withdrawn to hills east of town. According to the original orders from Alexander, this was as far as Ward was supposed to go. But by the time he got to Maknassy, new orders had come in. He was now ordered to seize the high ground east of Maknassy and send a light raiding party a short distance further on to tear up the enemy airfields at Mezzouna. But he was not to send any sizable forces beyond Maknassy.

Even before those orders arrived, it made sense for Ward, in order to protect his position in Maknassy, to push the enemy off the high ground east of town. He had the choice of making an immediate attack before the enemy could bring up reinforcements, or he could wait until he had organized his forces for a concerted, well-organized attack. Since, as he read his orders, he was under no pressure to hurry on beyond Maknassy, he decided to wait.

But even as he was moving toward Maknassy, the situation had changed. Montgomery sent an urgent message to Alexander asking for American armor to thrust through Maknassy all the way to the sea to cut the coastal road between Sfax and Gabès. Alexander, still unsure of the fighting quality of the Americans, thought this was too big an order. But Patton passed along new orders to Ward on March 22. He was to raid the enemy airfields, as already planned, prepare an armored force to be ready to harass the enemy as far as 50 miles beyond Maknassy, and, more immediately, to occupy the high ground east of Maknassy. He ordered the attack on three hills east of Maknassy to kick off that very night.

Two of the hills were quickly taken. But Djebel Naemia proved far more difficult. With help from a dense minefield, a German force of only 80 infantrymen managed to hold on through the night of March 22 and then to beat off a renewed assault on the following day until more German troops arrived.

On March 24, Ward concentrated a powerful force of three battalions of infantry, two companies of tanks, and four battalions of artillery to assault the hill from the north, west, and south. But tanks threw their tracks on the rocky ground, and the infantrymen simply couldn't make headway against the dug-in defenders, who now numbered some 350 men.

Patton was furious. He had counted on seizing the high ground east of Maknassy and then making a strong showing in his attacks on the nearby enemy airfields as a way of convincing Alexander and Eisenhower that he was capable of slashing through to the coast. He called "Pinky" Ward on the phone that night and ordered him not only to renew the attack on the following day, but to lead it himself. He warned: It must not fail.

General Bradley, then attached to Patton's headquarters, recalled hearing Patton's end of the conversation: "Pink, you got that hill yet? [Pause] I don't want any goddamned excuses. I want you to go out there and get that hill. You lead the attack personally. Don't come back till you've got it."

Actually, Ward had spent the entire morning on the first day of the attack on the front lines trying to rally his dispirited troops and get them moving forward. On several occasions, he found groups of men hiding in culverts and other depressions in the earth. They told the general they had been sent back for ammunition but as Ward's aide, Maj. William S. McElhenny, later reported, "they were not going back to the front." Ward organized the men in squads, assigned noncommissioned officers to command them, and sent them back into the line.

Ward moved on through an area under fire from German 88 mm guns and found a great many more stragglers who, as McElhenny reported, "claimed that they were pinned to the ground."

"We had walked to these positions and it was true that enemy small arms as well as artillery was sweeping the plain to our front. But the presence of the general, calmly moving from place to place, convinced the men that if we could move safely, they could as well," McElhenny wrote.

Ward sent the men up a railroad track toward the front and then almost immediately came on another group of about a hundred men.

"Reinforcements were unquestionably needed on the line and these men had no intention whatsoever of crossing the open field," McElhenny reported.

Again, Ward and his aides got the men moving out across the field in front of them.

"About halfway across the field enemy machine guns, small arms and artillery opened up and the soldiers all dropped to the ground," McElhenny wrote. "General Ward continued to advance . . . calling to the men, 'Come on! Come on! It's not hurting you! You've got to take that rise in the ground directly to the front.' Some of the men followed but it was again necessary . . . to go from group to group, showing them that the general was advancing and that it was their job to follow."

At half an hour after midnight on the morning of March 25, Ward—following his orders from Patton—led two companies in the renewed attack on Djebel Naemia. He was accompanied by Capt. Ernest C. Hatfield, who wrote his account of the battle shortly afterward.

"General Ward and [an aide] were continually walking among the troops, encouraging them forward with utter disregard to the machine gun fire going on around them," Hatfield wrote.

> One sergeant whom the general saw hesitating drew this searching rebuke:
> "Sergeant, could you go back home and face your mother, sweetheart and friends and tell them that you did your duty to your country and your comrades who are going forward, and look them in the eye? No, you couldn't. The thing for you to do is to move forward with your comrades."
> After the general had spoken to the sergeant, he seemed to take on new life and moved forward with the spirit of a person who is going into the battle with the idea to kill the enemy.

At one point, Ward and Hatfield came under heavy machine gun fire and hit the ground. Between them lay a battalion runner. One of the machine gun bullets hit the runner, seriously wounding him.

Through all this, Ward continued to move about among the troops as though he wore some kind of invisible armor that made him immune to enemy fire. But he wasn't. A shell fragment caught him in the eye near the bridge of his nose. Even though he was bleeding profusely, he continued to direct fire on the enemy. At one point, unable to reach his tanks by radio, he and Hatfield worked their way through enemy fire to a point where they found three tanks and directed them to fire their 75 mm guns at an enemy position on the hillside.

Ward was wounded sometime before 7:00 A.M. but refused to leave the front lines to find a doctor until he was assured the situation was under control about 10:00 A.M. He continued to monitor the situation, and at noon on March 25, he concluded that the hill could not be taken until after his troops had been rested and reorganized.

Apparently disturbed by finding many of his men hiding in fear behind the lines, Ward wrote a memo to all members of the division on March 27, warning against "skulking and straggling."

"Those who falsely believe that immediate personal safety is the best overall policy not only do not save themselves but jeopardize the lives of those who are doing their duty," Ward wrote. "Search your soul and make the enemy pay with his life for threatening the life of our country. Save your hide by bold, determined, aggressive action."

Before the division could be prepared for a renewed attack on the positions east of Maknassy, the situation in the valley to the south had become critical. The enemy was left holding the initiative in the Maknassy area, and a task force was hurriedly assembled to help out near El Guettar.

Moving at a fast trot, Darby's rugged Ranger battalion left a rendezvous point east of El Guettar about midnight on March 20—at about the same time Montgomery was launching a renewed offensive further south and Ward was maneuvering to take Sened Station. Although Darby's force numbered only about 500 men, the success of an attack by two infantry divisions depended to a considerable degree on whether Darby and his men could carry out their sneak attack on the north flank of an Italian unit holding a key position at Djebel el Ank on the Gumtree Road.

This was precisely the kind of warfare the Rangers had been trained for, but which they had had no chance to practice since their successful attack on the Italians in the same general area on February 11 and 12. In this second operation, Ranger scouts, scrambling through the mountains, had found a route that would permit them to sneak up on the Italians through terrain so rugged that it was not defended. Although the jump-off point was only five miles by the road from Djebel el Ank, the route chosen by the scouts covered 12 miles over rocks and through narrow gorges where a single machine gun could have stopped the Rangers cold.

The Rangers traveled light, carrying small packs, rifles, machine guns, grenades, knives, and lightweight infantry mortars. They were supposed to be accompanied by an engineer company with heavier 81 mm mortars. But the engineers soon fell behind the fast-moving Rangers. A full infantry battalion moved up the Gumtree Road prepared to make a frontal assault on the Italian position after the Rangers had made their surprise attack.

The moon was shining when the Rangers started out, but their route soon took them through a dark gorge where a man could see only the two or three men in front of him.

After more than an hour on the trail, they came into an open area where the long line of men could be seen by moonlight moving almost silently along the hillside.

Shortly before 6:00 A.M. on March 21, the Rangers were in position, hiding behind rocks along the edge of a plateau looking down on the enemy positions in the pass. At a signal from Darby, they began to fire with their rifles, machine guns, and light mortars. Darby later related how Corporal Robert Bevan, firing with telescopic sights on his Springfield rifle, knocked out an enemy machine gun.

"I ranged in with tracers and then put two shots right in the position," Bevan said. "The machine gun was quiet for a couple of minutes and then somebody threw a dirty towel or something over the gun and the crew came out and sat down."

Fixing bayonets, the Rangers swarmed down from the hill to knock out the enemy positions. But about 8:00 A.M., they were stopped by a fortified machine gun nest. It was too tough to crack with rifle and light machine gun fire, and they had run out of mortar ammunition. Darby had figured that the engineers would fall about two hours behind his Rangers. And then, just when they were needed most, the engineers arrived with their bigger mortars and quickly took care of the machine gun nest.

The Rangers scrambled among the rocks, rounding up prisoners at bayonet point. Father Albert E. Basil, the British chaplain who had been accepted as one of the Rangers, moved

Members of Company D of the 18th Infantry Regiment, 1st Infantry Division, dug in near El Guettar in March 1943 in preparation for the battle in which American infantry and artillery defeated a massive attack by the Germans' veteran 10th Panzer Division. (Source: National Archives)

among the Italians, speaking to them in fluent Italian. At his urging, they called out to their colleagues to surrender. They not only did so, but even lifted the mines in front of their positions.

The infantry battalion arrived at 10:00 A.M., and by 2:00 P.M. Darby was able to report that the entire area was in American hands and that they had more than 200 prisoners.

Early on the morning of March 21, as the Rangers were taking their roundabout march to attack the Italians at Djebel el Ank, Capt. Sam Carter and his heavy weapons company were climbing down from the trucks that had brought them out from Gafsa and delivered them to the plain southeast of El Guettar. Carter's outfit was one of four companies of the 1st Battalion of the 1st Infantry Division's 18th Infantry

Regiment. Also along on the march with Carter's D—Dog—
Company were the battalion's companies A, B and C.

The men were nervous as they looked out at the range of
hills about five miles away across the plain. They could make
out the hill mass and the taller peaks but could not yet distinguish their objective, designated on their military maps as
Hill 336, the numbers representing its height in meters. The
men quickly labeled it "Wop Hill."

"Definitely and most assuredly we had drawn the route
most dreaded," Carter later wrote, "—the plain with nothing
between bullets and us, if we were spotted, except a prayer."

Hoping to reach the cover of the hills before daybreak,
the men moved fast in two columns separated by 30 to 50
yards, with five to ten yards between men. By spreading out,
they hoped to reduce casualties if they were spotted and hit
by machine gun or artillery fire.

They had not gone far when they heard a short burst
from a machine gun hidden at the enemy position in front of
them. They were sure they had been spotted out there on
the open plain. But after a few moments, the firing stopped.
Carter later figured that the firing had been directed at a
patrol that worked through that area each night. The enemy,
apparently content that there was nothing out there but the
familiar patrol, settled down for the night.

While one column picked its way through a minefield to
approach the hill, Company C marched around to the rear
of Hill 336. At one point they were challenged by an Italian
sentry. But an Italian-speaking American gave him a reassuring response, and the column moved on into position at the
base of the hill about 15 minutes before the assault was
scheduled.

The company commander contacted the battalion commander by radio and asked for instructions. As he did so, his
company spontaneously rose up, as one man, and assaulted
the hill. The assault was such a surprise—as much to the
American commanders as to the Italians—that the hill fell to
the Americans almost immediately. The spontaneous assault
was one of those rare battlefield phenomena where soldiers,
acting without orders, see what needs to be done and do it.
The attack was reminiscent of the taking of Missionary

Ridge during the Civil War battle of Chattanooga on November 25, 1863. To the amazement of General Grant and other officers, soldiers of the Army of the Cumberland took it upon themselves to attack up the sheer slope of the ridge and smash through the strongest point on the Confederate line.

Almost as soon as Hill 336 was taken, it was hit by an artillery barrage—from the American side. The unit's artillery liaison officer radioed orders to cease fire. Another salvo landed. He shouted into the radio that there were Americans on the hill. Another salvo came in. The liaison officer and the battalion commander both got on the radio to the artillery and finally convinced them that the men they could see on the hill were Americans. Fortunately, some of the infantrymen had found foxholes. Others ran to the back side of the hill. There were no casualties from what the military euphemistically calls "friendly fire." About 175 Italians were taken prisoner, and 30 were killed or wounded.

Soon after the position was seized and Carter had set up the observation post of his heavy weapons company, he had visitors. General Patton, the II Corps commander, along with General Allen, the division commander, and members of their staffs arrived for a look at what was going on.

Carter gave them a succinct report on the situation along with a warning that all of these visitors would soon be spotted and become a target for enemy artillery.

"No sooner had this been said than, *wheeeeeee, boom, boom, boom, boom,* a battery salvo hit the road to our immediate left rear," Carter later reported.

He turned and dove into a foxhole that he had just finished digging right behind his observation post.

"Everyone else also made for the hole. Never before has the company commander of D Company had so many 'stars' trying to get to the bottom of his foxhole," Carter recalled. "We soon unscrambled and the Corps Commander said, 'It's too damned hot. Let's get the hell out of here.' Never again did the company commander of D Company have so many distinguished guests at his OP."

Shortly before noon on March 22, Carter's battalion commander received orders to seize a mountain range to the south of the Gafsa–Gabès road. This hill mass, known as Djebel Berda, was dominated by a jagged, towering column of rock designated as Hill 772, a metric measure indicating that it was more than 2,300 feet high, providing a key observation post for whichever side held it.

The battalion moved across an open area, suffering a number of casualties, including Carter's executive officer and mortar platoon leader, until it arrived in a protected crescent below the sheer cliffs of Hill 772. Plans were made for an attack on a lower hill by two battalions early the next morning, March 23.

About 3:00 A.M., everything became very quiet. And then, just about 4:00 A.M., the men heard a noise to their front that sounded like many motors. Ignoring the sounds for the moment, they prepared for their attack at 4:45 A.M. It was preceded by a heavy five-minute artillery barrage that ended with a round of white phosphorous shells as a signal for the infantry to advance. The artillery, falling above and to the rear of the Axis position, so demoralized the enemy that they quickly gave up and the two American battalions occupied the hill.

As the Americans were mopping up and preparing to dig in for defense, the plain below them erupted with tracer fire—red, white, blue, green, purple, yellow, and orange. It was still so dark that the men on the hill could see nothing but this wall of fire moving slowly across the plain toward them.

As dawn broke, the Americans saw what they later learned was the 10th Panzer Division—some 125 tanks. The German tanks, arrayed in a square box formation, came slowly forward. Infantry, interspersed among the tanks and out in front, moving just behind the rolling barrage, advanced with them.

The attacking formation, seeming to react to a prearranged signal, split up into three columns, one moving northwest, one following along the road, and the third—apparently the main column with some 30 tanks—headed to the south of the road around the base of Hill 336, the one the GIs had nicknamed Wop Hill, quickly overrunning the screening force out in front of a tank destroyer battalion.

As soon as it was light enough to see, the American artillery opened up on the advancing formation. "Soon," Carter reported, "the valley was just a mass of guns shooting, shells bursting, armored vehicles burning, and tanks moving steadily westward."

The German assault bypassed Carter and the other Americans on Djebel Berda, leaving them as fascinated spectators. He later described the scene:

> For the first hour we sat in awe watching the attack of the 10th Panzer Division. The precision and timing of the huge iron forts moving down the valley was a thing of magnificent beauty that few persons will only see once in a lifetime and the majority will never have the opportunity to view.
>
> Although we were stunned by such force for a short time we were soon realizing that if the unit flanking Wop Hill succeeded we would be cut off from all Allied units except the French forces south of Djebel Berda. The picture did not look good for our forces as the panzers were closing in on Wop Hill.
>
> The 3rd Battalion of the 18th Infantry, which was in position east of Wop Hill, was being overrun by tanks. The tanks would run their treads over the foxholes and as they cleared the foxholes two or three German soldiers would be pointing their guns at the occupants. Many of the soldiers were crushed by the tanks.
>
> Company K, 18th Infantry, was completely run over by the tanks but held their ground even among the tanks.

The enemy tanks seemed irresistible, especially since the Americans had no tanks on the scene to fight back. If they were to be held, it would be up to the infantry and artillery to do it on their own.

Then the tide turned. The advancing column was stopped by a minefield, and held there under a heavy artillery bombardment. As the American "spectators" watched from their vantage point, the attackers slowed, then stopped and began to retreat. The Americans could not help admiring the bravery of the German tankers who climbed out of their tanks, hooked up tow chains to damaged tanks, and pulled them back to points where they could be repaired. In all, they recovered 38 disabled tanks.

The German veterans gathered in the shelter of a hill east of Hill 336. Radio intercepts indicated a renewed attack would come at 4:00 P.M. Word was passed among the waiting American units. The time of the attack was later changed to 4:45 P.M. and, right on schedule, the enemy emerged from behind the hill. Darby, watching from the position his Rangers had occupied at the beginning of the battle, thought the attack looked like something that might have happened in the Civil War: "There was no running, just a relentless forward lurching of bodies."

When the Germans came within 1,500 feet of the American lines, artillery opened up with time shells that exploded just over the heads of the oncoming mass, blowing holes in the enemy column.

The new time shells, Darby noted, had arrived just a few days before the battle. But the fuze cutters used to set the timing devices on the shells failed to arrive. The artillerymen improvised, getting a blacksmith in Gafsa to fashion crude, but workable, fuze cutters out of horseshoes and scrap metal.

The enemy attack faltered, then stopped, and the threat to Hill 336 and the American line was ended for the moment. It was a bitter defeat for the Germans. Carter found some of the captured enemy soldiers actually in tears, frustrated that their 10th Panzer Division had been humiliated by infantry and artillery unaided by tanks.

The Americans, new to combat, were understandably elated at their feat. They were beginning to learn, however, that without infantry backed up by artillery, tanks are terribly vulnerable to enemy guns and antitank weapons. It is, apparently, a lesson every army has to learn on its own.

During this battle, Carl Lehmann, the Ranger sergeant, happened to be atop a hill overlooking the area. He had not gone with the other Rangers in their attack on Djebel el Ank. Instead, he had been on a patrol out in front of the American lines and was resting when the enemy attack came, in position to give a GI's irreverent commentary on the American generals conducting their side of the battle.

"We were on the pimple, a cone-shaped hill out in front of this mountain range," he recalled. "In the top of it was a rectangular excavation that had been used as a CP, obviously by the Italians, and now us.

"When I got back from patrol, I went to sleep up in the top of it. When I woke up, there were Allen and Roosevelt directing this battle and I was very unimpressed by their conversation. Neither one of them knew what the hell they were doing. Patton came up there but I didn't see him. I heard he was coming and I got the hell out of the way."

When the fighting ended on March 23, the Americans were left with a line extending across the valley from the pass seized by the Rangers to the positions held by the 1st Division infantrymen on Djebel Berda. But their hold was a tenuous one, with the 2nd Battalion of the 18th Infantry in an exposed position on the flank of Djebel Berda. On March 24, the Germans hammered the battalion with heavy artillery and, just after dark, opened fire at point-blank range with tanks and assault guns. When German infantry attacked, an entire American infantry company disintegrated, with many of the men killed, captured, or wounded.

During the night, elements of both the 1st and 2nd Battalions, including Sam Carter's Dog Company, pulled back a short distance to form a strong new defensive position. The commanders of the two battalions checked in with the regimental commander, trying to decide what to do next. The commander of the 2nd Battalion was afraid he couldn't hold his position and argued in favor of a retreat.

The commander of the 1st Battalion, which had had an uneventful day while its companion battalion was under attack, argued strongly for an attempt to hold the position. With reinforcements, he said, the Americans could take the entire Djebel Berda hill mass and pave the way for a tank attack all the way to the sea. If these positions, which had been seized relatively easily from the Italians, were abandoned to the Germans, he argued, the Americans would suffer serious losses if and when they tried to take them back again.

Orders came down from Patton's headquarters: The Rangers would move across the valley and screen the withdrawal of the two infantry battalions from Djebel Berda. The withdrawal was carried out during the night of March 24–25, but the Rangers remained in their exposed position on Djebel Berda until March 27, when they were relieved by troops of the 9th Infantry Division.

One can never be sure whether the 1st Battalion commander was correct when he argued that the American positions on Djebel Berda could have been held. But the experience of the troops of the 9th Infantry Division demonstrated how right he was about the difficulty of retaking that hill mass once it had been given up.

The task given the 9th Division, commanded by Maj. Gen. Manton S. Eddy, was incredibly difficult. Except for the division artillery, which had helped save the day at Thala after the German breakthrough at the Kasserine Pass, most of the troops had seen little or no combat. The division, which had never made any kind of an attack as a unit, was ordered to march at night across several miles of open plain into a rugged hill mass cut up into rocky crags and deep gorges. They started out with inadequate maps and without a chance to reconnoiter the terrain. All they learned from the 1st Division soldiers who had just retreated from Djebel Berda was that it was a natural fortress that could be held by just a few enemy troops.

From this inauspicious start, things went downhill. One battalion got lost and remained out of touch with the rest of the division for a day and a half. When contact was finally reestablished, the battalion reported that it had lost its commander and intelligence and communications officers, one entire company, and the commanders of two other companies. A reserve battalion, called forward to shore up the faltering attack, also got lost and remained out of contact for more than a day.

When the 9th Division men did manage to capture an enemy position, they found that during the brief time the Germans had held the hill mass, their engineers had brought up jackhammers and construction equipment to dig foxholes in the rock and construct heavily fortified machine gun and mortar positions. At this point in the war, the Americans had no such help from their engineers.

While the 9th Division was bogged down in the hills south of the Gafsa–Gabès road, the 1st Infantry Division, now concentrated north of the road, made good progress beyond Djebel el Ank, which the division and the Rangers had seized in the opening hours of the battle.

It was at this point that the operations by the 1st Armored Division near Maknassy were called off. General Alexander gave Patton detailed orders for the defense of Maknassy, Sened Station, and Gafsa and then ordered him to send an armored column to break through along the Gafsa–Gabès road. He was to do this even though the infantry had so far failed to clear enemy troops from the hills on each side of the road but especially on the south side, where the 9th Division was bogged down.

Instead of calling on Robinett's Combat Command B or one of the other existing combat commands, Patton chose to create a new armored force under Col. C. C. "Chauncey" Benson, an armored officer who was a personal friend and whose aggressiveness he admired. Benson was given a powerful force consisting of nine battalions of tanks, infantry, tank destroyers, artillery, and engineers.

As Benson launched his attack on the morning of March 30, he and Patton quickly had impressed on them the lesson the Germans had learned a few days earlier: Tanks are sitting ducks if the infantry hasn't taken out the enemy's antitank guns. This was the situation as Benson's force moved down the Gafsa-Gabès road. On the right side of the road, where the 9th Infantry Division had run into trouble, the German antitank guns remained in place and opened up with devastating effect when the Americans paused at a minefield blocking the road. Thirteen tanks and two tank destroyers were knocked out before Benson pulled back.

Attacks on the two following days were equally unsuccessful. But even though he had not been able to break through the enemy defenses, Benson had achieved one of the major objectives of his offensive, which was to draw enemy strength away from in front of Montgomery. The Germans threw both the 10th and 21st Panzer Divisions and much of their air power not only into repelling the Benson force but also into hammering elements of the 1st Armored Division on the other side of the mountain ridge at Maknassy.

For the first few days of April, the Benson force stood back and waited for the infantry to succeed in cleaning up the antitank positions that had blocked their way earlier. Then the enemy withdrew just enough for Benson to get

General Patton visited the front lines during fighting south of
El Guettar on March 30, 1943. (Source: National Archives)

beyond the Djebel Berda hill mass. Chances for a push to the
sea looked good.

After the failure of Ward to clear the enemy positions
east of Maknassy, Patton had decided to relieve him and
asked Harmon to leave his own 2nd Armored Division in
Morocco and take over Ward's 1st Armored. But Patton,
brave as he might be on the battlefield, was not good at firing people. He asked General Bradley, who by then had
become his deputy, to tell "Pinky" Ward he was going to be
replaced. When Bradley arrived at Ward's headquarters to
give him the word, he found Ward was not at all surprised.

"Though I disagreed with Patton's relief of Ward, the
relationship between them had become so demoralized by
distrust that it was better severed than patched up," Bradley
wrote in his memoirs. Ward returned to the United States
to command the Tank Destroyer Center at Camp Hood
and later distinguished himself as commander of the 20th
Armored Division in Europe.

Major General
Orlando Ward, who
was relieved of his
command of the 1st
Armored Division
by General George
Patton at the height
of the fighting in
Tunisia, is shown
in a 1945 photo.
(Source: National
Archives)

When Harmon arrived at the division headquarters after a hot, dusty drive from Gafsa, he found Ward waiting with his bedroll, ready to depart. He saluted as his replacement stepped out of the jeep and said: "The party is all yours, Harmon."

"I'm sorry, Ward, I had nothing to do with your relief," Harmon told him. "Can't you stay here tonight and show me the situation? General Patton didn't tell me anything."

Ward explained that he had been ordered to leave the minute Harmon arrived.

"We discussed the matter a moment," Harmon later recalled, "and then Ward said he would be glad to stay until morning if Patton okayed the delay. I telephoned Patton and he roared that he didn't give a damn what happened to Ward so long as I understood I was in charge. I edited Uncle George's assent in transmitting it: 'The general said he would be very happy for you to stay if you cared to.'"

Major General Ernest
Harmon arrives in
Tunisia to take over
command of the 1st
Armored Division from
Ward early in April
1943. (Source: National
Archives)

Harmon was just settling in when, on April 7, Benson's force was ordered to make a strong new drive down the Gafsa–Gabès road to force the enemy to continue the retreat already being forced by Montgomery's troops.

Patton ordered Benson to thrust through toward the coast, ignoring opposition along the way. Keeping track of the advance by radio, Patton became impatient and drove to the front in a jeep with an aide. He found the column waiting while engineers cleared a path through a minefield. Patton simply drove on, leading the way through the minefield until he reached a road sign indicating Gabès was only 70 kilometers—42 miles—further on. As he turned back, he ordered Benson to keep rolling "for a fight or a bath."

This business of smashing through, bypassing opposing forces, was dangerous and costly. A. Robert Moore, the tank officer who had just missed involvement in the debacle at Sidi Bou Zid and then fought in defense of Sbeitla until his tank was knocked out, was back in action with the Benson force in a new tank. Moore, who had been put in charge of a company, was promoted to captain during the Battle of El Guettar. He gave this description of his part in the battle:

"We started out, moving across the desert. The pass was seven or eight miles wide. We were spread out. We got down to a narrow pass where five German tanks and a bunch of artillery stopped the whole damn thing. There was only one place to get through and they had it mined and blocked, with infantry in the hills above it and artillery observers.

"In trying to do our battalion's job of getting through this pass, I got within about, I'd say, 400 yards of a little ridge that ran right along the front of the pass. I'm pretty sure it was a German Mark IV that fired at me. It knocked the track off on the right side. When that happened, the other track was still going and it spun the tank and for some reason it stopped and my 75 was pointed right at this German tank. My gunner got off about four rounds and then there was no more German tank."

But the enemy had not been knocked out. He had just moved around for another shot.

"So I'm sitting there with a busted track, can't go anyplace. And we're trying to figure out where this guy's coming from the next time. And when he did, we didn't see him. The second round came through the hatch that the driver and the assistant drivers get out of. They had their hands on both sides of the hole lifting their bodies out when I told 'em to bail out and run. The second round came between the thumb and the forefinger of the driver's hand. He had about 140 pieces of steel taken out of his hand when he got back to the hospital. He didn't stop running until he got there.

"Anyway, the driver and the assistant driver got out. The third round bounced off the top of our turret. When I say bounced, I mean it hit the beveled edge and it shattered the gunsight. The gunner looked up and said, 'The sight's gone.' I said, 'Let's bail out.' Well, I got out and the fourth round came through the gunsight. And the loader . . . was on his way out. He had his head up my butt on the way out. It cut him in half and it took the gunner's head off. So I lost two guys there. Three of us got out.

"That tank burned. I went back that night and got the half a body of [the loader]. He was still breathing but he did die before we got him to the hospital. The other guy, the gunner, the biggest piece of him we found was the hip. The rest of him burned in the tank.

"So I lost my job until I got another tank. I got another tank the next day, of course."

As Moore moved back up toward the pass blocked by the Germans, his radio operator was tuned in to the German radio traffic.

"He said, 'Captain, I just heard them say, "We all fire together."' I said, 'Oh, oh, they're getting ready to attack or pull out.' I knew pretty well they weren't going to attack because of the preponderance of material we had on this side of the pass. They fired and then it got quiet. We took off through the pass. That's the third time I saw Patton. I'm going down the road through the pass. He's in his car with his pistols on. He yells, 'Get going! Get going!' I waved to him."

And then, instead of going ahead, Moore swung his turret around and fired behind, up a side road where they had bypassed an enemy gun position.

"They were shooting at my rear and I didn't like that," Moore says.

Benson's tankers entered the British sector on the afternoon of April 7 and made contact with a British reconnaissance force between 4:00 and 5:00 P.M., thus linking the eastern and western branches of the Allied armies. The enemy pulled out of the passes at Maknassy and Faïd and joined in the column fleeing north toward a new line of resistance south of Tunis.

During these battles, the American GIs were fighting against some of Rommel's veterans and thought they were up against the Desert Fox himself. What they didn't know was that three days after the Battle of Medenine in early March, Rommel secretly boarded a plane and flew off to Italy and thence to Hitler's headquarters near the eastern front in Ukraine. Rommel was suffering from heart trouble and rheumatism. To Hitler, he seemed visibly ill, with a bandage covering sores on his neck. Rommel assumed that after a brief rest—a "cure," as he phrased it—he would hurry back to Africa. Hitler presented him with a rare award—a diamond cluster for his Knight's Cross—but then, concerned about what he perceived as Rommel's defeatist attitude, sent him home to rest. He was never to return to Africa.

The Germans managed to keep the secret of Rommel's departure for some weeks. Thus, even though the Desert Fox was gone physically, he remained present in the minds of the American soldiers and their leaders. And of course they associated him with the Afrika Korps, which they still faced, although Rommel, who came to Africa with the two-division corps, had long since assumed the baton of a field marshal and command of a German-Italian army.

On April 15, Bradley replaced Patton as II Corps commander and Patton was sent back to Morocco to plan for the invasion of Sicily. But as with Rommel, Patton's departure was kept a tightly held secret as part of the security surrounding preparations for the next phase of the war. Thus, within a few weeks, Rommel and Patton, the two most charismatic and well-known generals in Tunisia, had left the scene. Few on either side knew they were gone, and they remained for weeks as, in a sense, phantom commanders.

The next "meeting" of the two generals came in the summer of the following year, when Rommel headed an army group resisting the Normandy invasion. For two fatal weeks in June 1944, he held back reserves that might have repelled the invasion while he waited for a second landing by an army group headed by Patton. The "army group" did not exist. It was a fiction created by the Allies, made all the more believable to the Germans by the fact that Patton, whom they considered the enemy's best general, was not involved in the actual landings.

Patton did not take to the field in France until July—with the Third Army, not an army group. Rommel was in the hospital with a severe head injury suffered when his staff car was strafed by a British Spitfire on July 17. Three months later, still recuperating from his injuries, he was forced to take poison, at Hitler's orders, and died on October 14, 1944.

Soldiers of the 1st Armored Division pass the wreckage of a German fighter near El Guettar on April 11, 1943. (Source: National Archives)

In his brief five-week tenure as II Corps commander, Patton had undoubtedly shaken things up. But it would be an exaggeration to say that he had made much of a difference on the battlefield. When he took over, plans for the March offensive were well developed, and he made few changes. In the fighting at El Guettar and Maknassy, he was tightly constrained by specific orders from General Alexander's headquarters and had no chance to demonstrate the dashing brand of tank warfare for which he later became a legend in Europe.

Eisenhower's decision to pull Patton out of action and put him to work preparing for the next phase of the war indicated the confidence with which the Allied leaders were already looking beyond the battle for Tunisia to an invasion of Sicily before the winter storms. But the generals on both sides were aware that the clock was ticking: Every day the Axis held out in Tunisia raised the odds that an Allied landing in Sicily, Italy, or southern France would have to be delayed until the following spring. On the battlefield in the spring of 1943, it was not at all obvious that the Allies would win their race against the clock.

While the 1st and 9th Infantry and the 1st Armored divisions were fighting the Battle of El Guettar, the 34th Infantry Division was involved further north in the Battle for Fondouk Gap. A success there would put the Allies on the coastal plain in a position to catch the enemy fleeing from Montgomery's advancing army. But success there proved even more elusive than it had at El Guettar.

PART THREE

VICTORY
IN TUNISIA

18

Ordeal at Fondouk Pass

The enemy troops holding Fondouk Pass were neither very numerous nor very skilled as soldiers. One key German unit, in fact, was a punitive battalion made up of court-martialed soldiers being given a chance to redeem themselves in combat. But the enemy had that most prized of military positions—the high ground.

As the 125th Field Artillery Battalion—one of three gun units supporting the 34th Infantry Division—moved into position early on March 25 after an all-night, three-mile-an-hour drive in blackout conditions, Staff Sgt. Clem Miller looked around and didn't like what he saw. They were in an open field, with no trees or brush, not even a cactus plant. The enemy held the ridgeline in front of them and even had guns on the slope of a towering mountain to their left rear.

"We were like a pea on a plate," Miller says.

The gunners, still equipped with British 25-pounders, quickly set up their guns, occasionally casting a wary eye toward the high ground. They could almost feel the eyes of the enemy observers noting every movement. While the gunners were at work, Staff Sgt. Luke Krampovitch headed off into the no-man's-land between the American forces and the enemy with a four-man survey section. Their job was to determine the exact location of landmarks visible from the artillery

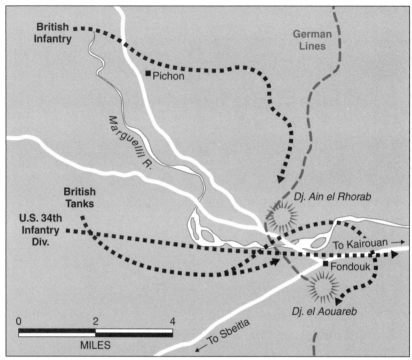

The 34th Infantry Division was tested in two battles for the key mountain pass at Fondouk between March 25 and April 9, 1943. The division performed so badly that British officers recommended it be sent far behind the lines to be retrained. However, at least part of the reason for the Allied failures at Fondouk was faulty planning on the part of British commanders.

position. Artillery spotters would use these known positions as reference points to help the gunners zero in on enemy troops and guns.

Clem Miller recalls that high school trigonometry was still fresh enough in the minds of the men with him in the survey section that they quickly caught on to the skill needed to mark the survey points for gunners. For the most part, the job was routine. But then there were those moments of sheer terror, like the one that morning.

Krampovitch was at the wheel when his jeep topped a rise in the road and came face to face with a German tank. Krampovitch spun the jeep around and headed back down the road as fast as the jeep would go. The surprised Germans took a moment to react before they got off three shots from their turret gun. The delay was just enough for the Americans to get away, and all three shots missed.

Despite the exposed position in which they found themselves, the morale of the 34th Division men was still high. The division was finally all together and about to launch its first offensive as a division after having been broken up and scattered about for most of the North African campaign.

General Ryder, the Abraham Lincoln look-alike who commanded the division, received his orders for the attack from Patton in a meeting at Feriana on the night of March 25. The attack by Ryder's division was part of the Allied plan to force the enemy to pull some of the troops confronting Montgomery's Eighth Army out of the line and send them to deal with an American threat from the west. The other parts of that plan, further south in the area of Maknassy and El Guettar, have been described in Chapter 17.

Patton's orders to Ryder, like those he gave to the 1st Armored Division at Maknassy, called for a limited offensive with limited goals. Ryder was to take the high ground at Fondouk Pass but not to press on to the east. The attack was what the military calls a "demonstration." He was to make a lot of noise but not to take unnecessary risks to seize significant amounts of ground.

Ryder decided to use two of his three regiments to make the attack while the third remained in reserve. The two regiments would attack on a five-mile-long front, with the 135th Regiment on the north side of a road running northeastward toward the pass and the 168th Regiment on the south side of the road. There would be about a thousand infantrymen to the mile.

Miller's outfit, the 125th Field Artillery Battalion, along with the 185th Field Artillery Battalion, supported the 135th Infantry. The 175th Field Artillery Battalion supported the 168th Infantry.

The 168th Infantry, which had lost its commander, Colonel Drake, and two of its battalions in the disaster at Sidi Bou Zid, was now commanded by Col. Frederick B. Butler, an engineer officer and West Pointer who had served earlier as a military aide to President Herbert Hoover. Its second battalion, the one that had managed to escape from Djebel Lessouda, was still commanded by Bob Moore, the Iowa drugstore operator, now wearing the silver maple leaf of a lieutenant colonel. Even though the 168th Infantry was still in the process of absorbing more than a thousand replacements for those lost at Sidi Bou Zid, it was marginally more experienced than the 135th Regiment.

The attack kicked off at six o'clock on the morning of March 27 and almost immediately ran into trouble. The first problem was the lack of transportation. Trucks carried $2^1/_2$ to 10 tons of ammunition. But the men were expected to march about 15 miles across the open terrain before they approached the high ground where the enemy was holed up.

Troops moving out in front of the 135th Regiment were surprised to find themselves in a minefield—laid, but not properly marked, by *Americans* a month and a half earlier when they feared a German attack through Fondouk Pass. Nearly a score of the attackers were wounded and eight or nine vehicles destroyed before the battalion worked its way through.

Once past the mines, hours passed with only occasional rounds of artillery to disturb the morning. Although it was still very early spring, the men advanced through fields of poppies and other wild flowers. General Robinett, the tank commander, later commented on the way the soldiers experienced the miracle of spring over and over as they moved through Tunisia: "There are many springtimes in that land, for it depends on altitude as well as upon soil and rain and proximity to the great Sahara Desert as well. A worshiper of the springtime would have difficulty in finding such a small area with so many."

In the early hours of the battle, the enemy artillery, directed by observers who could see all of the American units from their posts on the high ground, concentrated on knocking out the American artillery.

Miller, whose artillery outfit had staked out its position behind the infantry advance line, recalls that he could hear three guns firing at them. The soldiers first heard the *boom, boom, boom* of the guns. Time to hop into a foxhole and light a cigarette. Next came the shrill sound of the shells as they seemed to hang in the air and then scream downward. Time to throw away the cigarette and duck deep into the hole until the shell hit and the shell fragments and debris finished raining down. Then quickly shake off the fragments of hot metal before they burned through the uniform fabric.

Between rounds, Miller and several of his buddies pulled out a football and played catch, listening for the next *boom, boom, boom*. They played, that is, until the first sergeant shouted at them to knock it off before someone got killed.

As the 135th Infantry advanced, its 3rd Battalion was on the right, next to the 168th Regiment. Its 2nd Battalion stretched off to the left and rear. At about 11:30 A.M., a small German force, in armored cars and tanks, attacked the 2nd Battalion, which was also being hit by artillery from Djebel Trozza, the mountain to its left rear. The battalion halted while an artillery barrage was called in to drive away the German armor.

A patrol with six men in two jeeps was sent out to check the area toward Djebel Trozza. In midafternoon, one man struggled back into American lines to report that the patrol had been ambushed by German tanks. The lone survivor was so badly shaken that he couldn't tell where or when the ambush had taken place.

About the same time, enemy fire increased all along the line and the advance slowed and began to waver. The 3rd Battalion of the 135th Infantry moved to the right, across the road that was supposed to divide it from the neighboring 168th Infantry. It got only about 500 yards toward a ridge occupied by the enemy before fire became so intense that it stopped. Not only did it fail to take the ridge, but its move across the road opened up a gap between units. The Germans surged into the gap and caught the Americans in crossfire from the sides.

Twice during the night and again early the next morning, attempts were made to take the ridge or at least to infiltrate into the enemy positions. The attacks were made across flat land, without any cover, through barbed wire and minefields. The enemy fired their automatic weapons from positions that had been carved out of the solid rock with jackhammers and reinforced with railroad ties and steel girders. All three attacks failed.

First Lt. John G. Westover, a member of the 175th Field Artillery Battalion, was assigned as a forward artillery observer with the 168th Infantry. At one point, as the unit he was with fell back in the face of an enemy counterattack, he and his radioman jumped into a large hole that had been dug by the Germans. They were soon joined by several infantrymen. A machine gunner kept them pinned down while a mortar crew bracketed them with explosions. As an artilleryman, Westover knew the mortar men would soon correct their aim and drop a shell in the hole. He decided to run for it.

He waited until a mortar shell exploded, then dashed 30 yards to dive into a shallow ditch. He began crawling away from the hole, hoping his radioman would be able to make good his escape from the hole in the earth.

"Crawling through that grass, I suddenly came face to face with a wounded German who was crawling in the opposite direction," Westover wrote in his memoirs. "He seemed to be unarmed and was obviously scared. I had my .45 in my hand but I was not about to shoot an unarmed, wounded man. I said, 'Good luck, Buddy,' and kept on going. I wonder if he lived to tell that story to his grandchildren."

Westover crawled for about a quarter of a mile and finally reached his jeep. He waited there until his radio operator joined him. He said that when he tried to follow Westover's path, the machine gunner opened up, but missed. After the tide of battle turned, the two men returned to the hole to retrieve the equipment they had left behind. They assumed, from the fact that there were no bodies and no blood in the hole, that the infantrymen had also made good their escape.

Even before the firing had stopped, Sgt. Milo Green, who had continued to send a steady stream of "Brickbats" back to his hometown newspapers in Iowa, was assigned, along with the regimental chaplains, to the gruesome duty of recovering the bodies of those killed in combat. With a touch of gallows humor, they set out in a half-ton truck labeled, with white letters: "THE STUKA VALLEY HEARSE—DEATH RIDES WITH US."

"In those trying days some morbid sense of humor like that was all that saved us from going mad," Green wrote.

At Fondouk, bodies of men that had been dead for only a few days were so badly decomposed that Green and the others had to wear gas masks while doing their work. His worst day, he said, came during a later battle when he recovered the bodies of four close friends in as many days. Green also rescued wounded men from the field of battle and received the Silver Star award for gallantry in action at Fondouk.

On the morning of March 30—the fourth day of the offensive—the attack was called off. The troops were told to hold their positions and then, on the night of April 1–2, the entire division was ordered to move back two miles to a new defensive position.

Given its mission of making a "demonstration," the 34th Division had not done badly. It had, in fact, given the enemy something to worry about and diverted some troops from in front of Montgomery. But the failure to take the high ground at the cost of hundreds of casualties was a bitter disappointment for the division in its first offensive. Morale was abysmal.

The British officers who were in overall command of the fighting, under Eisenhower, muttered about the failure of the green Americans. But what happened next was, in effect, an admission that the first attack on Fondouk Gap had failed because the high command had sent too few troops to do too tough a job.

Lieutenant General Sir John Crocker, commander of the British IX Corps, was given the responsibility for carrying out a new attack—the second battle for Fondouk Pass.

This time, there would be enough men and machines to do the job. At least, that's what Crocker planned. Ryder's 34th Division would repeat its attack toward the pass. But Crocker would also throw into the battle the British 6th Armored Division, the 128th Infantry Brigade, and two additional squadrons of tanks. More artillery was moved up and placed in position all along a front extending for some 10 miles.

This time, too, the goal was different and more ambitious because the battlefield situation had changed. In the time since the first attempt to take Fondouk Pass, Montgomery had broken through in the south and the German and Italian armies were fleeing north between the Eastern Dorsal and the coast. Instead of a "demonstration," this time Crocker's job would be to sweep through Fondouk Pass and send his armor onto the coastal plain to intercept the retreating enemy. If he succeeded, the battle for Tunisia might end abruptly in the next few days.

Timing was crucial. The Allies would not be ready to go on the offensive until the night of April 7–8. But if they were to catch the enemy before he escaped to form a new line south of Tunis, they would have to break though the pass by April 10. Crocker was understandably impatient.

On April 6, the day before the attack was to be launched, Crocker and his staff came to Ryder's headquarters to outline their plans. It was the first time Ryder had a clear idea of what his division was supposed to do, and he was deeply disturbed by what he learned. His job was to attack straight across the flat, open land toward Djebel Aouareb, a sheer rocky outcropping rising to more than a thousand feet on the south side of the pass. His men could probably do it, although it would be tough. But then his attention focused on a similar mountain on the north side of the pass known as Djebel Aïn el Rhorab. His men could come under devastating flanking fire from that 957-foot-high promontory.

What about Rhorab? he asked.

Crocker and an aide assured him Rhorab was only lightly defended, or perhaps not defended at all.

Ryder asked for authority to shell Rhorab as he advanced.

No, the British officers told him. Their 128th Infantry Brigade would attack the village of Pichon and then move on south to mop up the few enemy soldiers who might be on Rhorab. Ryder could fire smoke shells toward Rhorab to cover his advance, but could not use explosive shells because Rhorab was on the British side of the line and their troops might be there.

Ryder, noting that the British infantry would have to fight their way south five miles before they even got to Rhorab, protested that his flank might remain unprotected for hours. General Koeltz, the French general whose troops had previously held the pass, echoed Ryder's concerns. So did a visiting American general. But Crocker and his aides again assured them Rhorab was no problem.

A military commander can dispute orders with which he disagrees up to a point. But if his appeals are rejected, he is expected to salute and carry on. That's what Ryder did. But he also changed his plans to make the best of a bad situation. He had planned to launch his attack at 5:30 A.M., just before dawn. Now he decided to move the kickoff time up to 3:00 A.M. This would mean setting his troops in motion in the dark. It also meant calling off a planned bombing attack on the enemy positions. Ryder wanted to use the bombers because he felt that aerial bombs would have a better chance than artillery shells of hurting the enemy, which was hiding among large boulders. But an aerial bombardment in the dark would probably not be accurate enough to produce the desired effect.

During the night, the division's 135th and 133rd Infantry Regiments moved up to a line about 1,500 yards—a little less than a mile—from the base of the mountain they were expected to attack. The 168th Regiment, which had taken part in the first battle of Fondouk Pass, was assigned to protect the division's flank and form a reserve.

Ryder was concerned about the ability of his men, who had little training in night operations, to get into position for a 3:00 A.M. attack. His fears proved justified. One battalion veered to the right, opening up a gap between it and the neighboring battalion. In the process, communications broke down. It was not until 5:30 A.M.—the time the attack would have started under the old plan—before the troops began their assault. A signal from the advancing infantrymen alerted the artillery to begin shelling the objective.

At this point, Ryder realized that the barrage had begun while his troops were still far from the mountain. He stopped the attack and even ordered some of the troops to move back from ground they had already covered. Now that it was daylight, he called for aerial bombardment of the objective for the half-hour from 8:00 to 8:30 A.M. The raid was postponed an hour and then another half-hour.

First Lt. Virgil E. Craven was executive officer of Company I of the 133rd Infantry Regiment, which was to the right of the 135th Regiment in the attack.

His company had gone only about 200 yards when a messenger ran up to the company commander with orders to halt while the neighboring unit caught up. The men, still wearing their overcoats and burdened with two extra bandoleers of ammunition each, waited for nearly half an hour before receiving the word to advance once more. As they did so, the sun came up from behind Djebel Aouareb, giving the men their first view of their looming objective and the terrain they would have to cover to reach it. All they saw was an expanse of flat, sandy soil covered with a sparse layer of grass and clusters of poppies here and there.

At 6:30 A.M., a rocket signaled the artillery to begin its barrage. But the lead platoon in Company I was still far from its objective. The troops moved forward slowly for the next hour and a quarter. They had not yet come under enemy fire. Then new orders came over the radio to wait for American bombers to attack the enemy positions. The men waited until 9:00 A.M., but the bombers never came. The reason given was that the ceiling was too low. The ceiling did not, however, prevent the Luftwaffe from carrying out its own dive-bombing attack on the American troops.

By midmorning, the company had advanced to within about 700 yards of the enemy positions, coming under increasing artillery and mortar fire. The advance ground to a halt, and light machine guns were brought forward to sweep the forward slopes of the mountain, focusing on likely enemy positions. But the Germans, with the advantage of the high ground, immediately rained down artillery and mortar shells on the machine gun positions, forcing them to cease firing.

While the men of the 133rd Regiment were receiving intense fire from the slopes of Djebel Aouareb, the 135th Regiment, on their left, was also under fire from Rhorab, the high ground that Crocker had assured Ryder would not cause him any trouble. It was not until late in the afternoon that the British, who were supposed to come down from the north and take Rhorab, got close enough so that the enemy troops noticed them and shifted their heavy mortars in that direction, and away from the Americans.

The I Company commander called for help to silence the German guns firing from Djebel Aouareb. He was told that tanks would arrive to assist him at one o'clock. While they waited, the men scratched shallow slit trenches in the hard soil with entrenching tools, bayonets, and the lids of their mess kits.

Ten tanks came rumbling up to the company position, as promised, and immediately attracted the most intense barrage of the day from the enemy guns.

Craven pressed himself into the ground as the shells rained down. He later claimed to have counted 30 rounds that landed within 25 yards of where he lay. But all but two were duds, and he survived unscathed.

In the midst of this barrage, the tanks advanced in front of Company I. Within minutes, four of them were hit and burning. The others turned and retreated back out of range. The Americans were still in the process of learning that tanks cannot survive without infantry support to dig out the enemy's antitank guns.

At 2:00 P.M., the company was told that a concerted attack would be made at 3:00 P.M.

When the signal for the attack was given, one of Company I's three platoons rose up and moved forward. It had gone only about a hundred yards when the officer leading the charge was killed by machine gun fire.

"This platoon was the only platoon in the entire battalion area that actually made an attempt to carry out the attack order," Craven later wrote. "The other platoons and members of the company did little more than look up from out of their slit trenches only to go back and dig a little deeper."

A new attack was scheduled for 5:00 P.M. This time, the battalion commander radioed, tanks would attack behind an artillery barrage. All officers were ordered to get out of their foxholes and lead the men forward with the tanks.

This time 15 tanks appeared from the rear and moved off toward the enemy positions, protected by the artillery. "Even with this supporting fire, the men of I Company could not be moved to join the tanks in the assault," Craven reported.

The tanks proceeded on about 200 yards beyond the infantry line. Then, as the American artillery shifted its aim to fire on the reverse slope of the mountain, the enemy gunners again opened with their guns hidden on the forward slope. Within minutes, six of the 15 tanks were burning. The others stopped and then retreated. To add to the confusion, as the attack was launched a British armored brigade came rumbling unexpectedly through the division area. The attack faltered and then collapsed.

The first day's attacks ended with the American infantrymen mixed in among the British tanks, with officers trying to bring some order out of the mixup under enemy fire attracted by the tanks.

With the coming of darkness, the men of I Company cautiously climbed out of their foxholes and stretched muscles cramped from the long hours huddled under the enemy barrage. About eight o'clock, men arrived carrying food from the kitchens set up behind the lines. But it was not a hot meal. Instead, the mess attendants handed out C rations packed tightly in heavy waterproof packaging. The sound the men made tearing open the packages was just enough to stir up the enemy gunners and bring in several rounds of artillery and mortar fire.

When the situation calmed down once more, the company commander set about reorganizing his command. In the process, it became apparent that each platoon was missing at least ten men, a total of 50 men missing from the company.

The mess sergeant heard this report and volunteered that he had seen some men from the company hanging around the kitchen area some eight miles behind the lines. Craven was ordered to go round them up.

He went back with the mess crew and found five men from the company. To avoid getting lost, he returned to the front lines over the same route the company had followed in the morning. When he reached the wadi from which they had started out, he found another 45 men from the company lurking there. Their excuse was that they had gotten lost and couldn't find the front lines. "Of course," Craven wryly noted, "it never dawned upon them that by going in the direction of the firing they would find the front line."

The stragglers were given a stern talking-to by the company commander and then sent back to their platoons.

During the night, the company commander sent out several patrols to find out where the enemy was. But the patrols, their morale shaken by the day's events, seemed to avoid, rather than seek out, the enemy. When they came back, they had nothing to report. On the other hand, the Germans were out there in the dark patrolling aggressively—to at least within 100 yards of the American lines. Proof of this was that when the Americans succeeded about 11:00 P.M. in retrieving the body of the lieutenant who had led the only platoon to carry out the assault, they found that his gold nugget ring had been taken from his finger.

The men were roused for a breakfast of C rations at 4:00 A.M. on April 9 and given orders for an attack at 6:00 A.M. Promptly at six o'clock, American artillery began to hammer the forward slopes of Djebel Aouareb, which seemed even bigger and more formidable as the sun rose behind it. The barrage was the signal for the attack to begin.

"Not a soul could be seen moving and furthermore enemy fire was not being received," Craven later reported. "Everyone continued to man their foxholes."

Another attack was ordered for 9:00 A.M. But just as it was scheduled to begin, enemy dive bombers arrived with 500-pound bombs, throwing the Americans into confusion.

"At 0930 the battalion commander contacted the company commanders by . . . radio and requested a report of progress of the attack," Craven wrote. "The company commander reported that his unit was going forward slowly but meeting stiff resistance when in reality hardly anyone had ventured to look up from his foxhole."

At 11:30 A.M., tanks arrived and moved out in front of the infantry. Artillery again struck the forward slopes of the objective. Encouraged by this assistance—and by the fact that there had been little enemy fire during the morning—the infantrymen finally rose up out of their foxholes and started forward. The artillery barrage was so intense that some of the Americans even began to feel sorry for the enemy soldiers.

Then, suddenly, the advancing Americans were struck with a withering combination of rifle, machine gun, and anti-tank fire, coming not from the mountain toward which they were advancing, but from their left flank. The tanks withdrew, leaving the infantrymen trying to scrape some shelter out of the bare ground.

For most of the afternoon, the men were pinned down by mortar, machine gun, and artillery fire, and casualties began to mount. Morale, already low, collapsed from the top down. The battalion commander told the regimental commander it was impossible to advance against the enemy fire and asked to be placed under arrest rather than be responsible for pushing his men forward. He was immediately relieved and placed under arrest.

At 7:00 P.M., Craven's company received orders to cover the withdrawal of the battalion as it moved back to the wadi from which the attack had begun. Shortly before midnight, the company pulled back to the original starting point after two days under intense enemy fire. When roll was taken, only 80 men remained in the company out of its original strength of 162 men.

During the early stages of the second battle of Fondouk Pass, the 168th Regiment, which had seen hard fighting during the first battle, was assigned to guard the right flank as the regiment's other two battalions made their attack. But as the attack faltered, Colonel Butler, the regimental commander, was ordered to send some of his men toward the front.

As he prepared to do so, the command post of the second battalion was hit by enemy bombers and Lieutenant Colonel Bob Moore, the battalion commander, was so shaken by the concussion that he had to be evacuated.

Butler turned to Ed Bird, the young officer who had distinguished himself in the fighting at El Guettar in late January, and had since been promoted to major. He said: "Major, get over there as quickly as you can. The 2nd Battalion is yours to fight."

Bird took off on foot with a crumpled map in his hand to find his new command post. He announced himself to the staff and then took off for the front, where one of his companies was supposed to be attacking.

He found the company commander waiting for an artillery barrage to lift.

"What are you doing back here?" Bird asked. "Why aren't you with the lead platoon?"

As the officer prepared to move forward, Bird joined him. They soon found a platoon leader who seemed to be at least as frightened as his men.

"Hurry them up. Get in among them, Lieutenant," Bird shouted. The men, firing their rifles, topped a crest and saw the enemy troops scurrying away.

From his position, Bird could see, off to the north, a confusing scene. Tanks were surging through the pass but the area was also dotted with many burning tanks. What had happened was, with the repeated failure of the 34th Division to take the high ground on the right side of the pass and with the unexpected resistance by the enemy on the left side of the pass, General Crocker, the British commander, felt that time was running out if he was to have any chance of intercepting the German and Italian troops streaming north toward Tunis. He ordered the British 6th Armored Division to charge through the pass even though he knew that the enemy minefields and antitank guns would take a fearful toll.

The German commander, whose task was to hold the pass until the 10th and 21st Panzer Divisions and other Axis units had passed Kairouan, rounded up as many antitank weapons as he could find. He assembled some 13 heavy antitank guns, including two 88 mm flak guns, south of the pass and two more on the north.

With British and American engineers working to clear a lane through the mines, the British Sherman tanks charged through the pass and began to emerge on the other side between 3:00 and 6:00 P.M. on April 9. Crocker, bitterly disappointed, concluded that it was already too late to catch the bulk of the enemy forces. But he also feared there might still be enough of them to cause him trouble. He ordered his tankers to hole up in the pass during the night before moving out the next morning on the 18-mile dash to Kairouan. When they arrived at Kairouan, they were just in time to glimpse the last of the enemy units disappearing toward the north.

The second battle of Fondouk Pass had been a costly failure. Not only had the Allies failed to catch the retreating enemy and end the fighting in Tunisia, but they had also paid a heavy price in men and equipment. It cost Crocker 34 tanks to crack through the pass without waiting for the infantry to clear the way. The 34th Division had lost more than a thousand men, counting dead, wounded, and missing in action. It had also suffered a severe loss in self-esteem—and in its reputation among the British officers.

Crocker complained bitterly to Eisenhower's aides about the performance of the division and recommended that it be withdrawn from the front for a thorough retraining—by British officers. His complaint was promptly leaked to the press and caused a serious crack in U.S.–British relations.

The Americans could hardly defend the performance of the 34th Division. But they correctly pointed out that Crocker also bore some of the responsibility for the Allied failure at Fondouk Pass by underestimating enemy strength on Rhorab and ordering Ryder to attack with his left flank unprotected.

Eisenhower believed, even after the war, that Crocker had complained directly to the press and caused "definite British-American recrimination." "Nothing," Eisenhower wrote in his memoirs about this incident, "creates trouble between allies so often or so easily as unnecessary talk—particularly when it belittles one of them. A family squabble is always exaggerated beyond its true importance."

Crocker, while not denying that he had had some caustic things to say about the 34th Division's performance, explained after the war that what he had to say was said to officers from Eisenhower's headquarters and that it was they who had passed his remarks on to American reporters.

For Allied leaders, the failure to disrupt the enemy's retreat toward Tunis was a serious disappointment. A success here would have stopped the clock and hurried the Allied victory in Tunisia. The failure to win the race to Kairouan meant the clock was still ticking and the chance for a landing in Sicily this year was still in doubt.

There was, however, a brighter side to the outcome of the battles at Fondouk Pass. Despite the friction between the Allies, the severe losses in the two battles, and the questionable performance of the 34th Division, the battles can, in retrospect, be seen as a turning point in the war. The Allies were, for the first time, operating on the enemy's side of the Eastern Dorsal and, perhaps most important, the Americans had, in a few bloody days, learned a great deal about how to fight a war.

As soon as the fighting ended, Ryder and his division moved back into a bivouac area near the town of Maktar. There, under their own officers, not the British, they began training intensively to overcome some of the shortcomings that had become so obvious in the two battles at Fondouk. In the next few days, they practiced working closely with tanks, following no more than 200 yards behind an artillery barrage, and patrolling aggressively at night. Special training was given to junior officers to teach them how to keep their men moving in an attack rather than let them hunker down and dig foxholes.

What the division had to do was quite clear. What was not so clear was whether this division, having been battered at Sidi Bou Zid and Fondouk, could ever be ready in time to be trusted to take part in the final battles for Tunisia.

19

Gaining the Upper Hand
in the Air

When the 33rd Fighter Group returned to action in early March after a rest of about three weeks, it was stationed at Bertaux, a small town southwest of Constantine in Algeria, more than 100 miles from the Tunisian border and even farther from the enemy, or the "bomb line," as the aviators marked the division between friendly and unfriendly forces.

The author of the war diary of the 60th Fighter Squadron was ecstatic about their new home:

> Great joy prevails! This area is the best that we have had since arriving overseas. A separate area for the men and for the officers has been established. We have now almost enough pyramidal tents for all the men to sleep in. There are grassy spots throughout the location, making it most pleasant to lie on and to walk in.

The pilots arrived in new planes. They had been hoping to be equipped with the new P-51 Mustang. Instead, they were provided with a later model of their old familiar P-40 Warhawk. For a few days, the pilots flew missions escorting the B-25 bombers also stationed at Bertaux or made long sweeps out over the Mediterranean looking for enemy aircraft or shipping. They saw a few enemy fighters, usually at a great distance. The field, far behind the lines, was spared the constant bomber and strafing attacks that had plagued them at Thélepte. Except for the frequent drenching rains that signaled the coming of spring, it seemed an almost idyllic way to fight a war.

And then, in mid-March, after only a few days at Bertaux, came orders to move. The ground crews were loaded into trucks and taken first to Thélepte. But instead of moving back into their old familiar dugouts, they continued on to the north to Sbeitla, where they were assigned to Sbeitla Number 2, nicknamed "Martha" by Spike Momyer, the group commander. This put the group once again, as it had been at Thélepte, at the American airbase closest to the enemy.

When the men arrived and set up their camp across the road from the landing strip, the field was still littered with the wreckage of planes left behind by the Germans who had used the field after their victory at Sidi Bou Zid. Engineers were still combing the field for the hundreds of mines planted by the enemy as they prepared to pull back onto the Eastern Dorsal.

Brigadier General D. A. Davison, an engineering officer, found that it was relatively easy to determine the pattern and draw a map of the mines laid by the methodical Germans. His men could then crawl across the area, removing one mine after another.

But after spending eight hours removing 1,788 mines from one field, he decided that if it took that long to clear a German field, it wasn't worth the effort: it was quicker to simply set his bulldozers to work carving out a new field. In fact, his men built five fields in the Sbeitla area in 72 hours.

Late on March 21, their first night at Sbeitla, the ground crews received a frightening reminder that they were back on the front lines. They had just gotten to sleep after their long truck ride from Bertaux when they were awakened and told that the Germans had broken through American lines only 30 miles away and were headed in their direction. They gathered their belongings, lined up gasoline cans to burn what they couldn't carry, and then waited. Finally, word came that there had not been a breakthrough after all.

During the following two days, the pilots flew in their planes from Bertaux. By this time the group, which had taken to calling itself the Nomads, had added a new nickname: "Momyer's Mob" or just "Moe's Mob."

At 9:15 A.M. on March 24, 12 planes from each of the three squadrons took off to escort bombers on an attack on an enemy airbase. As the American planes approached the target, a swarm of ME-109 fighters took off, climbing through the bursts of their own antiaircraft fire to try to repel the attack.

The Americans had the advantage of altitude and speed. In short order, they shot down four of the enemy planes still fighting to gain altitude and air speed. The Americans may also have benefited by the slightly increased maneuverability of their new P-40 Warhawks. Responding to complaints from pilots about the superior performance of the enemy Messerschmitt and Focke-Wulf fighters, the Curtiss engineers had removed two of the six guns from the P-40. They also took out a small gas tank. The pilots complained that this gave them less range and less firepower, but it also made them lighter and more maneuverable.

As the Americans finished their bombing run and turned toward home, four enemy pilots came right along with them. They were not necessarily very brave or aggressive; they may simply have been unable to extricate themselves from the moving aerial battle. Ground crewmen at Sbeitla stood in their foxholes, spellbound, as the swirling dogfight continued directly overhead. With the Germans added to the Warhawks in the American formation, there were some 40 planes involved in the wild melee in the airspace over Sbeitla.

The men on the ground struggled to tell friend from foe and then to pick out "their" pilots. At one point, they identified the plane of Capt. John M. Bradley, commanding officer of the 58th Squadron, as he struggled to shake off a Messerschmitt on his tail. Then they saw Capt. Charles A. Duncan swing in behind the German and shoot him down.

Lt. Robert Kantner roared over the field with flames streaming back from his burning plane. Instead of trying to land, he zoomed upward to empty his guns in the direction of the enemy planes. Then he banked sharply and came in for a crash landing in an area near the airfield. As the ground crewmen ran to his aid, he stepped out of the plane and then turned back to reach into the cockpit to retrieve his maps and helmet. He got away just before the plane exploded.

As the raid and dogfight of March 24 demonstrate, the new phase of the air war in which the group was now engaged was markedly different from the earlier phase in the nearly two months at Thélepte.

The most obvious difference was the sheer volume of air power the Americans were now able to put into the fight. No longer were the group's pilots sent off on lonely two-plane forays into enemy territory. No longer did they have to assume, each time they took off, that they would be outnumbered by the enemy. Now, with a dozen planes from each of the three squadrons, it was routine to send out imposing 36-plane formations. Sometimes, rather than flying in the familiar "V" formation, they flew in a long line abreast. This prevented the enemy from picking off the last man at the end of the "V." It also made it possible to swing the entire formation to face an attack, bringing the devastating power of 144 50-caliber machine guns to bear on the threat.

The targets, too, were now different. Instead of providing direct support for troops in contact with the enemy on the ground, most of the effort was now directed at two kinds of targets: the enemy's air power, preferably on the ground but also in the air; and the enemy's tanks and troops before they reached the battlefield. This reflected the strong opinion of Air Marshal "Mary" Coningham, the New Zealander who had commanded the Royal Air Force contingent during Montgomery's march from El Alamein into Tunisia and who was now in charge of tactical air and ground support operations under Eisenhower. It also reflected a policy change within the U.S. Army.

Providing maximum effective air support for the ground forces, Coningham said, "can only be achieved by fighting for and obtaining a high measure of air supremacy in the theater of operations. As a result of success in this air fighting our land forces will be enabled to operate virtually unhindered by enemy air attack and our air forces will be given increased freedom to assist in the actual battle area and in attacks against objectives in rear . . . "

At the same time, the American army was in the process of putting together a new field manual spelling out the relationship between air and ground commanders. It said exactly what the air arm had long argued:

> Land power and air power are coequal and interdependent forces; neither is an auxiliary of the other. The gaining of air superiority is the first requirement for the success of any major land operation. . . . Land forces operating without air superiority must take such excessive security measures against hostile air attack that their mobility and ability to defeat the enemy land forces are greatly reduced. Therefore, air forces must be employed primarily against the enemy's air forces until air superiority is obtained. . . . The inherent flexibility of air power is its greatest asset. . . . Control of available air power must be centralized and command must be exercised through the air force commander if this inherent flexibility and ability to deliver a decisive blow are to be fully exploited.

This meant, of course, that a ground commander could no longer hope to have airplanes standing by to come to his aid, to act, in effect, as airborne artillery. It meant that ground troops under attack from the air were on their own and could not expect to see friendly aircraft coming to drive off the enemy.

As these new policies took effect and the airmen flew raid after raid at enemy air bases, troops on the ground were taking a beating from the still-numerous enemy planes.

On April 1, while the fighting on the ground near El Guettar was at its height, a dozen Stukas bombed a frontline command post where General Bradley and Patton's aide, Capt. Richard Jenson, were checking out the situation. One of the bombs fell next to a trench where Jenson had taken shelter and killed him.

Patton, who was capable of sending men into battle in the certain knowledge that some of them would die, had grown fond of his young aide and took his death very personally. He was moved to tears by the young soldier's death: tears and anger. That afternoon, he wired Coningham's headquarters to complain of the lack of friendly air support, and the situation report for the day, sent out over Patton's name, enlarged on his complaint:

> Forward troops have been continuously bombed all morning. Total lack of air cover for our units has allowed German air force to operate almost at will. Enemy aircraft have bombed all division CPs and concentrated on units supporting the main effort.

Coningham was outraged and replied in a message that he broadcast to every senior commander in the Mediterranean theater:

> It is to be assumed that intention was not to stampede local American air command into purely defensive action. It is also assumed that there was no intention to adopt discredited practice of using air force as an alibi for lack of success on ground. If sitrep is in earnest and balanced against facts . . . it can only be assumed that II Corps personnel concerned are not battle worthy in terms of present operations.
>
>   In view of outstandingly efficient and successful work of American air command concerned, it is requested that such inaccurate and exaggerated reports should cease. 12 Air Support Command have been instructed not to allow their brilliant and conscientious air support of II Corps to be affected by this false cry of wolf.

Patton's biographer Carlo D'Este concluded that the affair "might easily have been the nastiest, most potentially damaging Anglo-American quarrel of the war."

Eisenhower, frustrated by the feeling that he could not control his own subordinates, almost resigned as Allied commander. But cool heads on both sides stepped in to tamp down the flames of bitterness.

On April 3, two days after the exchange of messages, Coningham visited Patton's headquarters to find him wearing his helmet and his ivory-handled revolvers, sitting scowling behind his desk. Patton, who had eaten early so he would not have to lunch with the New Zealander, neither stood to greet him nor offered to shake hands.

For a while, both men shouted and pounded on the desk. Finally, Patton demanded that Coningham send a new message retracting his remarks about the battleworthiness of the American troops. Coningham agreed and both men calmed down. Patton even invited him to lunch, they exchanged war stories, and they eventually discovered that they liked each other.

Both men were of course right. The American fliers were hammering away at the enemy—especially enemy air bases—with two or three missions a day. But on many days, the soldiers on the ground saw few if any friendly aircraft as the Stukas screamed down with their sirens blaring. It was understandable if they—and Patton himself—sometimes felt as though they had been abandoned by the air force.

Strangely, however, Patton's outburst came just a day after the planes of the 33rd Fighter Group had fought a series of spectacularly successful dogfights over the El Guettar battlefield.

Momyer led the raid, which involved fighters from his 33rd Fighter Group and a formation of B-26 bombers—a total of some 70 planes. As they approached El Guettar through scattered clouds in late afternoon, they were jumped by 30 or 40 German fighters. The American formation broke up into smaller and smaller units. Finally, individual pilots engaged in one-on-one dogfights.

One German plane got behind Lt. Eugene Grubbs and followed him as he dropped, out of control, toward the ground. Lt. Harold Wilson swung in behind the Messerschmitt and followed him down. He was too late to save Grubbs, but he did manage to shoot down the enemy plane, which crashed into the hills near a German artillery battery.

As Wilson dove, he passed the parachute of a German pilot who had jumped moments before after his plane was hit by Captain Duncan, the flight leader.

In another encounter, Lieutenant Kantner, the survivor of a crash landing a few days earlier, dove on the tail of a

German who was, in turn, behind another Warhawk. Kantner put one burst into the enemy plane, then dove and came up from below for another long burst. The burning plane went into a spin and crashed.

Watching his fuel, Momyer signaled for the Americans to break off and form back up into formation for the flight home.

"The B-26s that we were going to cover had been turned back and as I was starting home with a wingman, I saw this large formation," Momyer recounted later.

> It looked like about 20 airplanes above the mountains. I thought, "The B-26s are still there and there's no escort on them." I started over in that direction and the closer I got, I saw that their landing gear was down. It turned out that they were all Stukas. [The Stuka, which first came into service in the mid-1930s, had a fixed, rather than retractable, landing gear.] The B-26s turned around and the Germans had come in with this formation of Stukas to hit the tank formation that we had. . . . After I made the identify, I told the wingman that we would slide up the back end of the formation and work our way through. So, with that I started out to shoot the Stukas, and I shot four Stukas down real quick. *Bang! Bang!*
>
> In the meantime, the wingman got shot as we were coming in, so I pulled him off and took another shot and then started on back home. I really shot down that day, they think, six or seven or even as high as eight (four were confirmed) because the whole place was littered with them. I'd just sit right back there, from here to that wall and let him have it. . . . You couldn't miss. . . .
>
> I probably should have shot down more, on hindsight, but it was a pretty good day's work. When I got back I nearly ran out of fuel just as I turned into the parking place and it was just beginning to get dark, too. So, I was really lucky that everything lined up that I even got back. In any event, that is what stands out as the most vivid combat mission I flew in World War II.

Late that same afternoon, pilots of the 59th Squadron were sent to strike a concentration of enemy trucks near El Guettar. The unit history notes: "The 59th really hit the jackpot, knocking out at least 50 trucks."

On April 3, four days after the air battle near El Guet-tar—about the time Patton and Coningham were meeting—another American fighter group, flying British Spitfire fight-ers, intercepted a score of Stuka dive bombers, escorted by fighters, near Gafsa. The Americans shot down 14 Stukas to the loss of one Spitfire.

Except on those rare occasions when dogfights took place directly overhead, all ground crew members knew about what air combat was like was what they were told by the pilots. Major Woodworth, the 33rd Group's flight surgeon, was increasingly concerned about symptoms of combat fatigue among the group's pilots. But he didn't really know what it was like for them up there, and he couldn't find out by going along in a P-40 with its single cockpit. So on April 5 he went to a nearby bomber field and bummed a ride on a twin-engine B-25 bomber on an attack on one of the Americans' favorite targets: the German airfield at El Djem, halfway be-tween the coastal cities of Sfax and Sousse.

The 18 bombers climbed to altitude and headed east-ward. As they passed over Sbeitla, Woodworth's home base, he watched as an escort of 36 fighters from the 33rd Group rose to join the bombers. It was the largest formation Wood-worth had ever seen.

As the planes approached the target, the crew members took off their leather helmets and replaced them with metal helmets of the type worn by ground troops. Woodworth had forgotten to bring his, so he had no protection for his head. Standing behind the pilot's armored seat, Woodworth peered through a small window and watched as eight 250-pound bombs dropped from the bomb bay of the neighbor-ing plane.

He pressed his face against the Plexiglas window, trying to see the puffs of smoke as the bombs hit the ground. Sud-denly the window exploded in his face. A piece of shrapnel from an antiaircraft shell had torn through the roof of the plane, grazed the copilot's leg, just missed Woodworth's head, and gone out his window.

The flight surgeon asked the wounded copilot if he could do anything for him. He shook his head, No. There was not much Woodworth could have done, anyway, since he had also forgotten to bring along his medical bag.

The ship shuddered and Woodworth saw a large hole in the cowling of the left engine. The engine stopped, trailing black smoke, as the plane lost airspeed and dropped out of the formation.

Like hunters circling a wounded animal, German fighters made pass after pass at the crippled plane.

But as the bomber, still losing altitude, approached the fighter base at Sbeitla, the enemy fighters turned for home. Woodworth later learned that Major Chase had shot down two of the ME-109s and a second pilot had accounted for another.

The B-25 pilot used the butt of a flare pistol to enlarge the flak hole over his head and fired a flare signaling that the crippled plane was coming in for an emergency landing. With only one engine operating and the pilots fighting to keep lined up with the runway, the plane hit the ground on its right wheel and veered toward a P-40 that was being gassed up. Then it hit a rut that broke off the right wheel, sending the plane into a sideways skid past the fighter plane. As the bomber lurched to a stop, the pilots scrambled through an emergency exit above their heads. Woodworth tried to follow but then had to stop to remove his parachute before he could get out.

Members of the fighter group rushed to the scene of the crash and were surprised to see their shaken flight surgeon emerge from the wreckage. At last he knew what it was like to fly in combat.

James Reed, a pilot in the 58th Squadron, recalls flying two missions on April 7, pounding the enemy ground troops as they retreated toward Tunis. It was his good luck that he was not assigned to the third mission of the day, which ended in disaster. He recalled what happened:

> The mission planners at headquarters were wanting us to go down and strafe after we dropped the bombs. Our commanding officer refused to do this as the risk was too great compared to the damage we could do. I was not on the third mission, but our group was not *asked* to strafe after the bomb run, but was *ordered* to do so. The Italians had stationed armored units on both sides of the road and were just waiting for this stupid move on our part. The end result was that most of our planes were shot up and

came back over the hills in twos and threes instead of
in formation. Some had one landing gear hanging down,
others with oil covering the cockpit. Some of them had to
make crash landings and these planes never flew again.
Besides the lost planes, the 60th Squadron lost four pilots
and the 58th had one pilot missing. This was a case of
someone giving orders who did not know what they were
doing.

Even though victory seemed almost within grasp, such
difficult missions took a heavy emotional toll on the pilots.
The flight surgeon for the 59th Squadron summed up the
situation in a report to Woodworth, the group flight surgeon,
as he left for another assignment:

> At Bertaux, and at Sbeitla in particular, after crowding in
> numerous escort missions during which flak was very heavy
> and German planes were encountered, there were several
> pilots who became reluctant to fly, and one even refused
> to go on a third mission in one day. One developed a
> coarse tremor of the hands and admitted that he would re-
> fuse to fly if he could be exonerated of cowardice. Another
> pilot did refuse to fly and was transferred. After one very
> low altitude bombing mission from Ebba Ksour [where
> the group was stationed late in the conflict] with the worst
> flak ever encountered, many pilots could not sleep and
> kept visualizing flak most of the night during their insom-
> nia. These disturbances have calmed down fairly well now,
> and morale at present is good and strengthened by the
> imminence of victory in Tunisia.

Despite setbacks, in the weeks after returning to the battle line the pilots of the 33rd Fighter Group racked up an impressive series of victories in the air. The group's two leading
aces, Momyer, the group commander, and Levi Chase, the
commander of the 60th Fighter Squadron, set the pace with
multiple victories on several days. Even some of the rookie
pilots, brought in to replace veterans who had gone on to
other assignments, contributed to the string of victories.

Among those who had left were Bent, the old-timer
among the 58th Squadron's pilots. He was assigned to test
and develop tactics for the A-36, a P-51 fighter modified

to serve as a dive bomber. Cochran, still recovering from the fatigue that had gripped him at Thélepte, remained in Morocco and was assigned to train new pilots arriving from the States. He complained that squadrons and entire groups "were coming from the states poorly trained; in fact, they were hardly trained." Some of the pilots had never even fired their guns in the air.

He urged the army—to no avail—to spend more time training pilots in the States. It was foolish, he felt, to send poorly trained pilots to Africa and then ship fuel across the Atlantic so they could complete their training.

One of Cochran's most challenging assignments was to train the black pilots of the 99th Fighter Squadron, known as the Tuskegee Airmen. In the rigidly segregated army of that era, most black soldiers were assigned to support roles such as driving trucks or physical labor. Even though the Union Army had learned in the Civil War, 80 years before, that black soldiers could be highly effective fighting men, the belief persisted in the army of the 1940s that they could not be trusted in combat. It was thus with reluctance that the army agreed, under pressure from civil rights activists in the Roosevelt administration, to set up a special training program for black pilots at the Tuskegee Institute, one of the nation's leading black institutions of higher education.

When the young black pilots arrived in Africa, Cochran found them to be better pilots—better at landing, better at flying formation—than most of the white pilots. But they had had virtually no training in combat flying and even lacked such basic skills as navigation. Cochran found the pilots eager to learn and "a delightful group of guys to be with . . . a lot of fun." But he also found them "the least ready of any that we've ever seen."

Cochran was asked by his boss what should be done with this special group of pilots. To him, it seemed an open-and-shut case:

"Do with them the same way you do with any other kid that came over here in a P-40, any other American fighter pilot. Treat them as though they are replacements, and just put two of them in this experienced outfit, and put two of them in another experienced outfit, and let them come along just like we'd take any youngster, and introduce him into this combat business slowly, and let him get experience by going out with an experienced man. Then get him out and let somebody watch . . . his tail, and explain some things after he gets back on the ground."

Cochran's advice was of course ignored. The black airmen remained a segregated unit and learned about combat the hard way, through experience. Later, flying bomber escort missions out of Italy, the Tuskegee Airmen distinguished themselves as fighter pilots and boasted that they never lost a bomber to enemy fighters.

While the pilots of the 33rd Fighter Group were primarily engaged in the battle against the enemy's air power—strafing and dropping 500-pound bombs on airfields, dogfighting and escorting light and medium bombers—the heavy B-17 and B-24 bombers were carrying on an increasingly powerful campaign against the enemy's ports and other support facilities.

Often flying through heavy flak—on one occasion, medium bombers making a low-level attack on the marshaling yards at Sousse encountered a mile-long "box" of antiaircraft fire— the bombers attacked targets in Tunis, Bizerte, Sousse, and Sfax as well as facilities in Sicily and southern Italy.

One of the most spectacular raids was carried out on March 22 when the bombers hit the Sicilian city of Palermo and caused explosions that devastated 30 acres of docks. The force of the explosions—from the bombs and from ammunition and fuel stockpiles—was so great that it could be felt by air crews flying at 24,000 feet, more than four miles above the city.

Attacks on dock areas on the Tunisian coast were so frequent and so severe that the Germans were forced to avoid the ports and bring in supplies from transport ships by small boats, over the beach.

Even before the crucial battles at Sidi Bou Zid and Kasserine in February, Allied air commanders had begun putting together a plan to knock out the Axis aerial supply chain running from mainland Italy and Sicily to bases in Tunisia. Finally, on April 5, the time was deemed right and orders were given to launch Operation Flax. American and British bombers hit air bases in Sicily and Tunisia while fighters—most of them British—struck at Axis planes already in the air.

At the end of the day, the Allies claimed to have destroyed 201 enemy planes, all but 40 of them on the ground. The Germans admitted that 92 planes had been damaged or destroyed.

Five days later, in a smaller version of Flax, Allied fighters claimed to have knocked down 53 planes, most of them transports, which burst into flames and exploded. Another 26 transports and five fighters were added to the toll the following day.

By this time in the war, British fighters that had accompanied Montgomery in his pursuit of Rommel across Libya and into Tunisia were based at El Djem, the airfield near the coast between Sousse and Sfax that had so often been the target of the 33rd Fighter Group when the field was in German hands. This put the British fighters, guided by seaward-looking radar, in position to attack Axis air traffic in the Tunis area.

On the afternoon of April 18, in what came to be known as the Palm Sunday Massacre, about a hundred German transports managed to land at Tunis. But, as they took off for the flight home, they were hit by the British fighters. The Allies had difficulty counting the number of planes shot down but estimated the total at 50 to 70 transports plus another 16 escorts. The enemy admitted the loss of 51 transports.

To make up for the loss of the transport planes, the Germans turned to sending flights of giant six-engined ME-323 cargo and passenger planes on the perilous run across the Mediterranean. On April 22, the Allies caught a convoy of ME-323s and shot down 21 of them, plus 10 escort fighters.

By the latter part of April, with their aerial bridge from Europe to North Africa shattered and their perimeter around Tunis and Bizerte shrinking, the Luftwaffe was reduced to trying to sneak in flights of emergency supplies by night.

To the men of the 33rd Group, it was increasingly apparent that the fighting was moving rapidly toward a climax. Men made it a habit to stop by the operations shack several times a day to look at the map and see how the "bomb line" had moved, shrinking the area held by the enemy.

On April 12, the Nomads moved once again, this time to
a field still being graded by the engineers at the Berber village of Ebba Ksour, near the town of Le Kef. The pilots
found the skies crowded with Allied fighters and bombers
attacking the fleeing Axis armies. It was a far cry from the
situation only a few months before when the enemy fighters
"owned" the airspace over Tunisia. And on the ground, Allied
forces were moving into position for the climactic battles of
the North African campaign.

The dominance of the air by the Allies in the late winter
and early spring of 1943 was part of the growing Allied
superiority all across the board. American factories—the
"Arsenal of Democracy"—were pouring out a torrent of war
materials. It was not uncommon for a fighter squadron or a
tank battalion to be pulled out of the line for a few days for
every pilot to be issued a brand-new plane and every tank
crew a brand-new tank. Almost always, the new equipment
featured improvements over what it replaced. All along the
front, there were so many more Allied artillery pieces than
there were on the Axis side that some of the soldiers even
began to feel sorry for their adversary.

The near-miracles being worked by the American factories would have had no impact in North Africa, of course, if
the Allies had not been able to deliver the weapons to the
battlefield. But by this time, the American and British navies
were clearly winning the Battle of the Atlantic against the
German submarines, so the flow of weapons from the factories to the battlefields was virtually unimpeded.

20

A Hill Called "609"

In the few days between the end of the battles at Fondouk Pass, where the 34th Infantry Division had been so badly manhandled, and the opening of the final battle for Tunisia, the character of the confrontation changed dramatically.

In the battles further south, at Fondouk, Maknassy, and El Guettar, the Americans confronted a mixture of German troops and Italians, whose reluctance to fight was well known on both sides. In the north, things were entirely different.

Terry Allen, the 1st Infantry Division commander, summed up the situation:

"In Northern Tunisia, the defending forces were made up entirely of the toughest German combat units. They were fighting with their backs to the wall for a final do or die defense. . . . The Germans fought desperately here to defend this final hinge of their entire defensive system. When driven back from here, they were 'kaput.' . . . At El Guettar, the Germans were fighting for *time*. In Northern Tunisia, they were fighting for their very *existence*."

Omar Bradley took over from George Patton as commander of II Corps on April 15 as preparations were being made for what everyone on both sides expected would be the final battle for Tunisia. The only real question was how long it would go on. The change in command was kept secret so the enemy wouldn't know Patton had hurried back to Morocco to prepare for the next phase of the war: the invasion of Sicily. This is the situation confronting Bradley:

The enemy, having successfully slipped off to the north after the Allies' failure to crack through Fondouk Pass in time, formed up in a defensive semicircle swinging from the coast west of Bizerte down south along the mountain ridges and then east to the shore south of Tunis. It was similar to the line set up by the first Axis troops to arrive back in November, and in fact many of the place names were familiar to the Allied soldiers who had been involved in the First Battle for Tunisia in November and December: Green and Bald Hills, Longstop Hill, Chouigui Pass, Mateur, Beja, and Medjez el Bab.

General Alexander and the other British generals thought of the upcoming battle as a confrontation between the British and the Germans, with the Americans playing a supporting role, protecting the British flank while they raced for Tunis. But Patton and Bradley, with Eisenhower's backing, insisted that the American II Corps be given a starring, not a supporting, role—the job of anchoring the northern end of the attack and taking the city of Bizerte. This would not only be good for morale back home, they argued, but would provide the American army with essential on-the-job training for future battles against the Axis. Instead of about half the II Corps, which the British planned to deploy, this would mean committing the entire four-division Corps—the 1st Armored and the 1st, 9th, and 34th Infantry Divisions.

This decision raised a lot of eyebrows. The 34th Division? The division that, at least in the view of the British brass and even some members of Eisenhower's staff, had failed at Fondouk? The division so bad it should be sent far from the fighting for retraining?

It was Bradley who insisted on using the 34th, the Red Bull Division. In his memoirs, he tells of flying to Alexander's headquarters to make his case.

"Give me the division and I'll promise you they take and hold their very first objective. They'll take it if I have to support them with every gun in the corps," he told Alexander.

Eisenhower and Maj. Gen. Omar Bradley toured the battlefield near Bizerte in April 1943. (Source: National Archives)

The British general, a former division commander himself, laughed and replied: "Take them; they're yours."

This gave Bradley and the entire II Corps a key role in the battle. The only problem was that the Americans were all in the wrong place: south of the British, still down where they had been fighting at Fondouk, Maknassy, and El Guettar. Furthermore, the big American supply base was in Tébessa, way back in Algeria. To get the Americans into position to play a central role in Alexander's battle plan, Bradley had to shift four divisions and all of their supporting units—a total of some 100,000 men—about 150 miles to the north, across the lines of British moving eastward for the attack. At the same time, thousands of tons of ammunition, food, and other supplies had to be shifted from Tébessa to the area of Bradley's new headquarters near Beja—again, across the American traffic moving up from the south and the British traffic moving toward the east. And all of this had to be done in a period of less than two weeks.

Here, obviously, were all the ingredients for a world-class traffic jam. The British, with their own long experience moving men and equipment around North Africa, said it couldn't be done. Bradley's transportation experts said it could.

An elaborate system was set up to control the traffic. The troops moved north over several parallel roads, including highways back in Algeria. At some points, traffic going in one direction was halted while traffic moving the other direction had the right of way over the two-lane road. After two hours, the traffic pattern was reversed. At points where one road crossed another, military police controlled the flow, giving the right of way to traffic on one road and then to the other. As the deadline for the attack approached, Bradley ordered the drivers to use their headlights at night. He figured they would lose fewer trucks to enemy air attacks than they would to accidents in the dark. They flicked on their headlights, and the amount of men and supplies being moved increased.

The ability of the Americans to move men, weapons, and supplies was partially the result of a startling buildup in the number of trucks available to do the job. In his memoirs, Eisenhower tells how he complained to Gen. Brehon Somervell, who headed the War Department's supply and procurement branch, about a shortage of trucks. Somervell promised he could begin loading trucks at American ports within three days if the navy would provide an escort for the cargo ships. With a phone call to the navy, Eisenhower arranged for the escorts. Three weeks later, the first of 5,400 trucks began arriving in North African ports.

A couple of days before the attack was to be launched, Bradley was told that all his men and equipment would be in place in time. They had moved twice as much tonnage as the British said they could.

It was not a perfect system. When Ernie Harmon, the new commander of the 1st Armored Division, arrived at Bradley's headquarters near Beja, he was steaming about the delays his tankers had to put up with on the move north. He complained particularly about the British habit of stopping everything for afternoon tea.

Despite the halts for tea, Harmon was there and on time, eager for a fight. Shortly after taking over command of the division from General Ward, he had assembled his officers in a natural amphitheater near Sidi Bou Zid and Djebel Lessouda. The area was still littered with the burned-out hulks of the division's tanks. His thinking still colored by the chaos he had seen as he arrived at the culmination of the battle at the Kasserine Pass, he tore into the officers for the division's earlier failures and promised that things would change. As a signal of his seriousness, he slapped a $50 fine on some 70 officers who arrived late for the formation.

Eisenhower had told Harmon the British 1st Army carried the division on its books as "non-combat ready," and Harmon shared that news with the officers. This is his account of what he told them:

"I just don't believe that. I am confident that the 15,000 officers and men of this division are as good a cross section of fighting men as there is in the army. I don't want to hear any more talk of the defeat at Lessouda. This battlefield no longer is going to be the graveyard of the 1st Armored; it's going to be the symbol of its resurrection."

Many of the officers, with considerable justification, resented what they felt was the critical tone of what came to be known as Harmon's "resurrection speech." The disaster at Sidi Bou Zid, they could rightly argue, was the fault of the generals who had placed them in an impossible situation. And, they felt, it was the division's Combat Command B that held the line at Sbeitla while other units withdrew to the west, and that was largely responsible for turning back Rommel after he cracked through the Kasserine Pass. But many of the officers also had to agree that the still-green division had not done as well as it could have.

Bill Tuck, who had been seriously wounded in the early fighting west of Tunis, had returned to the division by the time of Harmon's speech. He had known and respected Harmon since he served under him in his first assignment as an armor officer. But the speech raised everyone's dander.

"I remember that speech," Tuck recalls. "It made everybody mad and I think it did me at the time. But we needed it. We had our tail between our legs. We needed to get out of the shock of being so badly defeated."

Impatient as Harmon was to go into action, he and his division would have to wait while the infantry cleared the way. The Americans were beginning to absorb the lessons of the earlier battles in Tunisia where tanks, sent onto the field before the enemy's antitank defenses were destroyed, were needlessly sacrificed. The 1st Armored would wait, like a loaded and cocked gun, for the signal to explode through into the enemy's rear.

Bradley put his three infantry divisions on the line. In the north, facing Bald and Green Hills, where the British had been stopped in December, was Manson Eddy's 9th Infantry Division. The division had not distinguished itself at El Guettar, where it failed to take the hills blocking the way toward the coast, but its reputation was relatively intact.

Anchoring the American line on the south was Terry Allen's 1st Infantry Division, which had done a creditable job at El Guettar and had helped turn back Rommel at the Kasserine Pass. Its task now was to drive down the Tine River valley and open the way for Harmon's tanks through a particularly narrow and dangerous area known as the Mousetrap.

In the middle, between the two other divisions, was Ryder's 34th Infantry Division. After two weeks of intensive training designed to repair some of the defects revealed in the fighting at Fondouk, the division was still moving into position near Beja on April 22, just a day before the attack was to kick off.

The men of the 34th Division didn't know what they were getting into as they approached the battle area, but what they saw was well calculated to make them apprehensive. Captain Larry McBride, of the 168th Regiment, recalls traveling through an area where a British reconnaissance unit had been chewed up by the Germans a few days before. He described the scene:

"Sgt. Paul Cavanaugh, my operations sergeant, from Neola, Iowa, was with me when we discovered the remains of a British reconnaissance group, one officer, a sergeant, and a corporal. . . . A round of artillery had dropped directly among them. One was disjointed at the hip sockets and was separated from his legs by some 12 or 15 feet. The officer's head and one leg were missing and a third was a torso completely without limbs or head."

The Americans buried the British soldiers as best they could and erected three crosses, surmounted by bullet-pierced helmets.

Nearby, they found a German tank. Beside it were five neat graves marked by swastikas. Helmets hung on three of them and the other two were marked by the cloth field cap of the Afrika Korps.

"It was a good thing that we did not often approach battle over the remnants of a prior engagement," McBride mused.

Bradley's thought was that by giving the Red Bulls a part in this ultimate battle, he would restore the confidence they had lost at Fondouk and from then on, as he put it, "no one will have to worry any more about the 34th."

At that point, the 34th Division was slated for relatively undemanding on-the-job training. Bradley seems to have thought that the main burden of the attack could be carried out successfully by the more experienced 1st Division while the 34th Division provided one regiment to protect the 1st Division's left flank but otherwise stood by in reserve. This seems to have reflected a flawed understanding of the geography of that portion of Tunisia and a faulty concept of the enemy's defenses. But these errors would not become apparent until several days into the offensive—and at that point the National Guardsmen from the Midwest would be called upon to carry out one of the most difficult assignments given to any unit in the entire war.

As the time for the offensive approached, the Allies concentrated an awesome array of artillery pieces for miles along the front, from Montgomery's 8th Army south of Tunis; through the area where the British 1st Army braced for the attack on Longstop Hill, where they had been stopped in December; along the area manned by the French and behind the American 1st, 34th, and 9th Infantry Divisions.

A British reporter, standing near an artillery position when the attack kicked off at four o'clock on the morning of April 23, described the scene as guns positioned in a long arc all spoke at once: "When the whole 12 miles of guns were firing together, a white flicker like summer lightning ran up and down the valleys and ridges, throwing the high ground into sudden relief, filling the hollows with light. It was as if the hill-waves were really pitching and rolling."

Terry Allen sent his three regiments moving to the east along a six-mile front to attack the Germans dug in on the hills overlooking the Tine River valley. By the end of the second day, several of the hills had been captured after intense fighting, including bayonet charges. In the process, the attack had swung toward the north and the regiment on the left had been squeezed out. This put the 16th Regiment on the left flank of the 1st Division, trying to move to the north to get in behind the enemy positions.

Col. George A. Taylor, commanding the 16th Regiment, said later that no one seemed to have realized the importance of the hill looming on his left: the 2,000-foot-high tower of limestone known as Djebel Tahent or, using the army's metric terminology, Hill 609.

When the importance of Hill 609 was finally realized, the fighting in that area had already been going on for two days. Taylor, even though he had inadequate maps and could not obtain an aerial photo of the area, assured Allen he could take the hill if he were given the troops. But there was an imaginary line along the slope of the hill that divided the 1st and 34th Divisions. Taylor was told to attack one of the lower hills, while the 34th Division was ordered to take Hill 609 and clear the way for the advance to the east.

It was not until April 26, three days after the big offensive had begun, that the bulk of the 34th Division moved up to begin its attack. From what the GIs could see, Hill 609 appeared to be a single massive mountain. Its sheer sides made it seem almost impregnable. What they could see, however, was the least of the challenge they faced.

Djebel Tahent was not only Hill 609. As the officers' maps showed, Hill 609 was just the highest point. Surrounding it were Hills 350, 400, 407, 473, 490, 523, 531, 545, and 575, each surrounded by a cluster of smaller hills. All these hills were in a football-shaped area about nine miles east to west and five miles north to south, with Hill 609 itself near the center. Unlike the widely separated hills on which the members of the 34th Division had been placed near Sidi Bou Zid, these were all close enough so that enemy troops

Hill 609 posed a formidable obstacle as the 34th Infantry Division attacked in the final stages of the fighting in Tunisia. (Source: National Archives)

on one hill could fire on anyone trying to take one of the neighboring hills. Dug in on those hills were Afrika Korps veterans plus members of two elite units: the Hermann Goering Division—a Luftwaffe infantry outfit that took its name from Hitler's obese, strutting field marshal—and the Barenthin Regiment, described by an American officer as "easily one of the finest fighting organizations that I ever saw."

The Germans had turned this whole jumble of hills into an intricately connected defensive complex. Machine gun nests, carved out of the rock with explosives and jackhammers, covered each line of approach. Mines lay hidden, thick along all the roads and trails. Distant guns waited to fire airburst artillery at any troops trying to take the hills. Even nature seemed to conspire with the enemy, providing an ancient earthquake fault to hide men and supplies moving into the defensive positions.

Today it is possible to drive on a winding road almost all the way to the top of Hill 609. The final few yards to the top are blocked by work at a quarry. From a vantage point just below the top, it is obvious why this was such an important

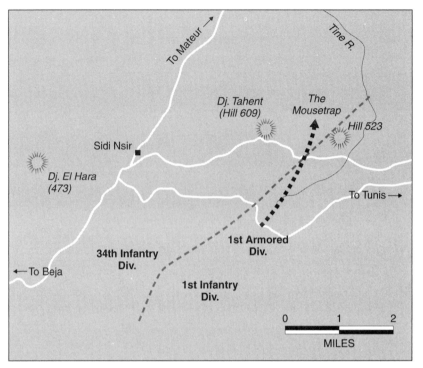

The 34th Infantry Division was given another chance by Maj. Gen.
Omar Bradley and succeeded in driving the Germans out of their
positions on the rocky crags of Hill 609 early in May. The 1st
Infantry Division fought along the southern slopes of the hill and
suffered the loss of an entire battalion before the two divisions
opened the way for a thrust to the east by the 1st Armored Division.

strategic point. German observers up there could see every
movement of American troops and weapons for miles in any
direction.

The line between the 1st and 34th Divisions, lying along
the southern slope of Djebel Tahent, was drawn before the
crucial significance of Hill 609 was realized. This created the
same kind of situation that had caused so much trouble at
Fondouk, where the attacking Americans suffered from mur-
derous crossfire from a hill in the British sector. In this case,
while Hill 609 itself fell in the 34th Division sector, several
hills that formed part of the interlocking German defensive
structure were in the area assigned to the 1st Division. At
best, coordinating the actions of two divisions is difficult.

In this situation, if anything went wrong—which it probably would—the result could be disastrous.

The 34th Division went into action on April 26 with a series of attacks on hills commanding the approaches to Hill 609. First came a battalion-sized attack on el Hara (Hill 473), a hill more than four miles west of Hill 609. The defenses were too strong, and that attack failed.

As this became apparent, Major Ed Bird, the commander of the 168th Regiment's second battalion, was ordered to throw his unit into a new attack that night.

On the afternoon of April 26, Bird and his company commanders huddled on another hill where they had a good view of el Hara. Bird outlined his plan: The battalion would move on the hill at night, avoiding the valleys where mines had helped break up the attack earlier in the day. Before daylight, he planned to have his troops "hard up against" the enemy before being discovered.

"If we aren't in those hills by daylight, right in among them, we'll be pounded all day long and there won't be much we can do about it," he warned.

At dusk, the men snaked out into the dark, each wearing a piece of white cloth on the back of his helmet to help guide the man behind him. They walked for most of the night, stumbling and cursing down a rock slope, across an open area, across a small stream, and then up the slope of el Hara.

As the first faint light of the new day began to brighten the eastern horizon, Bird concluded that he was just where he wanted to be: right in among them. An enemy machine gun opened up. Then another and a third.

The commander of the lead company stood up and shouted: "All right, guys, up and at 'em! Don't let a little machine gun fire stop you!"

Bird called in artillery, but the machine guns continued to fire. The attack faltered and then stopped. The men dropped to the ground, squirming into any depression that offered shelter from the bullets and fragments of exploding artillery shells.

Bird crawled to a point where he could see the Germans a short distance away. Again he called in artillery, this time pinpointing the enemy machine gun nests. Several of them were knocked out, but continuing the attack seemed fool-hardy. Two companies were ordered to keep the enemy occu-pied while a third was sent around to attack from a different direction.

When they signaled they were in position, artillery was directed at the very top of el Hara. The two companies who had been holding the enemy's attention charged forward while the third company, coming from an unexpected direction, caught the defenders by surprise. Late in the afternoon, the Americans were in possession of el Hara.

Before dark, Bird sent one of his companies to pursue the Germans and drive them off a neighboring hill. By the end of the day on April 27, the western approaches to Djebel Tahent were in American hands. But the bulk of Hill 609 was still several miles away, and the enemy still held it.

During the night, members of the battalion worked their way over the area of the day's fighting, bringing in the wounded and marking the locations of the dead by stick-ing each man's bayoneted rifle into the ground next to his body. One of the saddest notes was the death of Sgt. Lyle "Wimpey" Stephens. He was one of three Stephens brothers from Iowa who were members of A Company. His younger brother, Maurice H. "Morry" Stephens, was killed on April 1 during the fighting for Fondouk Pass. The third brother, Burdette, was transferred to a safer rear-echelon job and survived the war.

A similar situation provided the framework for Steven Spielberg's 1998 movie *Saving Private Ryan*. In the movie, Tom Hanks portrays an infantry captain who is sent, with seven men, to find, and remove from combat, a paratrooper whose three brothers have recently been killed in action.

About the same time Bird and his men of the 168th Reg-iment were preparing for their assault on the evening of April 26, men of the division's 135th Regiment gathered in the shadow of a hill about two miles southwest of Hill 609. They were excited and eager to go when they heard what a German deserter had to say about the defenses of Hill 609: It was held only lightly by disloyal German troops and could be stormed easily by about fifty men.

The report was apparently taken at face value at division headquarters. The regiment was ordered to attack in the dark that night, seize Hill 609, and then proceed to the north as fast as possible. The attacking force would consist of two battalions—twice the size of Bird's operation—with a third battalion in reserve. Relying on the report that Hill 609 was only lightly held, a single company was assigned to take the hill, laying a strip of engineer's tape to guide the units coming behind.

Almost as soon as the men set off about 7:00 P.M., it become obvious that the order to seize Hill 609 and quickly move on was, to put it charitably, overambitious. Stumbling through the darkness burdened by weapons and ammunition, they found the way blocked by rocks so large that one man would have to scramble to the top so others could hand equipment up to him before they could move on. Several men fell, breaking arms and legs.

When the lead company stopped about 5:00 A.M. on April 27, it was still more than a mile from Hill 609 and obviously too late to make a nighttime attack on the hill mass.

During the day, the company moved into a depression on a neighboring hill. Enemy observers up on the high ground spotted them. Not only did the unit come under enemy artillery fire, but the explosion of the shells in the confined area echoed and re-echoed off the rocks. Several soldiers suffered from concussion, and one was reported to have "gone crazy" because of the shelling.

Off to the north, Hill 609 loomed, still in enemy hands. But between the men of the 135th Regiment and their goal they found an imposing obstacle. Major Arnold N. Brandt, who was a company commander during the operation, later described what they saw:

"Hill 531 was a rock formation with jagged cliffs and crevasses. It was a huge fortress blocking all approaches to Hill 609. The slopes facing the 1st Battalion were steep except for a gradual slope in the center. This hill was in turn covered from the northeast by two slightly smaller but just as rugged hills . . . rising from the base of 609. In order to reach or flank Hill 609, these surrounding key fortresses would have to be eliminated."

On the following day, April 28, one battalion of the 135th Regiment succeeded in taking that imposing fortress, Hill 531, while another battalion took a key hill to the northwest.

Hill 609 itself remained tantalizingly close, but still in enemy hands.

Frustrated by the failure of the 34th to clear the enemy from his flank, Allen called off all attacks by his 1st Infantry Division on the 28th. That night, he and Ryder, commander of the 34th Division, made plans for a new, coordinated attack on the following day.

At 5:00 A.M. on April 29, the two divisions launched an attack from the north, south, and west, seeking not only to capture Hill 609 but to get around behind it to isolate the defenders and prevent reinforcements and supplies from reaching them. Bird and his battalion of the 168th Infantry were moved south from the hills they had taken two days earlier and were sent looping around Hill 609, moving from the west to the south and then to the east of the big hill.

At the same time, the 34th Division's 133rd Regiment attacked north of Hill 609, seeking to swing around behind the hill to meet Bird and his men. But this time, something new was added to the occasion. Desperate to end the delays and seize the hill, Ryder sent tanks with the 133rd Regiment, rumbling up the hills where no one ever expected to see tanks. The German defenses began to crumble as the tanks, from Harmon's 1st Armored Division, blasted out the dug-in gun positions.

On the afternoon of April 29, General Allen came to the command post of Colonel Taylor, commander of his 16th Regiment. He pointed on the map to Hill 523, more than a mile to the *east* of Hill 609, far out in enemy territory. That hill, he told Taylor, was the key to the enemy's defense of Hill 609: Take it and the 34th Division would be able to take Hill 609.

Taylor protested. His whole regiment was already fighting in a three-ring circus, he told Allen, and he had no reserves if anything went wrong. One of his battalions had already tried to take Hill 523 during the day and had been thrown back, he explained. Allen ordered him to try again that night.

Lieutenant Colonel Charles A. Denholm, commander of Taylor's 1st Battalion, got the assignment for a night attack. He, too, protested, but was told he had no choice.

Denholm led his men through a wheat field right up to the base of Hill 523. Although the brass thought Denholm would make a bayonet charge, that was not his style. Instead, he ordered his leading troops not to shoot until the enemy saw them and opened fire. "When the firing started, I arranged for the companies at the bottom of the hill to yell, fire into the air, and charge on signal. This action had the desired effect and the Germans pulled out at this sign of force. I do not believe in bayonets."

The Americans swept to the top of this key hill, blocking the enemy's access to its units on Hill 609. Denholm and his men quickly prepared for a counterattack. The hilltop was solid stone, so they had to erect parapets of rocks rather than digging foxholes. They then moved off even further east, trying to link up to a neighboring hill. But they found their way blocked by a crack in the earth that was too wide to jump and too sheer and too high to be climbed. This was the earthquake fault that had provided a sheltered path for the enemy moving up to Hill 609.

Hill 523 was too important to the Germans for them to permit the Americans to remain there. At dawn, enemy artillery, including fire from a captured American self-propelled gun, began to hammer the hilltop, cutting the telephone line connecting the unit to the rear and eventually knocking out all the battalion radios. The only link with Taylor's command post was by courier.

During the day on April 30, a thousand members of the Hermann Goering division, who had just arrived and were supposed to go to the front facing the British, were rushed in for an attempt to retake Hill 523. Their attack came from two directions and they were soon on top of the hill, where a wild free-for-all ensued.

Ed Paige, a 1st Division rifleman, was manning the phones at the regimental headquarters when Bradley arrived in a jeep to get a firsthand report on the situation. Paige later recorded the scene:

"The atmosphere around the CP was like a wake. Everyone was tired, dispirited and discouraged. There wasn't even a place for the general to sit. . . . With shock and some confusion I found myself in the middle of taking a message over the phone and sliding over to make room for the corps commander. . . .

"Captain Plitt, the S-3 [operations officer], set up his operations easel and proceeded to brief General Bradley. Any high hopes that the general was going to say something dramatic were soon dashed. The exchange went something like this:

"General Bradley: What about your regimental reserve?

"S-3: We committed that last week, sir.

"Gen. B.: What about the division reserve?

"S-3: That went to the 18th Infantry.

"Gen. B: Umm. What about the ten tanks we sent you yesterday?

"S-3: Two hit mines; three knocked out by direct fire; three by artillery fire; one lost a tread and the last one is pinned down.

"Gen. B: Umm.

"S-3: Couldn't the 34th provide some assistance?

"Gen. B: They are fully committed to taking Hill 609.

"S-3: We're going to lose that battalion shortly if something isn't done.

"Gen. B: Is there no way to withdraw them so they can regroup?

"S-3: They are totally pinned down and cut off.

"The general squirmed, rubbing his elbow into my ribs. I was tight up against a staff officer on my left and couldn't move.

"Gen. B: Umm. The only thing we can do is to await some development that might relieve the situation."

Allen did manage to obtain a company of tanks from the 1st Armored Division and send them to the rescue. But by the time the tanks arrived and drove the Germans from the summit, Denholm and about 150 of his men had been captured. The rest had been killed. The 1st Infantry Division had lost an entire battalion, and both sides were so bloodied by the fighting that neither had enough men to hold the hilltop.

While Denholm's men were fighting desperately, and finally, unsuccessfully, to hold Hill 523, the 34th Division was at last closing in on Hill 609.

This is the wall of rock that infantrymen of the 34th Infantry Division faced as they made their final assault on Hill 609.
(Source: National Archives)

On April 30, Bird's battalion managed to get around behind the hill and connect up with the infantry of the 133rd Regiment coming around from the north, accompanied by tanks. This put them athwart a water course that the enemy had used to resupply the defenders on Hill 609, thus cutting them off from supplies and reinforcements.

One battalion of the 135th Infantry Regiment got up close to the crest of Hill 609 on April 30. But then the battalion commander made the mistake of pulling back to feed his troops instead of pushing on to the summit. Perhaps he can be forgiven for his restraint: His men had found themselves up against a sheer cliff. German defenders, up above, tied together bundles of their potato-masher grenades—so-called because the grenade had a handle for ease of throwing—and dropped them on the Americans trying to find a way up the cliff.

On the following day, members of the 34th Division's 135th Infantry Regiment finally made it to the top of Hill 609, and all resistance in that area ceased on the following day.

Bradley's gamble on men of the 34th, so recently civilians in Iowa and Minnesota, had paid off, and the division went on to distinguish itself in bitter fighting in Italy. As A. J. Liebling, *The New Yorker* reporter, put it: "Many generals, in the course of history, have taken a hill at the cost of a division, and as many have lost a division without taking a hill. Bradley took a key hill and gained a division."

With the Americans and their French allies pressing in from the west and two British armies applying pressure from the south and west, the stage was set for a final Allied victory in Tunisia.

21

Victory in North Africa

L ate on the afternoon of May 4, Ernie Harmon was sitting on a hilltop near the key crossroads town of Mateur
planning his next move when a British brigadier from the
1st Army arrived to ask about his plans.

Harmon informed him he planned to sit there for another
day and a half while his engineers, infantry, and artillery had
a chance to study the battlefield and prepare for an all-out
attack on May 6.

"You mean you are going to sit here for thirty-six hours
and let the Germans get set in front of you?" the British officer demanded. Harmon told him that was exactly what he
was going to do. He assumed his visitor would hurry back to
his headquarters and try to get him fired. But Bradley arrived
a short time later and assured Harmon, "Whenever you're
ready to attack is okay with me."

Harmon's 1st Armored Division had finally been "unleashed" on May 3 after the 34th Infantry had driven the
enemy off Hill 609. But its advance through the dreaded
"Mousetrap" and into Mateur had been anticlimactic. When
the tankers of General Robinett's Combat Command B
swept into Mateur, they found most of the enemy had abandoned the town. The few remaining enemy soldiers quickly
surrendered.

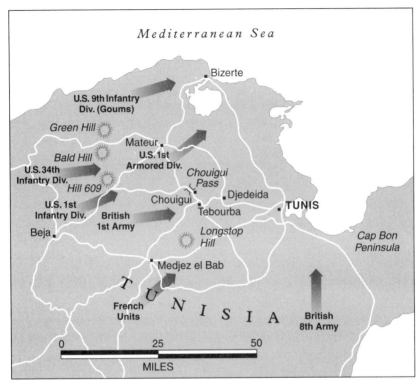

In late April and early May 1943, the buildup of Allied strength, on the ground and in the air, overwhelmed the Axis defenders, who were confined in a narrow strip of land around Tunis and Bizerte and then cut up into smaller fragments and forced to surrender. The fighting ended on May 13, 1943, six months and five days after the landings of Operation Torch, with the surrender of some 275,000 Axis soldiers.

The division's next job—the task Harmon was contemplating when the British officer arrived—was to drive northeast toward the sea, getting between the enemy forces clustered around Tunis and those in the Bizerte area.

In his account of the situation, Harmon makes a plausible case for taking the time to prepare carefully for his next move. The enemy, always skilled at erecting formidable defenses, had stripped the 88 mm antiaircraft guns from Bizerte and set them in the hills between Harmon and the sea in a formidable antitank defense. Even though they had been pushed back toward the coast, there still seemed to be plenty of fight left in the enemy. It did not make sense to rush ahead until you knew exactly what you were doing.

But the British officer's unhappiness with the delay in the attack was also understandable. General Alexander, the 18 Army commander in charge of the entire operation, had assembled four British divisions—two armored and two infantry—on a front less than two miles wide, to the south of the American positions. He was prepared to launch them on the morning of May 5, behind a massive air bombardment, in an attempt to smash right on through into Tunis. Harmon's delay in beginning his offensive meant, in the view of the British, that the enemy would not only have more time to prepare for the American attack but would also be able to concentrate more of their forces to resist the British advance.

Late in the afternoon of May 5 Harmon called his key officers together. By this time, the British had begun their offensive and were involved in a furious fight for the town of Massicault, which lay between their jump-off point at Medjez el Bab and Tunis. Harmon's plan called for Combat Command A to strike at the higher hills on the left. Combat Command B would take the lower hills on the right. Infantry would go straight up the road toward the northeast.

After the meeting, Paul Robinett, commander of Combat Command B, was returning to his command post when he and his driver were, as he later put it, "shot out of our peep," which the familiar jeep was still known as at that stage in the war. Robinett, who had been fighting almost constantly from the first encounter with the Germans in November until this final battle, suffered a severe wound to his left leg.

When Harmon visited him that evening, it was obvious to him that Robinett's part in the war as a fighting man was over. Colonel Benson, who had commanded a tank force in some of the bitterest fighting at El Guettar a few weeks earlier, took over Robinett's command.

Early the next morning, May 6, Harmon watched the battle unfold from his command post. The forces on the left moved ahead steadily and soon captured the high ground that was their objective. But the picture on the right was much less encouraging. Benson was far short of his objective, and 23 of his tanks were burning on the hillside.

Henry Gardiner, the battalion commander who had been shot out of his tank while protecting the Allied retreat from Sbeitla in February, again bailed out of his burning tank. He was first feared lost. But though wounded, he later rejoined his unit.

Harmon called Benson and his executive officer, Lt. Col. Hamilton H. Howze, to his command post. Harmon was an aggressive commander, but he could also be impulsive. When the division's advance guard had entered Mateur a few days earlier, the men had "liberated" a wine cellar and proceeded to get drunk. Harmon ordered them all to be shot. An aide delayed the execution until the next morning, by which time Harmon had cooled down enough to let the men off with a reprimand.

When Benson explained that his attack had bogged down because his men were tired, Harmon exploded:

"They can't be worn out. They've only been fighting for two or three hours. *You* must be worn out! You are relieved of command! Go back and sleep in the tent there."

He asked Howze what had gone wrong. Howze explained that they were blocked by a concentration of enemy antitank guns. Harmon put Howze in charge and told him to delay the attack until he had called in an artillery barrage on the enemy's guns. When the barrage lifted, Howze's tanks roared through the area that had been covered by the enemy guns and churned to the top of the hill.

But the tankers of Combat Command B had barely taken the objective when they radioed reports that they were receiving artillery fire from the neighboring hill that had been captured at noon by Combat Command A and was presumably still in friendly hands.

While the Americans were capturing the high ground on the right, the enemy had brought in a force of its big Tiger tanks and recaptured the hill on the left. The Americans fought most of the night before they finally reclaimed the hill about 3:00 A.M. and were in position to resume their offensive toward the sea on May 7. The battle to hold that one hill was a stern reminder that they still faced a determined and resourceful enemy.

As soon as Hill 609 had been seized, Bradley ordered the 1st and 34th Infantry Divisions to, in effect, change positions. He was concerned about the condition of General Allen's 1st Division, which had endured a week of hard fighting and had, in a single battle, lost an entire battalion. He ordered General Ryder to move his division over to the south side of the 1st Division and capture the Chouigui Pass, lying southwest of Mateur. As long as the enemy held the pass, he could move men and equipment between the forces opposing the Americans and those opposing the British and French forces driving northeast toward Tunis.

Allen and his division were ordered to assemble in an area near the pass and remain there on the defensive. With the enemy pulling back to a new line, the 34th Division quickly took its objective. From the pass, the troops could look off over the flat land stretching toward Tunis. They were sorely tempted to keep right on going. But the area they could see was in the British sector, and Ryder properly resisted the temptation to go charging off toward Tunis.

But Allen, who had a tendency to fight his own little war, was not content to remain on the defense while he could hear the guns of battle nearby. On May 6, he attacked into the Chouigui foothills and was thrown back with heavy losses. An irritated Bradley complained: "The gesture was a foolish one and undertaken without authorization."

While the 1st Armored Division and the 1st and 34th Infantry Divisions were busy in the southern section of the area assigned to the Americans, the fighting in the north fell to General Eddy's 9th Infantry Division. It was accompanied in its drive toward Bizerte by members of the Corps d'Afrique. This was a French unit made up of men who, for one reason or another, had been rejected when they tried to join the regular French army to fight the Germans. There were Jews, a Spanish doctor, and officers who had, in the view of their

Major General Manton S. Eddy, commander of the 9th Infantry
Division, enters the city of Bizerte after its capture by his troops.
(Source: National Archives)

former colleagues, "disgraced" themselves by trying to aid
the invading Allies back in November.

Added to this poorly armed but determined little army
were two tabors, or battalions, of Moroccan soldiers, Berber-
speaking natives of the mountains of Morocco who rode
sure-footed mules or horses. Each of their companies was
called a *goumier*, and the Americans referred to the men
themselves as Goums.

The Americans and their Corps d'Afrique and Goum
allies were confronted by Bald and Green Hills, the same
barrier that had blocked the British back in November and
December. Instead of trying to attack the hills directly—an
attempt that had resulted in disaster six months earlier—
Eddy sent his forces around the two hills.

This was, for the soldiers involved, some of the most
miserable work of the entire campaign. To get around Bald
and Green Hills, they had to work their way cross-country
through thick, five-foot-high brush. There were no roads, so
their supplies were brought forward on mules to the "mule-

head" and then carried by the soldiers. As they struggled under their loads, they marveled at how the Goums seemed to move almost effortlessly through the brush.

Progress was, understandably, slow. But the pressure paid off. Early in May, as they lost their hold on Hill 609, the enemy pulled back into new defensive positions, permitting the Allies to move forward on the offensive all along the line. Bradley urged the 9th Division to hurry on into Bizerte despite mines in the roads. He wanted them to prevent the enemy from destroying the docks and other facilities even though, as a British reporter noted, "the port, and the small town close round it, were as bomb shattered as any town has been in this war."

A tank destroyer unit entered the city at 4:15 P.M. on May 7. Together, tanks and infantry worked their way through, digging out or blasting snipers and antitank guns. They found Bizerte a largely deserted city, with few residents remaining to welcome them, most of them having fled to nearby towns or to Tunis. Most of the enemy soldiers had retreated back across a wide ship canal that runs from the Mediterranean into Lac du Bizerte, from which vantage point they continued to fire their artillery down the east–west streets.

The formal Allied entry into the city was delayed until the next day to give the French the honor of taking Bizerte. But the fall of the city—or at least the area on the west side of the ship canal—did not signal an end to the fighting.

On May 8, Colonel Benson, by now restored to command of Combat Command B, ordered Howze to form a 40-tank task force and surge forward to cut the road along the coast between Tunis and Bizerte, part of the strategy of cutting up and isolating units of the enemy army. Howze had two choices: take the shorter route across a low, rather swampy area, or go five miles north and make the steep climb over several hills to come in behind the Germans.

Howze chose the hill route. He managed to get his tanks over the hills, emerging on a hillside and catching the enemy completely by surprise. The Americans paused there during

Wrecked German tanks littered the battlefield near Bizerte as heavy fighting continued near the end of April 1943. (Source: National Archives)

the night and watched the fireworks show as the rapidly disintegrating enemy fired off ammunition and burned vehicles. At dawn on May 9, Howze swooped down toward the crossroads and the sea to cut the Tunis–Bizerte link.

Early that same morning, Harmon set off in a jeep for a tour of the front. At one point, he was assured that the area ahead was under American control and he continued down the road. He and his driver suddenly found themselves in the midst of a company of German soldiers huddling in a cut in the road trying to protect themselves from American artillery being directed by a light plane circling overhead. The two Americans jumped from their jeep and joined the enemy soldiers at the side of the road.

As he recounted the incident later, Harmon thought to himself: "Now I've really put my foot into it: a division commander captured by the enemy."

But the Germans apparently realized that for them, the war was over. Harmon and the enemy company commander rode back up the road, where Harmon ordered the artillery

When Allied troops moved into Bizerte, they found it, in the words of a British reporter, "as bomb shattered as any town has been in this war." (Source: National Archives)

to stop shooting and sent infantrymen down to round up the enemy soldiers.

Harmon's account of how he managed to extricate himself after stumbling into the enemy formation is far more modest than the citation, written a month later, recommending him for the Distinguished Service Cross. In that account, the enemy company becomes a battalion and Harmon, rather than coming upon the enemy unit by accident, "crossed through territory still in enemy hands and, with complete disregard for his personal safety . . . accosted a German battalion. . . . " The citation concludes: "His actions were over the call of duty and will long be remembered in the annals of our military history."

While Harmon was busy arranging the surrender of the German company, the German commander in the area between Tunis and Bizerte sent a message to von Arnim saying: "Our armor and artillery have been destroyed; without ammunition and fuel; we shall fight to the last." But half an hour later, at 10:00 A.M. on May 9, emissaries of the German

A grim-faced Col. Gen.
Jurgin von Arnim, com-
mander of the Axis Fifth
Army, was the highest-
ranking German officer
captured in North Africa.
(Source: National Archives)

commander arrived at Harmon's headquarters and asked for
surrender terms. He gave them the official word: "unconditional surrender." Shortly before 1:00 P.M., Harmon received
the surrender of the 10th and 15th Divisions, a total of some
40,000 men.

About the time the 9th Division soldiers were feeling their
way into the largely deserted city of Bizerte, the British were
receiving a quite different reception as they entered the
Le Bardo area in the western suburbs of Tunis. While Tuni-
sians stood expressionless or went about their business,
French residents of the city welcomed the soldiers with flowers and bottles of wine. At some points, enemy soldiers
opened up with rifles or machine guns and were hunted
down, but other Germans simply stood beside their vehicles
and observed the scene.

Allied pilots spotted an Italian ship outside the port at Tunis, apparently seeking to get away across the Mediterranean. What they did not know, as they bombed the ship and drove it back toward the harbor, was that it was loaded with 464 American and British prisoners, including Lieutenant Colonel Denholm and the survivors of his 1st Infantry Division battalion that had been captured on Hill 523 on April 30 during the fierce fighting around Hill 609. Denholm later gave this account of the attack on the ship:

> The ship sailed out of the harbor and anchored between two cliffs for protection while it waited for a German naval escort, which was to arrive the next morning. At daylight we were discovered by Allied airplanes and strafed, and the good word sent back for light bombers to take care of our ship. Our escort and the first flight of bombers arrived concurrently. The bombers took the escort as a better target (a destroyer, I believe) and sank it. Shortly thereafter another flight of bombers arrived and secured sufficient near misses to spring the sides of the ship so that it started leaking.
>
> The ship set sail back to Tunis harbor after the escort was lost and the ship was sinking. En route, we had a third bombing, which put a bomb in the forward hull, and secured several other near misses. As we were entering the harbor we took our fourth bombing; again a lot of near misses.
>
> The Italian crew, at this point, took axes and cut the life boats loose, and jumped in the water after them. . . .
>
> With little crew remaining, the captain beached the ship at La Goullette [at the entrance to the Tunis harbor] and the Germans departed in the one remaining lifeboat. Unfortunately, the ship beached on an even keel so that the planes could not realize it was grounded. At this point the prisoners took over the ship and by the use of red blankets and sheets put red crosses and PW signs topside. The air effort took these as a ruse and continued to bomb the ship hourly for the remainder of the day.

Finally, with the coming of darkness, the air attacks stopped. Several men got ashore to pass the word to the air force that they were bombing a prisoner-of-war ship and to obtain boats to rescue the men on the ship.

MM-VOS-43-1749   171632

Lieutenant Colonel Charles L. Denholm relaxed after his escape
from an Italian prison ship. Denholm and his 1st Infantry Division
battalion were captured during the battle for Hill 609, but he and
other members of his unit escaped after the ship on which they were
being taken to Italy was bombed. (Source: National Archives)

"The ship, we estimated, had received three or more
direct bomb hits and more than 4,000 holes from aircraft
cannon and machine guns," Denholm reported. "However,
only one prisoner was killed and three injured. When we were
ashore, we found the Germans rapidly evacuating Tunis.
Those we met readily surrendered to us."

With the fall of Bizerte and Tunis, the Allies expected the
enemy to follow the pattern set in earlier World War II battles when the situation was reversed and the Allies were on
the losing side.

One possibility was that they would do as the Americans
and Filipinos had done in the Philippines in the winter of
1941–42 when they pulled back into the Bataan Peninsula
and Corregidor Island and continued to resist the Japanese
for five months. The Cap Bon Peninsula, jutting out into the

Mediterranean south of Tunis, offered the kind of rugged terrain where a determined enemy might mount the same kind of last-ditch defense, holding out for months. The other plausible pattern was the withdrawal of the British army from Dunkirk after the German blitzkrieg attack through the Lowlands into France in 1940.

It was quite possible, of course, that the enemy might attempt to combine both a Bataan-type defense with a Dunkirk-style withdrawal. This is exactly what Rommel had contemplated as early as November, within a few days after the Allied landing in Morocco and Algiers. In a detailed plan, he proposed a strategy of retreating into the area around Tunis and then onto the Cap Bon Peninsula, all the while evacuating "increasing numbers of troops by transport aircraft, barges and warships."

"When the Anglo-American forces finally completed their conquest of Tunisia," he wrote, "they were to find nothing, or at the most only a few prisoners, and thus be robbed of the fruits of their victory, just as we had been at Dunkirk."

The British, with their humiliation at Dunkirk still very much in mind, organized what they called Operation Retribution. Its purpose was to prevent the enemy forces from gathering on the peninsula and then escaping to Sicily or mainland Italy.

What the Allies did not expect was what in fact happened: the sudden and total collapse of the Axis armies. As the German and Italian forces were cordoned off and lost contact with each other, the soldiers began to surrender, first by the tens, then the thousands, and then the tens of thousands. Von Arnim surrendered to the British about noon on May 12 after personally setting fire to the command trailer he had inherited from Rommel. The last to give up was Giovanni Messe, commander of the First Italian Army. He surrendered on May 13 as a field marshal—a rank to which he had been promoted just a few hours before. He wasn't braver than the other Axis generals; he was just more picky about whom it was he surrendered to.

Perhaps the Germans and Italians could have holed up on the Cap Bon Peninsula and held out there while withdrawing at least the key specialists, if not the entire army.

As the Allies entered Bizerte, German troops retreated to the thinly populated area on the east side of the canal that divides the city into two halves and continued shelling the built-up area on the west side of the canal. (Source: National Archives)

But Hitler and Mussolini seem to have concluded that this entire force was expendable.

As early as November 28 Rommel flew, without authorization, to Hitler's secret headquarters at Rastenburg in East Prussia and told *der führer:* "Africa cannot be held. The only thing left for us is to try and transport as many Germans out of Africa as we can."

It was not what Hitler wanted to hear.

"The Führer flew into a fury and directed a stream of completely unfounded attacks upon us," Rommel noted in his diary, and added: "I began to realise that Adolf Hitler simply did not want to see the situation as it was, and that he reacted emotionally against what his intelligence must have told him was right."

Hitler ruled out any talk of abandoning Africa and promised to send more men, arms, and supplies. In fact, troops continued to arrive in Africa until the last moment, although they were grievously shortchanged on fuel and other vital supplies.

Mussolini traveled to Germany on April 8 for his annual strategy conference with Hitler at Schloss Klessheim. By that time, he had been forced to give up all hope of hanging onto his North African empire and was increasingly concerned about the collapse of the Axis armies in Africa and the threat of Allied landings in Sicily, Sardinia, and Crete or in southern France or mainland Italy itself. He urged Hitler to make peace with the Soviet Union so the Axis could concentrate on preventing an Allied landing in Europe.

Hitler abruptly dismissed the thought of settling with the Soviets and insisted that Tunisia could be held indefinitely. As long as the fighting there continued, southern Europe would not be in danger, he contended.

This conference sealed the fate of the Axis armies in Africa. Hitler, whose obstinacy had resulted in the loss of the entire Sixth Army at Stalingrad in January, had now set in motion the chain of events that would lead to the loss of another army in North Africa.

If, in the final few weeks, the German and Italian armies had hurried onto the Cap Bon Peninsula and sealed themselves up there, it probably would have already been too late for either a Bataan resistance or a Dunkirk withdrawal. By that time they were, at least in some areas, desperately short of fuel—so desperate that they tried to run some of their vehicles on alcohol derived from wine. And it was reported that von Arnim was able to drive to the point where he surrendered only because his men had found a barrel of fuel washed up on the beach. But other Germans had enough fuel to drive their own trucks to the compounds where they were held after their surrender, and the troops observed by Howze and his men seemed to have plenty of ammunition for their final fireworks display.

The Axis troops' most serious deficiency was in air power, a total reversal of the situation just a few months before when the Messerschmitts, Focke-Wulfs, and Stukas ruled the air. As the Allies closed in during late April, most of the enemy's fighter aircraft were flown to bases in Sicily, where they were too far away to fight in North Africa, but close enough to be destroyed by Allied bombers. Troops attempting to hold out on the Bon Peninsula would thus have suffered from total Allied command of the air. They would also

Some of the Axis prisoners were assembled in this huge prisoner of
war camp south of Bizerte after the fighting ended in May 1943.
(Source: National Archives)

have had great difficulty withdrawing any sizable forces from
the peninsula, again because of the Allied fighter planes.

But a last-ditch resistance could very well have played
havoc with Allied plans for the next phase of the war. If the
Axis forces could have held out for another three months,
until August, it would probably have been too late for the
Allies to land in southern Europe in 1943. They would have
had to wait until the spring of 1944 brought weather suitable for landing on the Mediterranean islands or in Europe.
Perhaps the loss of an army would not have been too high a
price to pay for such a delay. But with the failure to retreat
into the Cap Bon Peninsula bastion in time, and with the
sudden collapse of their army, Hitler and Mussolini lost
both the army and the time they had been fighting for.

Some 275,000 Axis troops were gathered together in
huge prisoner of war compounds and then shipped off to
camps in the southern and western United States. For them,
the war was over. But for the victorious Americans, it was far
from over, although many of them apparently believed that

Soldiers of the 9th Infantry Division, here gathered around a half-track vehicle, were among the first to enter Bizerte as the fighting neared an end. (Source: National Archives)

they would soon be going home. When Eddie Rickenbacker, the legendary World War I ace, visited the 33rd Fighter Group shortly before the Axis collapse, he predicted that the war would go on for more than two additional years, until the fall of 1945. The airmen to whom he spoke thought he was being far too pessimistic, although, as it turned out, he was right on the mark.

Regardless of how long they thought the war would last, it was obvious to the American troops in North Africa that this was only a brief respite and that many of them would soon be back in the front lines. Their choice of recreation took various forms. One unit found a beach west of Bizerte and hundreds of soldiers cavorted in the waves, buck naked.

Men of the 34th Division's 168th Regiment gathered at a camp in the Tine River valley. There they had hot meals, used their helmets to wash and shave, cleaned—with five-gallon cans of gasoline—the dirty, bloody uniforms that were still wearable, and replaced the clothing worn out by weeks of hard fighting with new uniforms.

The division's 135th Regiment, the one that had taken Hill 609, was selected to represent the American army in the victory parade in Tunis on May 20. Marching with naked bayonets attached to their rifles, they came at the end of a parade that featured French Spahis on white Arabian horses and units representing the far-flung British Empire—from New Zealand Maoris and the King's African Rifles from Kenya to Scottish highlanders with their bagpipes.

Battery C of the 34th Division's 151st Field Artillery Battalion was assigned to military police duty in Tunis. Fran Vojta, a member of that unit, recalls one incident that the temporary MPs managed to overlook.

A young woman approached a group of soldiers who had been permitted to visit the city and were camped in a park. After some brief negotiations, the GIs set up a cot in a 6×6 truck and converted it into a bordello. A line quickly formed. After receiving 33 visitors during the afternoon, the woman departed with both money and a bagful of clothing she had received in payment for her services.

As soon as the fighting ended, the 33rd Fighter Group moved to a former German base at Menzel-Temime on the Cap Bon Peninsula. There they joined in the air force's effort to bomb the island of Pantelleria, which lies about a hundred miles west of the peninsula, into submission as proof that air power alone could force the surrender of an enemy strongpoint.

As that effort neared its climax, Momyer took a dozen new flight commanders, new element leaders, and a new wingman over the island. It seemed like a relatively safe, routine training mission. Most of the fliers were far more nervous about venturing far out over the ocean than they were about encountering enemy planes. After all, intelligence reported that most of the Axis fighters had been withdrawn to Sicily and Italy.

Then, suddenly, they were jumped by about 20 enemy fighters. Momyer didn't want to fight. All he wanted to do was to keep his planes together and get home safely.

"We started at about ten thousand feet, and we ended up clear down in the water," he recalled. "I can still see those

20 mm shells breaking all around the water. All I was trying to do was get these guys out of combat and back home safely. How we got home without anybody getting shot down, I think, is remarkable. It certainly wasn't any skill on my part. But I can still see those shells that were breaking all over the water."

The unexpected appearance of enemy fighters in the skies over Pantelleria was a reminder, if any had been needed, that the victory in Africa was not the final act in the war against the Axis but, rather, an elaborate, large-scale rehearsal by the American army of the acts yet to come.

In the six months from the landings on November 8, 1942, to the Axis surrender on May 13, 1943, the Americans had learned a remarkable number of lessons. They had learned how to make an amphibious landing. They had learned how tanks, infantry, and artillery should work together. They had hashed out a new doctrine in which the air force would concentrate first on knocking out the enemy's air power and striking at enemy tanks and troops before they could enter the battlefield. They had identified and promoted the officers and noncoms who had what it took to lead men in combat and pushed aside those who didn't.

Perhaps most surprisingly, they had found northern Tunisia an almost perfect training ground for the coming battles in Italy and northern Europe. Despite the image most of the troops carried in their heads of North Africa as a barren desert, much of Tunisia turned out to be a grassy Sahel, and the northern part of the country, with its fertile valleys and wooded hillsides, would have fit seamlessly into parts of France, Italy, or Germany.

To many American officers the decision to invade North Africa rather than striking directly across the English Channel at the Nazis was a foolishly time-consuming and round-about detour on the way to Berlin. But it is not hard to imagine the disaster that might have awaited if the green and untested American army had been landed on the Normandy

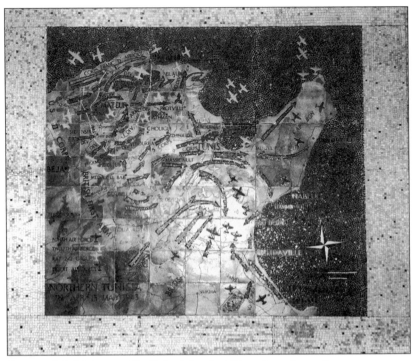

A map, inlaid in a wall of the North Africa American Cemetery, indicates with sweeping arrows the final battles in Tunisia as the Allies seized Tunis and Bizerte and forced the surrender of more than 200,000 Axis troops. (Photo by the author)

beaches in the spring of 1943 rather than waiting until, with the North African experience under its belt, it landed in France on June 6, 1944.

Churchill concluded that without the experience of fighting in North Africa, "the attempt to cross the Channel in 1943 would have led to a bloody defeat of the first magnitude, with measureless reactions upon the result of the war."

The most long-lasting, and probably the most valuable, lesson learned by the Americans in North Africa was how to fight in coalition with other nations. Only twice before—during the Revolutionary War and again in World War I—had the country been involved in coalition warfare, and in both cases the nation emerged with a deep-seated aversion to such cooperation. In North Africa, the Americans not only made their coalition with the French and British work, but began

1941 – 1945

IN PROUD REMEMBRANCE

OF THE ACHIEVEMENTS OF HER SONS

AND IN HUMBLE TRIBUTE

TO THEIR SACRIFICES

THIS MEMORIAL HAS BEEN ERECTED

BY THE

UNITED STATES OF AMERICA

A simple dedication, engraved on a wall of the North Africa American Cemetery, memorializes the Americans who lost their lives in World War II. (Photo by the author)

to see this as the right way to fight a war. This set the pattern for cooperation with allies in the North Atlantic Treaty Organization all through the Cold War, and in Korea, Vietnam, the Gulf War, the fight for Kosovo, and the war on terrorism.

With the North African experience behind them and with many of their leaders tested in that campaign, the Allies landed in Sicily on July 10, 1943, less than two months after the Axis collapse in Africa. That landing might have come several months earlier if the Allies had won the initial race for control of Tunisia. But delaying the Allies by those few months hardly justified Hitler's sacrifice of his North African army.

The Americans and British crossed over to mainland Italy on August 3, thus taking the fight to the European mainland. The Normandy invasion in June 1944 was followed by the Allied landings in southern France on August 15, 1944. Italy surrendered five weeks after the invasion in 1943, and the war against Germany ended two years after the victory in Tunisia, on May 10, 1945.

It is no exaggeration to say that were it not for the North African campaign, the war in Europe would have been longer and bloodier than it was and that its outcome might have been far less favorable to the Allies than it was.

A visitor to the quiet, sun-splashed cemetery at Tunis can surely agree that something very important happened here on Africa's northern coast in the last weeks of 1942 and the first few months of 1943.

A Note on Sources

For any student of the American part in the North African campaign in World War II, the essential starting point is George F. Howe's *Northwest Africa: Seizing the Initiative in the West* (Washington, D.C.: Center of Military History, U.S. Army, 1993). Fortunately, his masterful history of the six-month campaign, written shortly after the war, was reissued by the Government Printing Office in 1993 as part of the fiftieth anniversary of World War II and is now available, complete with an envelope containing detailed maps of the various landings and battlefields of the campaign.

Howe's research notes are on file at the National Archives in College Park, Maryland. These papers include voluminous correspondence with participants in the North African campaign, much of it concerned with clarifying conflicting accounts of what happened at certain points during the campaign.

For the landings themselves, Samuel Eliot Morison's *Operations in North African Waters: October 1942–June 1943* (Boston: Little Brown, 1947) is a useful complement to Howe's account of the campaign. The U.S. Navy's role in the campaign was, however, brief. After the initial landings, the navy was not involved in the subsequent battles except for the operations of a small group of torpedo boats. Morison was present at the landings and had the advantage of being an eyewitness to some of the events he describes.

The operations of the German submarines opposing the landings are described in great detail in Clay Blair, *Hitler's U-Boat War: The Hunted 1942–1945* (New York: Random House, 1998).

Air operations are covered, in broad detail, in W. F. Craven and J. L. Cate, eds., *The Army Air Forces in World War II: Europe—Torch to Pointblank, August 1942 to December 1943* (Washington, D.C.: U.S. Government Printing Office, no date).

The National Archives contains a remarkably well-organized and complete collection of wartime records maintained by the various units involved in the campaign, including the war diaries of the ships that delivered the troops to North Africa. Opening some of the maps and overlays used by soldiers in North Africa, one can almost feel the dust of the Tunisian Sahel clinging to the pages. The Archives collection also includes a number of German after-action reports that were captured or obtained after the Axis collapse and translated into American Army English.

In addition to the National Archives, documents relating to the North African campaign are available at the Military History Institute Archives and Library at the Army War College at Carlisle Barracks in Carlisle, Pennsylvania. The archives has on file the personal papers of a number of the officers involved in the campaign, and the library contains a number of first-person accounts of Tunisian battles, written by officers shortly after the war as academic exercises. Army Air Forces records and oral history interviews are available at the Air Force History Library at Bolling AFB in Washington, D.C., and at the Air Force Historical Research Agency at Maxwell AFB in Montgomery, Alabama.

A particularly revealing source of information about the campaign is the collection of the papers of Brig. Gen. Paul McD. Robinett, an armor officer who was involved in almost every important phase of the campaign. Articles and the manuscript of a book, along with voluminous correspondence, are on file at the George C. Marshall Archives at the Virginia Military Institute in Lexington, Virginia.

Bibliography

Books

Austin, A. B. *Birth of an Army*. London: Victor Gollancz Ltd., 1943.

Beevor, Anthony. *Stalingrad: The Fateful Siege: 1942–1943*. New York: Penguin Books, 1998.

Berens, Robert J. *Citizen Soldier: The Fighting Style of Brigadier General Edward W. Bird*. Ames, IA: Sigler, 1995.

Blair, Clay. *Hitler's U-Boat War: The Hunted 1942–1945*. New York: Random House, 1998.

Blumenson, Martin. *Kasserine Pass*. Boston: Houghton Mifflin, 1967.

Bradley, Omar N. *A Soldier's Story*. New York: Henry Holt, 1951.

Breuer, William B. *Operation Torch: The Allied Gamble to Invade North Africa*. New York: St. Martin's Press, 1985.

Chalfont, Alun. *Montgomery of Alamein*. New York: Atheneum, 1976.

Covington, Robert L. *The War Diaries of Sgt. Robert L. Covington, 60th Fighter Squadron, 33rd Fighter Group, U.S. Army Air Corps, November 1942–February 1945*. Blacksburg, VA: Pocahontas Press, 1998.

Craven, W. F., and J. L. Cate, eds. *The Army Air Forces in World War II: Europe—Torch to Pointblank, August 1942 to December 1943*. Washington, D.C.: U.S. Government Printing Office, n.d.

Darby, William O., with William H. Baumer. *Darby's Rangers: We Led the Way*. Novato, CA: Presidio Press, 1993.

D'Este, Carlos. *Patton: A Genius for War*. New York: HarperCollins, 1995.

Dupuy, Trevor N. *The Evolution of Weapons and Warfare*. Indianapolis: Bobbs-Merrill, n.d.

Eisenhower, Dwight D. *Crusade in Europe*. Garden City, NY: Doubleday, 1948.

Gauthier, Paul S., ed. *Brickbats from F Company, by Sgt. Milo L. Green, and Other Memorabilia Selections*. Corning, IA: Gauthier Publishing, 1982.

Hogg, Ian V. *Armour in Conflict*. London: Jane's, 1980.

Hougen, John H. *The Story of the Famous 34th Division*. Self-published, 1949.

Howe, George F. *The Battle History of the 1st Armored Division: Old Ironsides*. Washington, D.C.: Combat Forces Press, 1943.

————. *Northwest Africa: Seizing the Initiative in the West*. Washington, D.C.: Center of Military History, U.S. Army, 1993.

Irving, David. *The Trail of the Fox: The Search for the True Field Marshal Rommel*. New York: Dutton, 1977.

Knickerbocker, H. R., and others. *The Story of the First Division in World War II*. Washington: Society of the First Division, 1947.

Liddell Hart, B. H., ed. *The Rommel Papers*. London: Collins, 1953.

Liebling, A. J. *Liebling Abroad*. New York: Playboy Press, 1981.

Martin, Lewis, ed. *Guidebook to the Geology and History of Tunisia*. Tripoli: Petroleum Exploration Society of Libya: Ninth Annual Field Conference, 1967.

Miller, Clem. *Some Things You Never Forget: Five Battle Stars from Tunisia to the Po Valley*. Superior, WI: Savage Press, 1996.

Morison, Samuel Eliot. *Operations in North African Waters: October 1942–June 1943*. Boston: Little, Brown, 1947.

Mortensen, Daniel R., ed. *Airpower and Ground Armies: Essays on the Evolution of Anglo-American Air Doctrine, 1940–43*. Maxwell AFB, AL: Air University Press, 1998.

Reed, James E. *The Fighting 33rd Nomads During World War II: A Diary of a Fighter Pilot with Photographs and Other Stories of the 33rd Fighter Group Personnel*. Memphis: Reed Publishers, 1987.

Schmidt, H. W. *With Rommel in the Desert: In Victory and Defeat with the Commander of the Afrika Corps*. New York: Ballantine, 1951.

Starbuck, F. Randall, and Jerome J. Comello. *Air Power in North Africa, 1942–43: An Additional Perspective*. Carlisle Barracks, PA: U.S. Army War College, 1992.

Strawson, John. *The Battle for North Africa*. New York: Charles Scribner's Sons, 1969.

Thucydides. *The History of the Peloponnesian War*. Trans. Richard Crawley, ed. Ernest Rhys. New York: E. P. Dutton, Everyman's Library, n.d.

Vojta, Francis J. *The Gopher Gunners: A History of Minnesota's 151st Field Artillery*. Self-published, 1995.

Westover, John Glendower. *Selected Memories*. Tucson: Self-published, 1990.

Whiting, Charles. *Kasserine: First Blood.* New York: Stein and Day, 1984.

Willett, David. *Tunisia.* Hawthorn, Victoria, Australia: Lonely Planet, 1998.

Magazine Articles

Baldridge, Robert C., "How Artillery Beat Rommel after Kasserine," typed manuscript.

Berens, Robert J., "First Encounters: Facing the Germans, 1942," *Army,* July 1992, 45–48.

Betson, William R., "Sidi Bou Zid—a Case History of Failure," *Armor,* November–December 1982.

Blumenson, Martin, "The Agony and the Glory," *Infantry,* July–August 1967.

————, "Ike and His Indispensable Lieutenants," *Army,* June 1980.

Frisbee, John L., "The Lessons of North Africa," *Air Force,* September 1990.

Gardner, Henry E. (sic), "Kasserine Pass," *Armor,* September–October 1979, 13–17.

Hickey, James B., "The Destruction of Task Force Baum," *Armor,* November–December 1987.

Myers, Samuel A., "Random Recollections: The Gafsa Girls," *Armor,* March–April 1987.

Ogorkiewicz, R. M., "Facts and Figures: Tank Statistics of the Second World War," *Army Quarterly and Defense Review* 79 (October 1959): 63–67.

Oldinsky, Frederick E., "Patton and the Hammelburg Mission," *Armor,* July–August 1976, 13–17.

Robinett, Paul M., "The Axis Offensive in Central Tunisia—February 1943," *Armor,* May–June 1954.

Swezey, C. S., "Structural Controls on Quaternary Depocentres Within the Chotts Trough Region of Southern Tunisia," *Journal of African Earth Sciences* 22 (3) (1996).

Wolff, Kurt E., description of battle of Sidi Bou Zid in *Das Reich,* April 11, 1943, translated at the Command and General Staff School, Fort Leavenworth, KS, from Tactics Department, The Armored School, Fort Knox, KY, December 1943.

Newspaper Articles

"Attorney Clyde E. Herring Dies; POW of Germans During World War II," *Washington Post*, Sept. 26, 1976.

"Bluffs Lieutenant Winning DSC Has Humorous Memory of Occasion," *World-Herald* (Omaha, NB), June 4, 1944.

Buttry, Stephen, "From WWII to Vietnam, the Life of Our Nation Reflected in 4 Iowans," *Sunday World-Herald* (Omaha, NB), Nov. 8, 1997.

"Eisenhower Lists Regrouping Policy; He Pays Visit to Front," *New York Times*, Feb. 16, 1943.

"French in Tunisia Smash Tank Drive," *New York Times*, Jan. 5, 1943.

"Germans Stopped by U.S. Bayonets," *New York Times*, Jan. 6, 1943.

"John Knight Waters, Army General," *Washington Post*, Jan. 12, 1989.

King, William B., "Iowa Rangers, Led by Bluffs Man, Prefer the Front Line," Associated Press, February 1, 1943.

Kluckhohn, Frank L., "Armies Are United; Second U.S. Corps Meets British to Forge Arc Around Enemy," *New York Times*, April 8, 1943.

————, "'Front-Row View' of Sened Battle," *New York Times*, Feb. 3, 1943.

————, "Rommel's Crack Armored Division Halted by American Combat Team," *New York Times*, Feb. 23, 1943.

————, "U.S. Tanks Tackle Rommel's to Save Encircled Infantry," *New York Times*, Feb. 16, 1943.

Leonard, Bill, "One Small Town, One Huge War," *Des Moines Register*, April 10, 1994.

Middleton, Drew, "Allies Halt New Thrusts by Rommel," *New York Times*, Feb. 24, 1943.

————, "Americans Driven Back 22 Miles," *New York Times*, Feb. 18, 1943.

————, "Americans Retire; Yield Sbeitla and 2 Other Places After 5-Day Mauling by Axis," *New York Times*, Feb. 19, 1943.

————, "Germans Advance; Tanks and Infantry, With Artillery, Break U.S. and British Lines," *New York Times*, Feb. 22, 1943.

————, "Rommel Breaks U.S. Lines in Tunisia," *New York Times*, Feb. 16, 1943.

————, "Rommel Gains in Drive to Split Allies," *New York Times*, Feb. 23, 1943.

————, "Rommel Is Raided; Allied Planes Attack Foe in Central Tunisia—Land Fighting Scant," *New York Times*, Feb. 20, 1943.

————, "Rommel Repulsed," *New York Times*, Feb. 17, 1943.

————, "Sened Held Firmly," *New York Times*, Feb. 4, 1943.

————, "Sened Recaptured; Americans Take Town and Drive on Gabès and Maknassy," *New York Times*, March 22, 1943.

"News of Belated Victory Starts Parade Through Hanover Streets," *New York Times*, Nov. 19, 1940.

Sulzberger, C. L., "Americans and British Meet Beneath Frowning Djebels," *New York Times*, April 8, 1943.

Wilson, Richard, series covering operations of the 34th Infantry Division in North Africa, *Des Moines Register and Tribune*, August 15–18, 1943.

Official Records and Reports

Air Force History Library, Bolling AFB, Washington, D.C. "History of the 58th Fighter Squadron." (Covers period of Oct. 15, 1942, to Nov. 8, 1942).

The American Battle Monuments Commission, Arlington, VA. Annual Reports for 1997 and 1998.

Combat Studies Institute, Fort Leavenworth, KS. Combat Studies Institute Battlebook 4-D, "The Battle of Sidi Bou Zid," May 23, 1984.

George C. Marshall Archives, Lexington, VA. Robinett Papers. Combat Command B Operation Report for Bahiret Foussana Valley Operations, March 1, 1943, for the period February 20 to 25.

————. El Guettar operation, intelligence report for March 30 to April 8, 1943.

————. Memo from Maj. Gen. Orlando Ward, March 27, 1943, warning against skulking and straggling.

————. Proceedings of a board of officers for recommendations for changes and improvements in organization, tactics and equipment. Signed by Lt. Col. William B. Kern, Capt. Thomas W. Hoban, and Capt. Walter R. Geyer. December 21, 1943.

Military History Institute Archives, Carlisle Barracks, PA. Orlando Ward file. Document awarding Distinguished Service Cross to General Ward for action at Djebel Naernia. (Contains his service record and other decorations including Silver Star in

World War II and Oak Leaf Cluster for Silver Star for action at Maknassy in April 1943.)

————. Memo, October 11, 1943, in which Lt. Col. Hamilton H. Howze tells of action around Mateur involving tanks.

————. Sworn statement from Capt. Ernest C. Hatfield, March 27, 1943, concerning General Ward's heroic behavior March 24–25 during attack on Djebel Naemia.

————. Transcript of Conference, June 16, 1943 (location not given) in which Brig. Gen. Robert V. Maraist and Col. Peter C. Hains reported on the operations of the 1st Armored Division in Tunisia.

National Archives. Statistical Section Headquarters, 33rd Fighter Group. RG 18. "33rd Fighter Group, Operational History, Vol. I, from 10 November 1942 to 29 February 1944: Mediterranean Theater of Operations."

————. "Report of 33rd Fighter Group Intelligence Officer on Statistics. July 29, 1943." (Reports destruction of 52 enemy planes between March 3 and April 5.)

National Archives. Records of the Office of the Chief of Naval Operations, World War II. RG 38. "Action Reports of 41st Fighter Squadron Aboard USS *Ranger* in Action off North Africa."

————. War Diaries of the USS *Chenango,* USS *Ranger,* USS *Santee,* and USS *Suwannee.*

National Archives. RG 407. "A Brief History of the Second Battalion, Sixth Armored Infantry, from October 11, 1942, to May 12, 1943, including the North African Campaign."

————. "History of the 168th Infantry for period November 12, 1942 to May 15, 1943."

————. "Report of 1st Lt. Harry P. Hoffman of activities of third battalion, 168th Infantry, from 7 February to 20 February 1943."

————. "Report of 1st Lt. Marvin E. Williams of the activities of the 168th Infantry in the Sidi Bou Zid area 14–17 February 1943."

————. "Report of Maj. Robert R. Moore, commander of 2nd battalion, 168th CT [combat team]." (Report covers activities of the unit from Feb. 3 to 19, 1943. Describes movement of regiment to Sidi Bou Zid area and disposition of forces.)

————. "Report of Operation, 1st Armored Division, Sbeitla, Tunisia 3 February 1943 to 18 February 1943."

U.S. Air Force Historical Research Agency, Maxwell AFB, AL. "60th Fighter Squadron War Diary, July 1943."

U.S. Army Center of Military History, Washington, D.C. "Combat Operations of the 1st Infantry Division During World War II."

Monographs

World War II Infantry Monographs prepared at the Advanced Infantry Officers Course, on file at the library of the Military History Institute at Carlisle Barracks, PA:

No. 2. Anderson, Roland, 1947–48 #603-135-1947 135th Infantry Regiment, 34th Division, Vicinity of Fondouk El Okbi, North Africa, 26 March–11 April 1943.

No. 12. Brandt, Arnold N., 1947–48 #603-135-1947/3a 1st Battalion 135th Infantry Regiment, 34th Division Hills 609 and 531, Mateur, Tunisia, 26 April–2 May 1943.

No. 14. Carter, Sam, 1947–48 #603-18-1947/2a 1st Battalion 18th Infantry, First Division, El Guettar, Tunisia, 17–25 March 1943.

No. 24. Craven, Virgil E., 1949–50 #603-133-1949a Co. I, 133rd Infantry, 34th Division Fondouk Gap, Tunisia, 8–9 April 1943.

No. 90. Wilson, Lloyd G., 1947–48 #603-509-1947a 509th Parachute Battalion in North Africa 8 November 1943–February 1943. First Airborne Combat Operations of U.S. Army.

Monographs Available at the Air Force Historical Research Center, Maxwell Air Force Base, AL:

The Armored School, Fort Knox, KY. "Armor in the Invasion of North Africa," A Research Report, 1949–1950. Foreword by Maj. Gen. Ernest N. Harmon.

Committee 11, Officers Advanced Course, the Armored School, Fort Knox, KY. "The 1st Armored Division at Faïd-Kasserine," a Research Report. May 1949. Preceded by a letter from General Howze complaining that citations in the manuscript were taken from a paper he wrote about Sidi Bou Zid.

Maj. Robert T. Cooper, USAF, "The 33rd Fighter Group: Fire from the Clouds," an Air Command and Staff College Student Report. Report number 88-0600.

Ann Larson, Project Director, "Citizen Soldiers: the History and Contribution to American Democracy of Volunteer 'Citizen Soldiers' of Southwest Iowa (1930–1945)," A project funded by the National Endowment of the Humanities Youth Grant Division, Project #Ay 20265, 1981.

National Archives. Historical Division, Air University Library, Air University. RG 319, Box 228. "Proposed Mission Against Fondouk Gap, Tunisia, 7 April 1943," February 7, 1951.

Lt. Col. Alan M. Russo, "Kasserine: The Myth and its Warning for Airland Battle Operations," Maxwell AFB, March 1985.

Dr. Richard W. Stewart, "The Training and Battlefield Employment of the 34th Infantry Division in World War II: The First Two Years," paper presented at the Conference of Army Historians, March 29, 1990, Washington, D.C.

Diaries and Memoirs in Possession of Author

Leighton, Charles F., of San Diego, CA. Diaries concerning his experiences as a member of Darby's Rangers in the Arzew landing and the Sened Station raid.

McBride, Lt. Col. (Ret.) Larry, of Riverside, CA. Materials, including article manuscripts and memoirs, relating his involvement with the 168th Regiment of the 34th Infantry Division.

Moore, A. Robert, of Bloomindale, IL. Memoirs relating his experience with the 1st Armored Division in North Africa.

Paige, Edmund M. (also known as Edmund M. Wheeler), of Bloomfield, NJ. Memoirs relating his service as a member of the 1st Infantry Division.

German Records I

Source: National Archives, Dr. George Howe research records, Record Group 319, Stack Area 270, Row 19, Box 225:

Fifth Panzer Army headquarters. "Order for the conduct of operations in the south sector." Contains orders for the Fifth Panzer Army and the 21st Panzer Division. January 24, 1943.

————. "Order for the Operation 'Fruhlingswind.'" February 8, 1943.

10th Panzer Division, Orders from General Fritz von Broich for Operation Fruhlingswind. February 9, 1943.

————. Report by Dr. Menges on prisoners and captured matériel, for period of February 14 to 22, 1943.

—————— . Report by Dr. Menges gives order of battle of Americans and British. February 25, 1943.

—————— . Report of the activities of the intelligence section covering period March 22–April 24, 1943.

21st Panzer Division. Memo by messenger. "The fight for Sbeitla is harder than expected. Defense well organized; about 50 enemy tanks. Seven-hour tank fight. Sbeitla firmly in our hand . . . " February 21, 1943.

220th Panzer Engineering Battalion. Report on work from January 30 to February 5. Lists number of mines laid (3,528 panzer mines, 454 S mines). In same period, removed 1,053 British and French mines. Also refers, on page 2, to work in Maknassy area. February 6, 1943.

Bayerlein, Brig. Gen. Fritz, who was attached to Italian General Messe. Memorandum for war diary, May 5, 1943: "General Messe is a very haughty and conceited officer who understands little of the conduct of operations but is great on theories."

Copy of radio message of February 21, 1943, on supply situation of Gruppe Rommel on evening of February 20.

Greiner, Hellmuth (officer on Rommel's staff). Diary notes from August 12, 1942, to March 17, 1943.

Hitler, Adolf. Letter to Mussolini, November 20, 1942. Hitler talks of reinforcing in North Africa: "I believe that the coming week will be critical." "As soon as the problem of transportation is solved I am convinced that all will be all right."

Luftwaffe commander, Tunis. Memo, December 18, 1942, spelling out plans for Operation Riga, parachute-glider attacks on bridges, railroad lines, in Allied rear.

Luftwaffe commander, Tunis. Memo, December 26, 1942, with detailed plans for Operation Riga.

Mussolini, Benito. Letter to Hitler from Duce headquarters, Rome, December 29, 1941. Stresses importance of control of Tripolitania.

Order for the defense of the Tunis position, April 11, 1943.

Report of sorties flown by bomber and fighter aircraft during Operations Fruhlingswind (plan for attack on Sidi Bou Zid) and Capri (plan for attack on Medenine) from February 14 to March 8, 1943.

Report on "evidence of shortages in ammunition, fuel and rations." March 11, 1943.

Report: "The repulse of a large-scale enemy attack is impossible with the amount of ammunition on hand." April 14, 1943.

Retzlaff, Captain. April 2, 1943, Report No. 4. Describes visits to various units. Praises tactics of American planes. Allies now have air superiority. "Our air force at the time is plainly inferior." Comments on fighting ability of Americans and Italians.

Rommel, Gen. Erwin, February 18, 1943. Message to Comando Supremo requesting more troops, urging attack on Tebessa.

"The Struggle for the African Outpost: the Balance Sheet of the Campaign in North Africa." Unsigned summing-up of the situation.

German Records II

Source: National Archives, Dr. George Howe research records, Record Group 319, Stack Area 270, Row 19, Box 226:

21st Panzer Division. Diary of operations, January 1, 1943 to March 31, 1943. Contains detailed account of fighting at Faïd Pass and Sidi Bou Zid.

Brief biographies of German officers: Fritz von Broich, Martin Harlinghausen, Koch, Rudolph Lang, Hans Lederer, Joseph Moll, Heinz Pomtow, Harald Stolz, and Gustav von Vaerst.

Comando Supremo. Radio message from General Ambrosio to the German-Italian P. Army and Fifth Panzer Army. February 8, 1943.

————. Order to von Arnim and Rommel, 2339 hours, February 18, 1943. Orders Rommel: "Will attack over the general line Sbeitla-Tebessa, Maktar-Tadjerouine, next on el Kef."

Deutsches Afrika Korps [DAK] war diary. Twenty pages cover period of February 19 to 24, 1943, including battle of Kasserine Pass.

German-Italian Panzer Army. Message from operations section, command post, 0030 hours, February 23, 1943. Describes decision to break off attack and withdraw troops.

Kesselring, Field Marshal Albrecht. Message from O. S. Sud to Rommel and von Arnim personally, February 18, 1943. Favors drive toward Tebessa. "Will speak to Duce and Amborsio [sic] today."

Report of conference at 0945 hours, February 19, 1943, involving Kesselring, von Arnim, others.

Report of conference at 1745 hours, February 20, 1943, between Kesselring and von Arnim at Tunis airfield.

Rommel, Gen Erwin. Report to Comando Supremo, February 18, 1943, recommends move into Feriana-Thélepte area.

————— . Message to Comando Supremo, 1420 hours, February 18, 1943, recommending "an immediate enveloping thrust of strong forces from the southwest on Tebessa and the area to the north."

Supply list for the plan of attack, February 18, 1943.

Telephone message to Rommel's advanced command post, February 19, 1943. Order for Operation Sturmflut (Storm flood). Rommel to "immediately push forward over the general line Sbeitla-Tebessa northward in the deep flank and rear of the British forces standing in front of the North Tunisian Front."

Von Arnim, Gen. Juergen. "Commentary on the 'plan' 'thrust on Tebessa,'" February 18, 1943.

Correspondence

Alger, Col. J. D. Letter to Maj. Gen. Orlando Ward, Feb. 4, 1951. National Archives, Record Group 319, Box 226.

Clark, Gen. Mark W. Letter to Gen. Harmon, Dec. 12, 1943, urging soldiers to smash the Germans. Very tough talk. Harmon sent it to all unit commanders. National Archives, Record Group 319, Box 228.

de la Meza Allen, Maj. Gen. Terry. Letter to Dr. Howe, April 16, 1951, concerning battle of Hill 609-Tine River valley. National Archives, Record Group 319, Box 228.

Denholm, Lt. Col. Charles A. Letter to Dr. Howe, Feb. 20, 1951, describing his escape from an Italian prisoner-of-war ship. National Archives, Record Group 319, Box 226.

Devers, Jacob L. Letter to General Harmon, April 16, 1943, from Headquarters, Armored Force, Fort Knox, KY. Refers to Robinett as "a trouble maker without a lot of foundation." Most of letter deals with plans for use of tanks. National Archives, Record Group 319, Box 228.

Drake, Col. Thomas D. Letter to Maj. Gen. Orlando Ward, Jan. 15, 1951. National Archives, Record Group 319, Box 226.

Eisenhower, Gen. Dwight D. Letter to Gen. George C. Marshall, Feb. 21, 1943. He says he wanted to retain Thélepte airfields [note plural] and confine enemy to narrow corridor from Fondouk southward. Orlando Ward file, Military History Institute Archives, Carlisle Barracks, PA.

——— . Letter to Gen. Marshall, March 3, 1943. Refers to Robinett. "Another puzzling man is Robinett. He has made the best fighting record of any combat commander on the front. However, I will never recommend him for a promotion until he learns to control his tongue. He seems intelligent but entirely without judgment, except in a tactical sense. For the moment his ceiling is brigadier—but I hope he begins to develop." Ward file, Military History Institute.

——— . Letter to Maj. Gen. Ward, March 12, 1943. The letter refers to Robinett as difficult, tells Ward not to let anyone doubt who is in charge. Ward file, Military History Institute.

——— . Letter to Brig. Gen. Robinett, September 15, 1967, refers to Robinett as "always one of the able subordinates in that nasty African war, where we were so often fighting at a great disadvantage." Military History Institute.

Hains, Col. Peter C. Notes of interview, undated. National Archives, Record Group 319, Box 226.

Harmon, Maj. Gen. Ernest. Memo dated May 21, 1943, commenting on tanks. National Archives, Record Group 319, Box 228.

——— . Memo dated May 24, 1943, praising Col. Hamilton H. Howse and Col. Louis V. Hightower. National Archives, Record Group 319, Box 228.

——— . Letter to General Marshall, August 13, 1943, referring to discipline problems. National Archives, Record Group 319, Box 228.

——— . Letter to Brig. Gen. Robinett, June 23, 1971, Robinett Papers, box 5, folder 29. George C. Marshall Archives, Lexington, VA.

Howe, Dr. George F. Letter to Lt. Col. Donald C. Landon, Dec. 27, 1950, requesting information about Battle of Hill 609. National Archives, Record Group 319, Box 226.

Irwin, Maj. Gen. S. LeRoy. Memorandum to Brig. Gen. Robinett, June 23, 1949. National Archives, Record Group 319, Box 226.

Latham, Brig. H. B. Letter from British cabinet office, historical section, to Dr. George F. Howe, July 17, 1950, responding to questions from Howe concerning second attack at Fondouk el Okbi, April 7–10, 1943. National Archives, Record Group 319, Box 228.

————. Letter to Dr. Howe, September 13, 1950, with statement prepared by Lt. Gen. Sir Gordon MacMillan on the events prior to and during the battle of Fondouk in April 1943. Includes cover letter from General Sir John Crocker. National Archives, Record Group 319, Box 228.

Marshall, Gen. George C. Letter to Maj. General Orlando Ward, May 5, 1943. Warns Ward against pessimism. Ward file, Military History Institute.

McQuillin, Brig. Gen. R. E. Comments on Chapters VII, IX, and XII of Howe manuscript. Undated. National Archives, Record Group 319, Box 226.

Miller, Col. Robert P. Letter to Dr. Howe, Jan. 14, 1951, describing his role as commander of the 1st Battalion, 135th Infantry, 34th Division, at Hill 609. National Archives, Record Group 319, Box 226.

O'Daniel, Maj. Gen. John W. Letter to Brig. Gen. Ward, Jan. 5, 1951, describing operations of the 168th Infantry in the landings at Algiers. National Archives, Record Group 319, Box 226.

Potter, Col. H. E. Letter to Lt. Col. A. F. Clark Jr., Sept. 4, 1947, with five-page attachment, undated, containing responses to questions from Dr. Howe by General der Flieger Paul Deichmann. National Archives, Record Group 319, Box 226.

Robinett, O. L. "Dick." Letter to Brig. Gen. Robinett March 16, 1943. Refers to letter from Treasury Department asking for $32.14 due on 1941 income tax. Tells of difficulty getting decent farm labor, mentions possibility of buying 313-acre farm for Paul. Robinett Papers, box 3, folder 27, George C. Marshall Archives, Lexington, VA.

Robinett, Brig. Gen. Paul McD. Letter to his brother O. L. "Dick" Robinett from North Africa, Dec. 24, 1942. Robinett File, box 10, folder 6, George C. Marshall Archives, Lexington, VA.

————. Letter to F. H. Bowticou, Dec. 31, 1942, describing French and British buying pack animals. Robinett Papers, Box 3, George C. Marshall Archives, Lexington, VA.

————. Letter to his sister, Opal (Mrs. E. C. Webb), Jan. 19, 1943. Tells of visit by local "caid," all turned out in finery. Robinett Papers, Box 3, George C. Marshall Archives, Lexington, VA.

————. Letter to Col. A. B. "Monk" Dickson, Janaury 25, 1943. Asks for good French maps and photographs, reports from pilots. Calls field glasses and telescopes "trash." Robinett Papers, Box 3, George C. Marshall Archives, Lexington, VA.

————. Memo to Commanding General, Allied Forces headquarters, Feb. 7, 1943, complaining about rear echelon troops getting candy, mirrors, pencils, brushes, ink, etc. Robinett Papers, Box 3, George C. Marshall Archives, Lexington, VA.

————. Memo to Commanding General, Allied Forces headquarters, Feb. 10, 1943, complaining of lack of crosses to mark graves. "We do not even have a supply of markers and our chaplains have to use ration box boards, sticks, or anything else immediately available." Robinett Papers, Box 3, George C. Marshall Archives, Lexington, VA.

————. Letter to "Dick" Robinett, Feb. 14, 1943, about bill from government for $32.41 income tax. Asks his brother to pay it under protest. Robinett Papers, Box 3, George C. Marshall Archives, Lexington, VA.

————. Letter to his father, Feb. 26, 1943, just after Kasserine. Robinett papers, box 10, folder 9, George C. Marshall Archives, Lexington, VA.

————. Memo to Commanding General, Allied Forces headquarters, March 1, 1943, with urgent request for light horse cavalry to carry out reconnaissance. Robinett Papers, Box 3, George C. Marshall Archives, Lexington, VA.

————. Letter to Gen. Malin Craig, March 26, 1943. Notes that casualties from burns and mines are lower than World War I. Notes that "frankness and forthrightness are not always appreciated, but when one is responsible for one's own conscience, it is best to keep his own self-respect." Robinett Papers, Box 5, George C. Marshall Archives, Lexington, VA.

————. Letter to collector of internal revenue, May 1, 1943, returning uncompleted tax return. Robinett Papers, Box 3, George C. Marshall Archives, Lexington, VA.

————. Letter to Maj. Gen. Harry J. Malony, May 21, 1943. Tells of getting shrapnel in legs, missed final "kill." Robinett Papers, Box 3, George C. Marshall Archives, Lexington, VA.

————. Letter to Maj. F. M. Burton, May 21, 1943, thanking him for operation on his legs. Robinett Papers, Box 3, George C. Marshall Archives, Lexington, VA.

————. Letter to General Fredendall, August 8, 1944. Says his official record does not cover some of the "most interesting and difficult part of my service." Contains details of fighting in North Africa. Robinett Papers, box 10, folder 5, George C. Marshall Archives, Lexington, VA.

————. Letter to President Eisenhower, September 12, 1967. Military History Institute Archives, Carlisle Barracks, PA.

————. Letter to Gen. Harmon, June 5, 1971, commenting on book by Harmon. Robinett Papers, Box 5, Folder 29. George C. Marshall Archives, Lexington, VA.

Rosen, David V. Letter to Gen. Mark Clark, June 25, 1947, describing his role in the landings at Algiers. National Archives, Record Group 319, Box 226.

Ryder, Maj. Gen. Charles W. Answers of questions submitted by Dr. Howe, March 18, 1949. National Archives, Record Group 319, Box 226.

Stack, Col. I. R. Letter to Dr. Howe, March 8, 1951. National Archives, Record Group 319, Box 226.

Stark, Col. Alex. Letter to Brig. Gen. Ward, Jan. 21, 1951. National Archives, Record Group 319, Box 226.

Taylor, Brig. Gen. George A. Letter to Dr. Howe, November 22, 1950, describing his role in the fighting near Hill 609. National Archives, Record Group 319, Box 226.

Thompson, John H. Letter dated July 12, 1948, to Senator James P. Kem, R-Missouri, urging belated recognition of the role played by Combat Command B in the Kasserine battle. "Like the other American correspondents who were there at the time, I know that it was General Robinett and Combat Command B which turned the tide in the valley, and which caused the Germans to refer to them as the victors of Kasserine." Thompson was military editor of the *Chicago Tribune*. Robinett Papers, Box 3, George C. Marshall Archives, Lexington, VA.

Ward, Maj. Gen. Orlando. Letter to 13-year-old Richard Harrison of Garrison, KY, October 19, 1942. Richard had written "To a Soldier in Ireland" and his letter was received by Ward. Ward file, Military History Institute.

————. Letter to Brig. Gen. W. B. Smith, November 16, 1942, complaining that a newspaper picture credits Rangers rather than 1st Armored Division for action at Oran. "This is a personal letter to you and please destroy it." Ward file, Military History Institute.

————. Letter to Gen. Eisenhower, March 7, 1943. "George Patton is taking over with a vim and I look towards a united front in this Corps. Personally, I am a new man." Ward file, Military History Institute.

————. Handwritten letter dated April 4, 1943, relinquishing command of 1st Armored Division to General Harmon. Ward file, Military History Institute.

————— . Letter to "Bobby," undated. Bobby appears to be commander of "your landing on the west." Letter was not sent.
But it emphasizes Ward's strong objections to sending destroyers (he calls them corvettes) into Oran. Ward file, Military History Institute.

Battlefield Staff Ride

In 1993, the U.S. Army Center of Military History collected many
of the records relating to the fighting in Tunisia in preparation for
a "staff ride" of the battlefields for veterans of the battles and
younger officers. Brig. Gen. Harold W. Nelson, chief of military
history, was the staff ride director, and Lt. Col. Roger Cirillo was
the staff ride leader. The materials were published by the Center
of Military History in two volumes, each containing two or three
parts, plus an appendix containing maps and sketches. The volumes are:

Kasserine Pass Battles, Readings, Vol. I, Part 1, containing book ex-
cerpts, articles, and both German and American combat diaries,
reports of operations, and operational orders.
Kasserine Pass Battles, Readings, Vol. I, Part 2, containing additional
war diaries and operational reports.
Kasserine Pass Battles, Doctrines and Lessons Learned, Vol. II, Part 1.
Kasserine Pass Battles, Doctrines and Lessons Learned, Vol. II, Part 2.
Kasserine Pass Battles, Maps and Sketches, Appendix.

Oral History Interviews

Source: Air Force Historical Research Agency, Maxwell AFB, AL.

Adler, Maj. Gen. Elmer E. May 4, 1966. Was in North Africa
early, stationed in Cairo, observed El Alamein.
Austin, Maj. Gen. Gordon M. May 18–20, 1982. Commanded a
B-26 group.
Black, Col. Percy, C.S.C., March 26, 1943. Member of General
Patton's staff in the North African invasion.
Cochran, Lt. Col. Philip G. June 3, 1943. Good description of
operations out of Thélepte.
Cochran, Col. Philip G. Oct. 20–21 and Nov. 11, 1975.

Dahl, Maj. Gen. Leo P. July 7 and 9, 1982. Set up weather fore-casting for Operation Torch and then monitored replacement aircraft across the Atlantic.

Davison, Brig. Gen. D. A., who calls himself "Tooey Spaatz's Engi-neer," June 1, 1943. Tells how he built airfields in North Africa.

Dean, Lt. Gen. Fred M. February 25–26, 1975.

Dixon, Lt. Col. Palmer. June 10, 1943. He was an intelligence officer involved in planning for and involvement in North African Campaign.

Doolittle, Gen. James H. September 26, 1971.

Engler, Colonel Howard E. General Doolittle's operations officer, May 27, 1943.

Klocko, Lt. Gen. Richard P. October 29–30, 1987. Commanded 350th Fighter Group, equipped with P-39 fighters. Was shot down February 23, 1943, spent rest of the war as a prisoner.

Low, Col. Curtis R. July 23, 1943. Describes operations in sup-port of the British in Egypt.

Mears, Col. Frank. August 10, 1943. Good description of opera-tions with the British from Alamein to Tunisia.

Miller, Col. Robert S. Report of paraphrased interview, March 18, 1943, on his return from a tour of duty as an army ground force observer in North Africa.

Mitchim, Maj. Kelly. P-38 pilot, 82nd Fighter Group. December 8, 1943.

Momyer, Gen. William W. January 31, 1977. Part of Corona Ace Series involving qualities of fighter pilots.

Oliver, Maj. Gen. L. E. Commander of Combat Command B, Feb-ruary 5, 1943.

Waters, Gen. John K. Senior Officers Oral History Program, Proj-ect 80-A, Vol. II and IV, Carlisle Barracks, PA.

Interviews with North Africa Veterans

Bent, John T. "Jack." Rochester, NY. Telephone interview by author, July 20, 1999.

Berens, Robert. Springfield, VA. Personal interview by author, Octo-ber 14, 1999.

Cavanagh, Paul. Grand Junction, CO. Telephone interview by author, March 2, 2000.

Dellavedova, Dominic. Davenport, IA. Telephone interview by author, January 19, 2000.

Eineichner, Clarence W. East Detroit, MI. Telephone interview by author, May 18, 1999.

Lehmann, Carl H. Upper Marlboro, MD. Personal interview by author, October 1, 1999.

Miller, Clem. Duluth, MN. Telephone interview by author, January 12, 2000.

Moore, A. Robert. Bloomingdale, IL. Telephone interview by author, November 5, 1999.

Moore, Robert. Atlanta, GA. Son of North Africa veteran. Interview by author, October 20, 1999.

Pirnie, Bruce. Springfield, VT. Telephone interview by author, March 6, 2000.

Popejoy, Elmer. Greensburg, IN. Telephone interview by author, February 1 and 2, 2000.

Tillery, Donald D. Lynnhaven, FL. Telephone interview by author, October 8, 1999.

Tuck, William. Houston, TX. Telephone interview by author, November 1, 1999.

Vojta, Francis J. Edina, MN. Telephone interview by author, September 8, 1999.

Index

p. 46 - Invasion Plan
p. 100 - Berbers
German Control of air, (Green Troops)
p. 125 - German Fighter Planes Superior